The American Baker

Exquisite Desserts from the Pastry Chef of
The Stanford Court

By

JIM DODGE

with Elaine Ratner

Foreword by Maida Heatter

Illustrations by Susan Mattmann

Photographs by Michael Lamotte

SIMON AND SCHUSTER   NEW YORK

Designed by Eve Kirch
Photographic Stylist: Liz Ross
Photographic Assistant: Bruce James
Manufactured in the United States of America

1   3   5   7   9   10   8   6   4   2

Library of Congress Cataloging-in-Publication Data

Dodge, Jim, date.
The American baker.

Includes index.
1.Desserts.   I.Ratner, Elaine.   II.Title.
TX775.D63   1987   641.8'6   87-13060

ISBN: 0-671-61158-5

For James A. Nassikas,
founder and guiding spirit of the superb Stanford Court Hotel,
who gave me the opportunity to create and grow there

Contents

5. Basic Sponge Cakes and Meringues 89

White Sponge Cake (Génoise)
Chocolate Sponge Cake (Génoise)
Jelly Roll Sponge Cake

Chocolate Jelly Roll Sponge Cake
Hazelnut Meringue
Almond Meringue

6. Creams, Sauces, Glazes, and Decorations 101

Pastry Cream
Chocolate Pastry Cream
English Custard (Crème Anglaise)
Lemon Cream
Chocolate Cream
Chocolate Butter Cream
Custard Butter Cream
Egg White Butter Cream
Swiss Butter Cream
Fondant
Chocolate Fondant
Chocolate Sauce
Lemon Sauce
Strawberry Sauce
Cranberry Sauce

Apricot Sauce
Raspberry Sauce
Caramel Sauce
Rum Caramel Sauce
Butterscotch Sauce
Bourbon Sauce
Rum Sauce
Apricot Glaze
Currant Glaze
Chocolate Glaze
Candied Ginger
Candied Orange Peel
Chocolate Ganache Shells
Chocolate Butterflies
Chocolate Truffles

7. Tarts 129

Field-Ripened Pineapple Tart
Coconut-Pineapple Tart
Vanilla Plum Tart
Rum Plum Tart
Almond Apple Puff
Cranberry and Almond Puff
Cinnamon Apple Tart

Gingered Dutch Apple Tart
Apple and Walnut Tart with
    Butterscotch Glaze
Almond Apricot Tart
Ginger Crumb Apricot Tart
Strawberry-Apricot Tart
Strawberry Goat Cheese Tart

8. Pies, Cobblers, and Crisps   163

9. Cakes   191

10. Puddings 241

11. Pastries 253

12. Cookies 279

Foreword

Years ago hotel food was, to put it kindly, not the best. We checked into a hotel and, unless there was a hurricane or a tornado outside, we went someplace else to eat. Times have changed. Now, even if we're not staying there, we go to certain hotels to eat—because the food is so good. It is often as good as in the best restaurants; occasionally it is even better.

When we are lucky enough to be in San Francisco we head straight for The Stanford Court, the most beautiful and luxurious hotel I know. The man responsible for this work of art is James Nassikas, the owner, the creator, and the man-on-the-job almost day and night. James Nassikas was recently named Independent Hôtelier of the World (the world!) by Hotels and Restaurants International. Incidentally, James Nassikas graduated from the very prestigious Ecole Hôtelière, on the banks of Lake Geneva in Switzerland. Another student there at the same time was Craig Claiborne. They have been good friends ever since.

James Nassikas's life appears to be a total commitment to his hotel; he's like a mother with a new baby (although he has had this baby for eighteen years now). He wants everything to be perfect, which is why he hired Jim Dodge as pastry chef.

I first met Jim Dodge many years ago when he was vacationing in Florida and came to visit us. He is young, handsome, and charming. He is quiet and reserved, but when we talked about gingersnaps, he was illuminated and his eyes twinkled. I could quickly see that we were talking his language. I had a marvelous time and felt as though we were old friends. Since then, on many visits to The Stanford Court, I have watched Jim and his assistants in the bake shop at 5 A.M. And I have tasted most of Jim's desserts.

The first word to describe these desserts is simple: pure and clean in design, and natural and undiluted in taste. This collection of very personal recipes is an outstanding example of very good taste, both to the palate and visually. This wonderful book is like a relaxed and lengthy visit with an outstanding chef/artist in his kitchen, watching him work and listening to his strongly felt philosophy (fresh, plain, and not gussied up). I share those sentiments.

Some of these recipes are classics; as Jim says, there are some things that just can't be improved on. But most are extraordinarily creative and exciting combinations of mouth-watering ingredients: strawberries with green peppercorns, oranges with tarragon, honeydew in chile (you make a sweet sugar syrup that includes a fresh hot pepper and then pour that over the diced melon), pears with anise. And new techniques—did you ever hear of a fruit tart made like this? A tart shell (this one is different and divine) is baked empty, then it is filled with a mixture somewhat like a butter cake and baked again. When the juicy pineapple is placed on top, you know the bottom crust will stay crisp (see page 132). The fruit tarts alone could fill a book—mouth-watering, tempting, colorful: a strawberry and goat cheese tart, a cranberry caramel tart. And pies: banana cream pie—the best there is! Pastry crusts and doughs that I have never seen before. Many delicious cobblers and crisps that are quick and easy. Spectacular chocolate cakes. And cookies like little jewels.

All through this book you will learn new and professional techniques and time-saving methods. I often make bite-size pastry tarts that are baked before they are filled. I had always cut aluminum foil rounds and patiently pressed them into the unbaked pastry. One day in Jim's kitchen I watched him roll and cut the pastry, place it in the forms, and then place in the forms paper cupcake liners that had been filled ahead of time with a layer of dried beans. It took only seconds to line many pastry shells. It was quick and easy, so I tried it when we got home. I found that the pastry shells baked to a more even and beautiful color than ever before. I'll never do it any other way (see pages 73–74).

Dessert making is an individual and personal art. Each artist does it differently. Jim Dodge generously and patiently shares all his original ideas, creative techniques, and sensational recipes, in great detail.

I can't wait to make most if not all of the recipes in this book. Jim, congratulations.

Maida Heatter

1

The Secrets
of a
Great Dessert

The most compelling reason for dessert is pleasure, pure and simple. We may argue that dessert is traditional, that it rounds out a meal, or even that it's nutritious, but in our heart of hearts we know that we look forward to dessert because it's fun. What's more, making dessert is fun. It's an opportunity to be creative; to work with luscious, rich ingredients; and to please an audience, whether it's a table of admiring friends or business associates or just the family.

I never get tired of making desserts. The tried and true ones I've been making for years are like comfortable old friends. I know they'll do what I expect them to do, and I know they'll please. The new ones I invent excite a sense of adventure, and challenge me to stretch in new directions. They don't always come out great the first time, but they always get my creative juices flowing and make me glad I chose, back when I was a teenager, to become a pastry chef.

I have been fascinated by good food since I was a small child, spending hours in the kitchens and dining rooms of my family's hotels in New Hampshire and New York. My father, a skillful chef, purposely began developing his children's palates early, teaching us to appreciate and enjoy wholesome, carefully prepared American and Continental food. Later my classical training and apprenticeship with Swiss pastry chef Fritz Albecker, at the Strawbery Court Pastry Shop in Portsmouth, New Hampshire, taught me to re-create the full range of traditional European desserts. As soon as I had a firm grip on those techniques, my

19

New England-bred independent spirit insisted that I could and should apply them to a pursuit of my own instincts and tastes.

Over the years I made my share of mistakes in attempting to combine ingredients in new and interesting ways, but I also made many wonderful discoveries. Bit by bit I developed a philosophy of dessert making that seems right for the lives we live today. The result is a repertoire of desserts that are based on solid classical technique (you simply can't improve on some things) and my own ideas of how to use the exciting ingredients, especially the fresh fruits, we have at our fingertips in lighter, less sweet, and intensely flavorful desserts.

SEASONAL INGREDIENTS

Because I have responsibilities to a year-round restaurant menu that requires a nucleus of dependable, unchanging desserts, I have a small selection of "regulars," signature dishes that my staff and I turn out daily. Chocolate Beret Cake, Cheesecake, Dacquoise, cookies, and French pastries are always on the menu and always popular. Once those items are baked and ready to go, I am free each day to create the rest of the dessert menu with whatever ingredients and inspiration come my way.

I always start with a trip to the kitchen storeroom to check out the day's deliveries of the season's best fruits. Why would anyone want to use a mealy, out-of-season apple when the figs are sweet and juicy or the nectarines are fairly bursting with rich flavor? For that matter, why pay for and use any ingredient that is not absolutely at its peak in flavor and appearance? Of course, the wonderful hidden bonus here is that produce at its peak of ripeness is also at its peak of abundance—and at its lowest price.

I have suppliers who know I am always on the lookout for the best fruits of the season, so they send over the best they have each week. You have suppliers too, in your local produce market or department. Be a fussy shopper. Let it be known that you want only the best, and when your grocer goes out of his way to steer you toward it, show your appreciation. Let him know that the peaches were outstanding this week, and next week he'll be waiting to tell you about his terrific new shipment of plums or nectarines.

Most important, select the recipes you make according to what's fresh and delicious in the market today. Don't pass by the sweet, juicy strawberries because you came looking for grapefruit. The grapefruit may have passed its peak, while the strawberries will never be better. Notice what's fresh and ripe each time you shop, and plan your next dessert around it.

COMPLEMENTARY TASTES AND TEXTURES

Most of my desserts start with one predominant flavor: The magnificent strawberries or peaches or pears that are irresistibly ripe and sweet today dictate my direction. Then I think about other flavors that will enhance and underscore that main flavor, make it shine even more than it does by itself. I usually settle on just one flavor to add; occasionally I choose two. I may go for a background flavor with pastry cream (vanilla) or lemon cream; or play with a tried and true combination, like cinnamon and apple; or create an unexpected pairing, like cranberry and caramel or blackberry and lime. Whichever approach I take, my concern is always balance; I don't want to add any ingredient that will overwhelm or compete with the main flavor. A dessert with four or five main ingredients is confusing and inevitably disappointing. Your taste is pulled in too many directions, so you don't enjoy the full impact of any one flavor.

I also think about texture when searching for a complementary ingredient. If a fruit is particularly soft and lush, like a ripe papaya, I might team it up with firm, spicy blueberries. Peaches and pistachios is one of my favorite combinations—a delightful contrast of taste, texture, and color.

The ingredients I decide to combine have to be more exciting, more flavorful together than any of them is separately. If they are, I know my dessert will be exciting and flavorful too.

CLARITY OF FLAVOR

Since I go to a great deal of trouble to select the best ingredients I can find and to put them together in exciting combinations, the last thing I want to do is muddy their flavors. I am careful in all my desserts to keep sugar to a minimum. Too much sugar will mask the rich, lively flavors of fresh fruit with the result that you taste sweetness instead of that wonderful fruit flavor you started with. (The same goes for nonfruit flavors such as chocolate, nuts, and even vanilla.)

For the same reason I refuse to put anything artificial or second-rate into my desserts. My flavorings are all pure. The colors in every dessert come naturally from the fresh ingredients. The liqueurs are of the highest quality, and so are the cocoa, chocolate, butter, eggs, and cream. Any ingredient with even a slightly off flavor will affect the overall taste of the dessert. That includes the preservatives that are added to ultrapasteurized cream and the additives in imitation vanilla or imitation anything else.

SIMPLICITY

Once the concept is clear and the ingredients are gathered, all that's left is to let those ingredients, individually and in combination, speak for themselves. I don't mean to imply that dessert techniques are not sometimes painstaking or that it's not necessary to pay enormous attention to detail. I've spent most of my life developing the skills necessary for producing fine pastries. What I mean is that it is very important to let the ingredients in a dessert determine how it should look. The hardest thing for many beginning pastry cooks is to let go of the idea that in order to be impressive a dessert must be "fancy," that regardless of what's inside, it needs some sort of artistic design on the outside to make it eye-catching and exciting. Nothing could be further from the truth. The most impressive desserts are the simplest. Clean lines and understated decorations are always more striking than elaborate embellishments.

My favorite way to decorate a cake is to cover it with plain, unsweetened whipped cream or a simple, incredibly flavorful butter cream and top that with fresh berries or slices of fruit. I like to add an interesting texture to the sides with chopped, toasted nuts or curls of grated chocolate. My tarts are finished with just a light glaze to make them shine. I serve my fruit ices in a simple cookie wafer cup or scooped into a dessert dish and garnished with a sprig of fresh mint. When I'm feeling really extravagant, I might put a ring of chocolate truffles atop a chocolate cream pie or decorate an individual pastry with a delicate chocolate butterfly.

Whatever I use on the outside of a dessert is as fresh and natural — and as delicious — as the ingredients inside. Nothing is ever just for show. Nothing is sugary or made of paper or otherwise inedible. A dessert is not a work of art to be admired from a distance; it is an invitation to pleasure, the promise of a delightful eating experience.

PROMISES OF PLEASURE

A well-made dessert communicates with those who are going to eat it long before they take the first bite. Its first appeal is visual. What appears on the outside is a promise of what awaits within. The pastry cook should always be aware of this promise. Once you have created anticipation, you either fulfill that anticipation or you disappoint.

A cake decorated with berries promises berries inside. A cake topped with clouds of whipped cream promises lightness. Chopped nuts suggest a delightful crunchiness, and a tart's border of golden crust sets up the expectation of a dry, crisp, buttery contrast to the fruit it holds. If you decorate a chocolate cake with fresh cherries but there are no cherries inside, people will be disappointed, even if it's a very fine chocolate cake. But if there is a hidden treasure of succulent cherries between the layers, their effect is heightened because the pleasure began with the first sight of cherries and the anticipation of eating them.

Sometimes the pleasures of a particular dessert announce themselves not through appearance but through smell. A cake that has been saturated with rum or crème de cassis will create its own excitement. That excitement will hold through the last bite if the spirits used are of the highest quality and have been applied generously.

The presentation of any dessert is part of the pleasure it gives. In The Stanford Court restaurants the desserts are displayed near the entrance so that people can see them as they are led to their tables. At home you can display desserts on a sideboard. Even if a dessert needs to be refrigerated until shortly before serving, bring it to the table whole, set on a simple but elegant plate, and let your guests enjoy the way it looks. Arrange your cookies or pastries attractively on trays. Serve your poached fruits in a clear glass bowl that shows off their rich colors.

Part of the pleasure of a great dessert, after all, is the admiration and appreciation that comes to the cook.

2
The Most
Important
Dessert Ingredients

FRESH FRUIT

The better the fruit you put into your desserts, the better the desserts will look and taste. Baking will not improve the flavor of fruit that is overripe or that was picked prematurely. Always buy the best seasonal fruits you can find, treat them like the fragile objects they are, and use them when they are at the peak of ripeness.

Fruits that need to continue ripening after you buy them, such as pears and mangoes, should be kept at room temperature until fully ripe and then refrigerated to keep them from spoiling, though ideally they should be used once they reach their peak. Bananas are an exception and should always be kept at room temperature.

The following guidelines will help you to select the best of each season's crop.

Apples: The best apples for your desserts are whatever tart varieties are grown locally. Sweet apples are fine for eating but not good for baking. My favorite varieties are Pippin, Winesap, McIntosh, and Ruby Blush Gravenstein. When buying apples, reject any that are obviously underripe (green and hard) or obviously old. The underripe ones don't have enough flavor; the old ones tend to be mealy. Choose apples that look fresh, have good color for their variety, are firm and crisp, and have smooth, unbruised skin.

Apricots: The best apricots are a uniform, rich, deep orange color, with a dark orange blush. Avoid any that are green or yellowish. Look for plump apricots that smell ripe and fragrant and that feel firm yet tender. If they are soft, dull-looking, or dry, they are probably old.

Bananas: You seldom see ripe bananas, golden yellow and lightly firm, in the market. They bruise too easily and overripen too fast. The bananas you are most likely to see, and those that are best to buy, are mostly yellow with green tips. Bring them home and let them ripen for a few days at room temperature.

Blackberries, Blueberries, Boysenberries: See Raspberries.

Cantaloupes: Select a cantaloupe with thick, coarse netting over beige, not green, skin. The blossom end should yield slightly when pressed. Check the stem end for a smooth scar, which shows that the melon was allowed to mature (and sweeten) before it was picked. And by all means, smell it. A sweet, ripe cantaloupe will have a sweet, ripe aroma.

Cherries: I use Montmorencies when I can get them, and otherwise Bings. Montmorencies have bright red skins and are pleasantly tart. Choose Montmorencies that are plump and fresh-looking, with glossy skins. Look for Bings that are dark maroon, plump, and glossy. All the cherries you buy should be firm and have fresh, flexible stems. Don't buy cherries that have turned brown.

Coconuts: The coconut is the seed of the coconut palm and therefore is technically a fruit (more specifically a drupe), not a nut. When you buy a coconut, it is virtually impossible to tell if it is good or has begun to go rancid. The best way to find a fresh one is to shake it. You should hear its milk sloshing around inside. Don't buy any coconut that has no milk or that has wet or moldy eyes. Even after taking these precautions, you may occasionally find that you have a rancid coconut. Always smell the coconut juice when you open the coconut. If it smells rancid, throw the coconut away.

Cranberries: Since cranberries come in sealed packages, you can't pick and choose except to accept or reject an entire package. Look for berries that are plump, glossy, firm, and brightly colored. Don't buy them if they're soft or have begun to turn brown or moldy. If you find a particularly fresh-looking batch at a good price, buy several bags and freeze them. The buying season is short, but cranberries keep for months frozen. Do *not* defrost before using.

Figs: There are a great many varieties of figs but only a few that show up regularly in markets. The one most commonly available in northern California is the Black Mission, generally considered the best all-purpose fig. When ripe it is very dark, almost black. Figs need to be fully ripe to have good flavor. Choose those that are plump, soft, and evenly colored. If they are giving off liquid or if they smell fermented, they are overripe and will taste sour. Since fresh figs are fragile and don't ship well, they may be hard to find.

Grapefruits: Pink grapefruits are sweeter than white and therefore best for desserts. My first choice is Star Ruby grapefruit from the Bahamas. If you see some, try them; they're a special treat. Pick up a grapefruit before you buy it. It should feel firm and heavy for its size. Look for brightly colored thin skin that looks fresh. Well-rounded grapefruits are usually better than those that are pointed at one end.

Honeydews: Honeydews should be creamy white or pale yellow rather than green or greenish white, and should give slightly at both ends when pressed. The best way to select for sweetness is to feel the skin. If it is tacky rather than smooth, the melon will be ripe and sweet (the sugar rises to the skin as the melon ripens). As a final test, smell it—it should smell about the way you hope it will taste.

Lemons and Limes: Look for lemons and limes that feel firm and heavy for their size. Those that are plump and have bright, smooth, thin skins will be the juiciest and most flavorful. Avoid lemons with green on their skins; they tend to be overly acidic.

A note on zest: The zest of a citrus fruit is the colorful thin outer skin. It contains a great deal of citrus oil and a pleasant concentration of citrus flavor. When a recipe calls for grated zest, be sure you take only the zest and not the bitter white pith that lies directly beneath it. You can remove zest from the fruit with a grater or a hand-held zester. If the pieces are large, finely chop them with a knife or cleaver.

Mangoes: It is best to buy mangoes when they are still firm but give slightly when pressed. Let them soften at room temperature. Look for smooth skin that is mostly red and yellow. A little green is all right, but avoid any that are all green. Mangoes with shriveled skin, dark spots, or a fermented smell are overripe.

Nectarines: Ripe nectarines are firm and give slightly when pressed; they are a little softer at the stem end. Look for those that are plump, with smooth, yellow-orange skin and a red blush. Avoid any that are hard or green or dull. Nectarines that are a bit too firm to eat will get softer if left out at room temperature, but they will never get any sweeter than they were when picked.

Oranges: Before you buy an orange, hold it in your hand. It should feel firm and be heavy for its size. It should have smooth skin (thin is better than thick) and look fresh. You can't judge an orange by its color because some are dyed orange; they are required by law to carry a label that says color has been added. I most often use Valencia, an excellent all-purpose orange.

Papayas: Try to find medium-size papayas that have solid or speckled yellow, smooth, unbruised skin. They should be firm but give slightly when pressed and should give off a pleasant, fruity aroma. Dark spots or wetness means the fruit is overripe.

Peaches: Peaches should be bright yellow with a red blush. Look especially at the indentation around the stem (or where the stem used to be). If the skin there is green, the peach was picked before it ripened, and it will never get sweet. Choose peaches that are relatively firm but give slightly when pressed. They should smell ripe and sweet. Never buy peaches that are green, hard, or dry-looking.

Pears: I prefer Anjous and Bartletts for pastry making. Pears will ripen at room temperature. Since they tend to bruise very easily, especially in the store, your best bet is to buy them a few days before they are fully ripe and let them ripen at home. Buy pears that are firm, with just a little give. Avoid any that are very green or are bruised. Even when underripe, pears should smell like pears.

Pineapples: Once a pineapple has been picked, it will not ripen any further, which means it will never get any sweeter. So, obviously, the sweetest pineapples are those that were allowed to ripen in the field; they are usually labeled "field-ripened." Although they tend to be very expensive, they do taste significantly better than ordinary pineapples. Field-ripened or otherwise, look for pineapples that are round rather than oblong and that are more golden brown than green. They should feel firm but give slightly when squeezed. A pineapple that feels soft or smells fermented has started to spoil. Pineapples should look fresh and have a pleasant, fresh pineapple smell. Fresh-looking, deep-green leaves are a sign of freshness but, despite a common belief, the ease with which you can pull center leaves from a pineapple doesn't tell you anything about the sweetness or ripeness of the fruit. See illustrations for peeling a pineapple on pages 32–33.

Plums: The best plums for baking are Laroda, Friar, and Casselman. I have also used Santa Rosa plums because I like their tartness, but they give off an excessive amount of juice when cooked. Whatever variety you prefer, look for plums that are plump and have good color. They should feel tender yet firm and should be a little soft at the ends, a sign of maturity. Plums do not ripen after picking.

Quinces: A delicious autumn fruit, the quince is almost always cooked before eating. Ripe quinces look like big, hard, yellow or yellowish-green apples. Avoid any with dry-looking stems, bruises, or brown spots.

To peel a pineapple: Cut off the top and bottom. Stand the pineapple upright and, using a sharp knife, cut away a strip of skin about 1½ inches wide. Follow the curve of the fruit and cut deep enough to remove the eyes completely. Turn the cut side toward you and cut another strip. Continue until all the skin is removed.

Raspberries: Raspberries are expensive and extremely perishable, so it's important to choose them carefully. They should look plump and fresh and have deep, rich color. Although raspberries almost always come wrapped, you can still smell them for a fresh berry aroma. Check the bottom of the basket to make sure there is no mold or leaking. Raspberries should be firm, juicy, and sweet. The only way to tell for sure is to taste one—if your market will let you.

Rhubarb: Although it is a vegetable, rhubarb is usually cooked as if it were a fruit. The two major types available are field-grown and hothouse. I much prefer the field-grown for its dark red color and full,

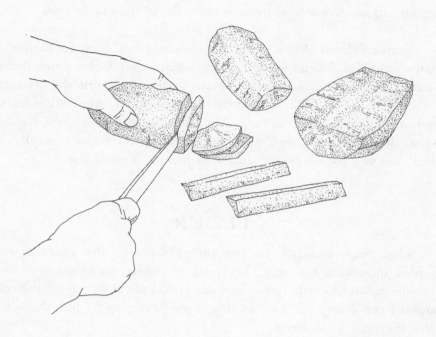

Cut the peeled pineapple into quarters. Before slicing, lay each quarter on one flat side so that it won't slip under the knife. Cut out the core, then slice crosswise. (For choosing a ripe pineapple, see page 31.)

tart flavor. Hothouse rhubarb, pink or light red, has a milder and less interesting taste. Choose rhubarb stalks that are firm, crisp, and deep cherry red. Don't buy any that look wilted or flabby. Fresh-looking leaves are a good indication that the rhubarb is fresh. Always discard the leaves before eating the rhubarb; they contain a heavy concentration of oxalic acid, which is extremely poisonous.

Strawberries: Your grocery store may have its strawberries already packaged in a basket, but that doesn't mean you can't examine them. Look for solid-colored dark red berries with fresh-looking leaves. Pick up the basket and check the bottom; it should be dry and show no signs of mold. Make sure the berries are firm and that none of them, or at least none you can see, have mold. Choose a basket that smells like ripe, sweet strawberries. No aroma usually means very little flavor. Small and medium strawberries tend to have more flavor than large ones.

Watermelons: When selecting a watermelon, look for dull rather than shiny skin. When buying a whole watermelon, look for one that has a rich, fruity fragrance and a yellowish underside, and is slightly soft at the blossom end. Still, it is impossible to know what's inside. Cut watermelons are easier to judge. In addition to aroma, look for firm, moist, deep-red flesh with no white streaks. Cut melons usually cost more, but you have a better chance of picking a good one.

FLOUR

Flours vary greatly in the percentage of protein they contain, which in turn influences the way they perform when combined with other ingredients and baked. Regardless of type, I always prefer unbleached flours. I think they have noticeably more flavor, and I like the natural color they give to desserts.

Pastry Flour: Pastry flour, which is 6 percent protein, is the best of the soft flours. It is difficult to find, however, and for that reason I have not used it in the recipes in this book. Pastry flour is especially good for tart doughs and cookies because it produces the softest crumb of any flour.

Cake Flour: Cake flour, with 8 percent protein, is the best flour for delicate cakes. While it is still somewhat soft, it has enough protein to provide a stable structure and keep a cake from falling.

All-Purpose Flour: All-purpose flour ranges from 11 percent to 13 percent protein. It is perfect for rich cakes because it produces a somewhat coarse and firm crumb, sturdy enough to carry the weight of the other ingredients.

Bread Flour: Bread flour, with 14 percent protein, is the best flour for layered doughs and for breads. Its high protein content allows doughs to stretch and to effectively hold moisture.

Storing Flour: Store flour in an airtight container in a cool, dry place. If you live in a warm, humid area or if you don't use your flour very often, it is wise to store the container in the refrigerator.

Measuring Flour: To measure flour, dip your measuring cup into the flour container and scoop up a rounded measureful. Use a knife to scrape off the flour above the rim of the cup.

Sifting Flour: If you live in a humid climate where flour tends to clump, you should always sift your flour before using it. Otherwise, the need to sift depends on how the flour is to be used. If you are going to incorporate it into a delicate, thin batter, such as for a sponge cake, sift it. If you are going to use it in a rich, creamed batter, there is no need to sift unless there are noticeable clumps. When you do sift flour, sift first and then measure.

CHOCOLATE

Bittersweet or Semisweet: I use bittersweet chocolate most because I like its slightly bitter edge. Semisweet chocolate is a bit sweeter, and some people prefer it. You can substitute semisweet for bittersweet in any of the recipes in this book. The main thing is to find the chocolate that is most suited to your own personal taste. In many parts of the country bittersweet chocolate is hard to find, so semisweet may win by default.

The best way to buy bittersweet or semisweet chocolate is in bulk, so that you can see and perhaps even taste what you are getting. If the only chocolate available is packaged, buy the smallest amount possible of several kinds, take them home, and decide which you like best. Then go back and buy a larger quantity of the one you've chosen.

When evaluating bittersweet or semisweet chocolate, first look at its color; it should be deep, even, and glossy. Don't buy chocolate that has begun to turn white or gray. Break off a piece and listen for a clean snap, which indicates that the chocolate was tempered well. Look at the break; if there are round "oyster shell" cracks, the tempering wasn't done properly. Next, smell the chocolate. It should have a rich, full aroma.

Now you're ready to check for texture and flavor. Eat a piece. It should melt quickly in your mouth and have a smooth finish. High-quality chocolate is never chewy or grainy. Notice the balance between sugar and cocoa. They should combine in a full, round flavor. Don't buy chocolate that tastes either acidic or overly sweet. There should be a lingering aftertaste of chocolate, not sugar. If chocolate tastes smoky, don't buy it. It's probably from the rain forests of South America, where smokers are used to keep the picked beans dry. Cocoa beans pick up odors very quickly. (For that reason you should always store chocolate wrapped in paper or foil, but not in plastic wrap. The fats in the chocolate will pick up the taste of plastic.)

For the best flavor, bittersweet or semisweet chocolate should be aged three months. The package will not tell you if the chocolate's been aged, so your best guarantee is to find a manufacturer whose product is consistently of high quality and stick to that brand. It's wise to avoid buying chocolate around holidays. Chances are it will not be aged because it's been rushed to market to fill the large demand.

Unsweetened: Unsweetened chocolate comes already packaged. Find a brand that is consistently good and stick to it. If the quality of the unsweetened chocolate you're using now isn't consistent, change brands.

Cocoa: Any powdered cocoa you like the taste of is fine. Dutch processed cocoa is not as acidic as ordinary cocoa because of added alkali, but it's simply a matter of taste.

White Chocolate (also called Cocoa Butter Covering): For good flavor it's important to use high-quality white chocolate made with real cocoa butter, not vegetable fats, and real vanilla. Read the labels. Avoid any white chocolate that has artificial flavoring in it. The best white chocolates are imported from Europe. Buy your white chocolate in a store that sells a lot of it. That way it is most likely to be fresh. Check to see that it is a creamy ivory color and that it smells fresh; if it's yellow or has a slightly rancid odor, it's probably old.

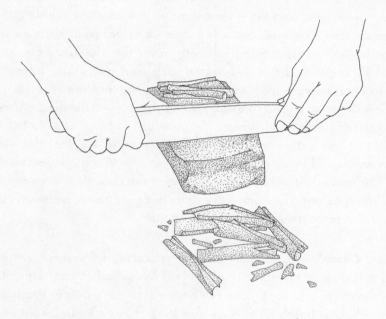

Raking chocolate produces long, delicate, tubelike curls. It requires a large block of chocolate. Stand with your apron and hip against the table to steady the chocolate. Hold the knife with two hands, setting the blade at a right angle to the surface of the chocolate block. Starting at the far end, press down and draw the blade toward you. Although it is not necessary, you will find raking easier if you let the chocolate stand in a warm place for one day before you begin.

Storing Chocolate: Store chocolate in a cool (65° to 70° F), dark, dry place with good air circulation (not in the refrigerator). Properly stored chocolate will keep for at least a year.

Tempering Chocolate: Although chocolate is tempered in the manufacturing process, you must temper it again before using it as a coating or glaze. Tempering is the only way to keep it from becoming grainy and to get a good shine and fine texture. Recommended temperatures for tempering vary from manufacturer to manufacturer. The following procedure should give good results. If you want the precise tempering temperatures for the chocolate you are using, write to the manufacturer.

Use a double boiler that fits together snugly. If even a small amount of water or steam gets into your chocolate, it can ruin the whole batch. Chop or grate the chocolate. Set a few ounces aside. Melt the rest over boiled (not boiling) water. Stir frequently until the chocolate comes to about 100° F. Replace the boiled water with cool water and allow the chocolate to cool, stirring frequently. Gradually stir in the chocolate you set aside; it will act as a seed to establish the right crystallization pattern. Continue stirring until the chocolate drops to 85° to 86° F (83° to 84° for milk chocolate) and is the consistency of thick frosting. Replace the water with warm water and bring the chocolate up to a working temperature of 88° to 89° (86° to 87° for milk chocolate). Keep the chocolate between 83° and 90° all the time you are working with it. If it goes above or below, you should start the tempering process over again.

Grating Chocolate: Chocolate should be warm and soft for grating; otherwise, it will splinter rather than peel off in curls. Let your chocolate stand in a warm (not sunny) place for one or two days before grating it. I grate a good-sized batch all at once and keep it covered in a cool place so that I always have some ready to use.

Chocolate Equivalents: 1 ounce of chocolate equals 2 tablespoons ⅛ cup) melted or ¼ cup grated.

DAIRY PRODUCTS

Butter: Use only unsalted, grade AA butter for pastry making; it has a cleaner flavor than salted butter. Buy your butter from a store where there is good turnover and where the butter is not kept frozen. The fresher the butter, the better. Notice the quality of the butter you buy, and when you find a brand that is consistently excellent, stick with it. Besides tasting good, it will break clean when it's cold and will be smooth, not grainy, and free of lumps. Because there is no salt to act as a preservative, unsalted butter is extremely perishable. If you suspect the butter in your store isn't fresh, smell it. Even through the wrapper you will be able to tell if it has gone rancid. If you watch your butter carefully, you will notice that the texture varies with the season. In winter, when the cows are grain-fed, the butter is harder. During the months the cows graze on green grass, taking in a lot of amino acids, it is softer. Both are fine. Always store your butter, wrapped, in the refrigerator; it will keep up to four days. If a recipe calls for soft butter, be sure you let it come to room temperature before using it. Only soft butter will whip to its maximum potential. On the other hand, it's important to use cold butter in many dough recipes to avoid activating the gluten in the flour. Cold butter helps to keep the gluten relaxed and keeps the dough from coming together too quickly. The recipes in this book always indicate whether the butter should be cold or soft.

Cream: Cream should contain only cream. Period. Read the ingredients listed on the carton. Pure heavy cream (sometimes labeled heavy whipping cream) has a fresh, sweet flavor. It is not ultrapasteurized and does not have added preservatives, which give cream a bitter edge. Fresh, pure cream needs no sweetening or flavoring. To use it as a topping, simply whip it to soft peaks and enjoy it. (Whip it in a cold bowl or at least one you have cooled by running it under cold water.) If all you can get is processed cream, you'll need to add sugar to round off the taste of the preservatives. For every cup you whip, add 1 teaspoon of sugar. Cream, especially cream without preservatives, will turn sour if kept too long or stored improperly. Keep it refrigerated until you are ready to use it, and be sure to use it before the pull date printed on the carton.

Eggs: All the recipes in this book should be made with large, grade AA eggs. The color of the eggshell has no connection with the quality of the egg. In some parts of the country white eggs are preferred; in other parts brown eggs are. The eggs inside are exactly the same. Buy your eggs in a store that has good turnover and keeps its eggs refrigerated. Eggs kept at room temperature can deteriorate more in one day than they would in a week under refrigeration. Open the carton and make sure the eggs you buy are clean, uncracked, and odor-free. At home you can store them up to two weeks in the refrigerator. Keep them in their carton to cut down on loss of moisture. And keep them away from foods with strong odors, or you may end up with eggs that taste like onions or cabbage. You can store leftover yolks submerged in water in a covered container in the refrigerator for two or three days. Store leftover whites in a tightly covered jar in the refrigerator for up to a week or in the freezer for up to six weeks.

Milk: Don't substitute low-fat or nonfat milk for whole milk in a dessert recipe. The lack of butter fat will affect the body of whatever you're making. Your dessert will probably come out watery and may taste bland.

SUGAR

Sugar contributes to both the structure and texture of baked goods. It tenderizes during the baking process and adds color because it browns (caramelizes) when cooked. It serves not only to sweeten but also to subdue and balance assertive flavors, effectively rounding them off. But sugar also can be cloying to the palate. Too much will quickly dominate a dessert, overpowering and masking the flavor of other ingredients.

Brown Sugar: I use light brown sugar when I want a subtle brown sugar taste, and dark brown when I want the flavor to be more assertive. The distinctive color, texture, and flavor of brown sugar come from added molasses; the sugar is not raw or unprocessed as some people assume. When measuring brown sugar, pack it firmly into the measuring cup.

Powdered Sugar (also called Confectioners Sugar): I use powdered sugar whenever I want a finer, smoother texture than I can get with granulated sugar. About 3 percent cornstarch has been added to the sugar to make it smooth. Powdered sugar tends to clump, so always sift it before using it, and measure after sifting.

Refined (Granulated) Sugar: I use extra-fine (or superfine) sugar because it dissolves much more quickly than regular refined sugar. In some places it's hard to find. If your market doesn't carry it, you might try looking in a liquor store. They sell it for mixing drinks (it's also called bar sugar). It comes in 1-pound boxes. You can, of course, use regular granulated sugar in any of the recipes in this book.

Caramel: Caramel is refined sugar that has been cooked until it melts, turns brown, and develops a rich, pleasantly bitter taste. Sometimes water is added to the sugar during the cooking process; I usually cook the sugar alone. Few people think of using caramel as a sweetener, but carefully used it adds a wonderfully rich color and an assertive, balanced, bittersweet flavor to desserts.

Maple Syrup: As a true New Englander I have a special fondness for maple syrup. When I was young, my family had a sugar house that produced maple syrup for the inns they owned in New Hampshire. I have vivid memories of climbing through the deep snow to get to our row of maple trees to collect the buckets of sap. And I have very fond memories of sitting in the sugar house afterward while that sap was boiled down and filtered into syrup. I remember being enveloped by the warm steam and the wonderful smell. The best maple syrup is produced in a season when there is a string of cold nights and warm, sunny days. The first run of sap is light amber in color and delicately flavored. That is grade A maple syrup. Much of the maple syrup sold in supermarkets is made of poorer grades of sap; it is darker in both color and flavor. When you buy maple syrup, look for the grade on the label. The best syrup is expensive, but the delicious, clean flavor is well worth it.

Molasses: Molasses should be used sparingly. It has a very concentrated, assertive flavor and can easily dominate or totally overwhelm the other ingredients in a dessert. When used carefully and paired with appropriate ingredients, it adds an appealing heartiness and depth of flavor. Stored in its bottle in a cupboard it will keep indefinitely.

OTHER BASIC INGREDIENTS

Baking Powder: Baking powder is the leavener most often used in American baking. When mixed with a liquid and heated it produces carbon dioxide gas, which makes the batter rise. I've found only one commercial brand of baking powder that is aluminum-free, and that is Rumford. Read the labels, and if at all possible, buy a brand that does not have aluminum in it.

Baking Soda: Baking soda also produces carbon dioxide gas and leavens baked goods. It's important to use it with an acid such as buttermilk or cream of tartar to balance the alkaline taste of the soda.

Cream of Tartar: Cream of tartar is a residue left over from the wine-making process. It is used in conjunction with baking soda to leaven baked goods. A pinch added to beaten egg whites makes them more stable.

Salt: Like many professional cooks in San Francisco, I first learned the difference between table salt and kosher salt from my good friend Barbara Tropp, who delights in presenting salt tastings for friends and fellow cooks. Now I use kosher salt exclusively. It is much more palatable than table salt, lighter on the tongue, and not as salty. It also does not have the chemicals that are added to table salt during processing that give it an assertive off-flavor. All of the recipes in this book are based on kosher salt. If you haven't tasted table and kosher salt side by side, I suggest that you do so. I predict that you, too, will want to bake and cook with kosher salt. If you decide to make your desserts with table salt, use only half as much salt as is called for in each recipe.

Vanilla: The recipes in this book use two forms of vanilla, extract and beans. Look for a pure, high-quality extract with a strong, smooth flavor. Good vanilla extract is aged six months, during which time the sugar that has been added caramelizes, and the vanilla and caramelized sugar round out each other's flavors. When you buy vanilla beans, look for beans that are plump, not dry, and that give off a wonderful aroma. The best vanilla beans are cured by a natural sun-drying process that intensifies their rich flavor. Keep your vanilla beans at room temperature in a tightly closed container, alone or buried in sugar. (If you store the beans in sugar, you will always have a supply of fragrant vanilla sugar.)

3
The Efficient
Pastry Kitchen

Equipment

Tips for Using This Book

Equipment

Most of the equipment you need to make fine desserts is probably already in your kitchen. When you decide to replace some things or fill in gaps in your collection, I strongly recommend that you buy the best-made, sturdiest equipment you can find. And remember that price alone may not be the best indicator of quality. If an expensive tool feels flimsy, don't buy it. If an inexpensive one seems solid and durable, it's your best bet. Always try out a hand-held tool to make sure it feels comfortable in your hand. If it doesn't, you won't be happy with it.

I buy stainless steel whenever possible. It doesn't give off metallic odors or pick up food odors, and it will not react chemically with acidic foods that can cause off-flavors and staining. I also like wood and wood-handled tools, and I am careful to keep them in peak condition. Never leave wood or wood-handled tools in water. The wood will absorb the water; then, as it dries out, it will warp or crack. Always keep wooden handles well oiled.

Because I work in a professional kitchen, I tend to like professional equipment. You will probably find high-quality home cooking equipment in your local kitchenware and specialty food shops. If you have trouble finding what you're looking for, see if there is a restaurant supply house nearby that sells to the public. Their equipment is more often utilitarian than beautiful, but it is dependably well constructed and durable.

Following is a list of recommended equipment for an efficient home pastry kitchen:

BAKING PANS

Baking Dish (2½-quart, shallow, earthenware or Pyrex): For baking cobblers and crisps. If you plan to serve your cobblers and crisps onto dessert plates in the kitchen, any baking dish will do. If you intend to put the whole cobbler or crisp on the table and dish it out there, you should buy an attractive baking dish that you'll feel comfortable placing before your guests.

Bread Pans (two pans approximately 9 x 5 inches, about 2¾ inches deep): Use whatever kind of bread pans you like best, but if they are not made of a nonstick material, be sure to keep them seasoned (see below). For baking Brioche I use pans with flat covers that slide into place, but any bread pan will work. If you don't use a covered pan, simply trim the bread flat before slicing it for bread pudding.

To season bread pans (or any other new pans): Wash the new pans with mild detergent and dry them thoroughly. Rub the insides with a thin layer of vegetable oil. Set in a 350° oven for 30 minutes. Seasoning will keep the pans from rusting and keep food from sticking to them. After using seasoned pans, wipe them clean with a dry cloth or towel. Do not wash them unless absolutely necessary. If food begins sticking to a pan, it's time to season it again.

Cake Pan (9-inch round, 2 inches deep): I recommend a heavy aluminum cake pan. Aluminum is easier to care for than tin and works just as well. Make sure you get a pan with straight sides. If you bake a cake in a pan with sloping sides, you'll have to trim its edges straight before you can ice it. It's easier to have a straight-sided pan. Unless you plan to bake several cakes at once, one pan is all you need.

Cookie Sheets (two): Choose heavy aluminum cookie sheets with good strong sides. Thin cookie sheets warp in the oven. Two will be enough if you make cookies or pastries only occasionally. The busy baker should have four. It is sometimes necessary to stack two pans together to keep the bottoms of cookies or pastries from burning before the rest is fully baked; with four sheets you can still bake two sheetsful at a time. I also use cookie sheets in place of jelly roll pans for baking jelly roll sponges.

Custard Cups: Bake your crème caramel in porcelain or Pyrex custard cups, set in a water bath. You should have at least eight 5-ounce cups. Metal custard cups are fine, too. I tend not to recommend them simply because they are hard to find.

Pie Pans (two 9-inch, two 10-inch): My method of blind baking or prebaking a pie shell requires two pans the same size. You line one pan with dough, then place the second pan on top, invert the two, and bake the shell upside down. This gives you a light, crisp crust. I prefer aluminum pie pans because they are lighter, thinner, and easier to handle than Pyrex.

Ramekins: If you want to make Crème Brulée, you'll need at least ten 4- or 5-ounce porcelain ramekins. The shape doesn't matter—some are round, others oval. As in the case of the soufflé dish, I prefer the European ones because they are made from better porcelain.

Soufflé Dish (8-cup): I bake my bread puddings in a soufflé dish. I recommend the European ones, although they are more expensive, because they're made out of better porcelain. I've found that the rims of less expensive soufflé dishes chip very easily.

Springform Pan (10-inch): When you buy a springform pan, be sure you get one that opens easily, locks securely, and has a bottom that fits snugly in place. Loose bottoms have been known to fall out between oven and cooling rack, with disastrous results.

Tart Pan (10-inch): The best tart pan is tin-lined with a strong ring and a removable bottom. Avoid washing your tart pan unless absolutely necessary. Simply wipe it clean with a dry cloth or towel. The pan will stay seasoned, and your tart shells won't stick. Always remove a tart to a serving dish or cardboard circle before slicing. If you cut on the pan bottom, you'll cut right through the tin lining.

Tartlet Molds: To make individual tartlets and pastries (such as Chocolate Cups and Rum Corks) you'll need small (2⅜ inches diameter, ½ inch deep), smooth-sided (not fluted) tartlet molds. Since most of the pastry recipes in this book make twenty-four to thirty pieces, you should have thirty molds.

Water Bath Pan: Some desserts, such as cheesecake and custards, have to be baked in a water bath, which means that you need a pan large enough to contain them. A lasagne pan or roasting pan works fine.

TOOLS

Bowl Scraper: A flexible plastic scraper allows you to empty mixing bowls thoroughly. It may be either round or square and has no handle. Be sure you get heavy rather than thin plastic; the thin plastic tends to crack.

Cherry Pitter: For pushing the pits out of cherries without mutilating the fruit, you need a cherry pitter. As with other tools, make sure you get one that fits very comfortably in your hand. The best cherry pitters are the ones that resemble paper punches. You squeeze them rather than push a plunger. Since you'll probably be pitting many cherries at once, avoid the pitters that fit over your fingers; after a while they hurt. And because they keep your fingers closer to the cherries, they tend to get more juice on your hands. Choose a punch-type pitter with a hammer that glides smoothly and doesn't wobble. Wobbling will tear up the fruit.

Chinese Knife (Cleaver): A Chinese knife with a stainless steel blade is a perfect tool for chopping nuts, cutting cookie doughs, and cutting frozen napoleons and sometimes even cakes. Because it has a thin, square blade, it is easy to control and very accurate. Choose any cleaver that feels comfortable in your hand, as long as it has a thin blade (you'll probably want a size 2 or 3).

Cutting Pin: Use about an 18-inch length of wooden dowel or unpainted broom handle to trim the excess dough from tart shells before baking. The edge of a tart pan is very sharp. If you roll a rolling pin around the edge to trim doughs, the pan will ruin the buffed surface and may even make cuts in the surface of the pin, which will cause doughs to stick to it.

Dough Scraper (also called Bench Scraper): A good dough scraper is invaluable in a pastry kitchen. You'll use it for cutting and lifting doughs and for working fondant, as well as for scraping your work surface clean. The wide, thin blade lets you lift dough and move it, keeping it close to the table so it doesn't stretch very much. When you make fondant, you'll use your dough scraper to work the fondant against a marble slab. Choose a dough scraper with a strong stainless steel blade that doesn't bend easily. Make sure the blade is tightly anchored in its handle—if it's loose it's going to weaken and become wobbly. It's very important to try out a scraper before you buy it to make sure it fits comfortably in your hand. When scraping wooden work surfaces clean, be careful not to cut the wood with the blade.

Food Thermometer: For tempering chocolate or making fondant you need a food thermometer. I use a Cuisinart instant-reading thermometer, which has a range of 40° to 260° F. Some other brands of instant-reading thermometers go only to 220° F, which isn't high enough. I prefer an instant-reading thermometer because of its convenient size and because you don't have to leave it in the saucepan while your liquid cooks. You dip it in and get a reading at once. The plastic holder the thermometer comes in has a pocket clip, like those on fountain pens, that doubles as a holder. You slip the thermometer through the loop in the clip and hold the cool plastic while the thermometer dangles into the pan. However, if you already have an accurate candy thermometer, there's no need to replace it.

Icing Spatulas: You'll need two icing spatulas, one with a short (4- to 6-inch) blade for icing fine pastries and one with a long (12-inch) blade for icing cakes. Having a blade at least as long as the cake is wide allows you to spread icing in one long stroke across the top of the cake and thus achieve a smoother finish. Make sure the blades fit tightly in their handles and that the handles are comfortable in your hand. The blades should be rather stiff.

Knives: For making desserts you need three knives—a French knife for general chopping and cutting (you can use a Chinese cleaver if you prefer), a paring knife for cutting up fruit, and a thin-bladed slicer for slicing cakes into layers and slicing serving portions of finished pastries and cakes. Your slicer should have a blade at least 10 inches long to enable you to slice with long, clean movements and get smooth cuts. Some people prefer to slice with a serrated bread knife because they feel more comfortable with a sawing movement than a smooth slicing movement. But bread knives tend to have thicker blades than slicers, so when you cut a cake or pastry they make a wider and messier cut. You'll notice when you use a slicer that the blade doesn't accumulate as much cake on it as a bread knife. When you use a slicer, don't saw; draw the full blade smoothly through whatever you're slicing. Once you get used to using it, I think you'll prefer it and find it extremely versatile. It's important to keep all your knives clean and the handles oiled. For safety, use only very sharp knives. A sharp knife cuts easily while a dull knife has to be pushed. The more force you use, the more tendency there is for the knife to slip.

Large Metal Colander or Strainer: A large metal colander or strainer will protect you from splashes when you pour liquids through it into hot caramel. Stainless steel is best. Make sure the colander or strainer has strong handles and small rather than large holes.

Measuring Cups: Stainless steel measuring cups are best for measuring dry ingredients. They're stronger and last longer than plastic, and they don't dent like other metal cups. You'll need one four-piece set (including 1 cup, ½ cup, ⅓ cup, and ¼ cup). A 2-cup Pyrex measuring cup with a pouring spout is best for measuring liquids. Being able to see through it is important for accuracy, and 2 cups is a good all-purpose size.

Measuring Spoons: I recommend a five-spoon metal set including 1 tablespoon, ½ tablespoon (a helpful innovation), 1 teaspoon, ½ teaspoon, and ¼ teaspoon. I was always losing my measuring spoons, so I finally put them on a key ring.

Melon Baller: A melon baller is very useful for removing the cores from halved or quartered apples and pears. It's easier to work with than a knife or a corer, and it minimizes waste. A melon baller with two cutters of different size is most versatile. Make sure the cutter bowls are solidly connected to the handle and that the cutting edges are sharp.

Metal Grater: The best grater is one that's versatile. I recommend a four-sided stainless steel box grater that includes a fine grater; a large, round-hole grater; and a horizontal-hole zester. Choose one that is sturdy and has a good stance, that is, one that is not wobbly. Rub your hands carefully against the cutters, to check that they're sharp.

Metal Spoons: You should have two large, long-handled metal spoons for stirring while cooking. Get one with a solid bowl and one that has holes or is slotted. The solid one is handy for spooning out pastry creams and butter creams; the perforated one is good for lifting fruit out of its cooking liquid. The spoons can be all-metal or have wooden or plastic handles. Just make sure they don't have any sharp edges and that they feel comfortable in your hand. Long handles are important because they keep your hands away from the heat.

Pastry Bag and Tips: You should have a sturdy cloth pastry bag that feels comfortable in your hand. For most people that means a large size. Buy your tips individually rather than buying a set. Those sold as sets are usually meant for home cake decorating and are smaller than the professional tips called for in the recipes in this book. There is no need to have a full range of sizes; buy the tips for the recipes you plan to make. Always rinse your pastry bag immediately after using it and, if possible, hang it up to dry.

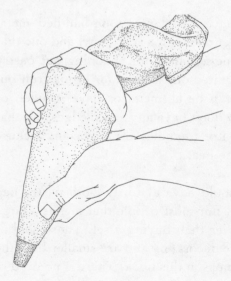

To use a pastry bag:

(1) Insert the desired tip.

(2) Twist the bag just above the tip and tuck the twisted cloth into the tip; this will keep the cream from leaking out while you're filling the bag.

(3) Fold over the top of the bag about 3 inches to form a cuff.

(4) Hold the bag with one hand under the cuff and fill it no more than two-thirds full.

(5) Twist the top of the bag tightly closed.

(6) Hold the bag firmly with one hand just above the filling. The other hand will guide the tip.

(7) Release the twisted cloth from the tip.

(8) Position the bag where you want to begin piping. Squeezing only with the upper hand, gently force the filling out through the tip.

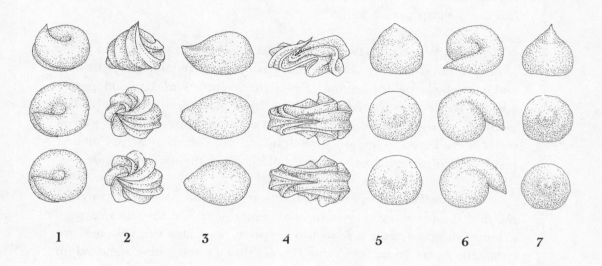

Piped shapes: 1. pointed dome 2. rosette 3. tear drop 4. shell 5. mound 6. apostrophe 7. candy kiss

Pastry Brushes: Your pastry kitchen should have three brushes — one for brushing flour off doughs, one for glazing, and one for egg washes. Before you buy any pastry brush, brush it against your hand. It should feel very soft. If it scratches your hand at all or if it feels the least bit rough, do not buy it. It will tear your dough. A wide (2- or 2½-inch) brush is good for brushing flour off doughs and tables. If you plan to make a lot of puff pastry or other big doughs (Danish or croissants), you would do better to get a large soft-bristled brush the size of a dustpan brush. It doesn't matter what it's made of or how much it costs as long as it's very soft. Small pastry brushes, about 1 inch wide, are fine for glaze and egg wash. Don't use the same brush for brushing flour and for glaze. A glazing brush will get sugar stuck to its bristles and soon be too stiff and inflexible for brushing flour off doughs.

Pastry Cutter (1-inch, round): Look for a pastry cutter that is soldered, not spot welded. Soldered cutters are stronger and last longer. If you can't find a cutter or can't get one without buying a whole set, you can use a sharp paring knife.

Pastry Wheel: A pastry wheel is the best tool for cutting thin pieces of dough for latticework, cutting puff pastry, and trimming deep-dish pie and tart shells before baking. Small pizza cutters make good pastry wheels. Make sure the wheel fits snugly in place and rolls freely. If it wobbles, you will find it difficult to cut a straight line. If it doesn't roll freely, it will tend to get stuck or drag and not cut accurately. For best results when using a pastry cutter, hold it tilted slightly to the side.

Propane Torch: An ordinary hardware store propane torch provides the fastest and easiest way of browning meringue and the surest way to achieve an appetizing, golden brown color. It is also the best tool for caramelizing the sugar on Crème Brulée. Buy a torch with a standard tip that concentrates the flame, not a flame spreader. Adjust the flame to medium and hold the torch with the tip of the flame just touching the meringue or sugar you want to brown. Move the flame constantly in small circles until the entire surface is browned.

Rolling Pins: Every pastry cook should have two rolling pins, one a tapered dowel-type French rolling pin and the other a heavy ball bearing type with handles. The French pin is for rolling out pie and tart shells and small pieces of pastry. The thick center of the pin pushes the dough out to the edges quickly. The slender, tapered shape allows you to see what's happening to a small piece of pastry. The heavy ball bearing pin is for rolling out puff pastry and other large pieces of dough. The weight of the pin helps to distribute the dough quickly, without a lot of force. Since you don't have to worry about pushing hard enough, you can concentrate on rolling the dough level. Both French and ball bearing rolling pins should be made of maple; the ball bearing pin should have maple handles and roller. Before buying any pin, rub your hands against its surface; it should be polished smooth. If it's porous or rough, doughs will stick to it. Pick up the ball bearing pin and spin the roller. It should spin freely and smoothly. Always wipe your rolling pin clean with a dry cloth or towel as soon as you're done using it. The fats in the dough will keep it seasoned. Don't immerse a rolling pin in water. If something sticks to it, use your plastic bowl scraper to gently scrape it clean, then wipe it. Never allow dough to dry on it. If you have to wash it, use only a little water and dry it right away. A good maple rolling pin is as good as any pin available. Marble rolling pins work well because they have smooth surfaces and they have weight, but I don't think they're any better than maple.

Rubber Spatula: Use a wide-blade (about 2½ inches) rubber spatula with a strong handle for scraping down bowls during the mixing process. Buy one with a slightly stiff blade; it will soften as you use it. Don't use a rubber spatula to stir hot sauces; it will eventually melt or crack. Use a wooden or metal spoon instead (wood if your pan is aluminum).

Scissors: Keep a pair of sharp, all-purpose scissors in the kitchen. You'll use them for cutting jelly roll sponges, trimming pie shells, making parchment circles, and many other tasks.

Sieve: I like using a fine sieve for sifting flour, and it's certainly a good tool for straining pureed fruit. Make sure it has a strong handle and a strong frame.

Sifter: Every kitchen should have a sifter, but it's especially important if you live in a humid climate where flour tends to clump. If you live in a dry climate, it's not as much of a problem, but you'll still need to sift your flour for delicate cakes. A simple, old-fashioned, hand-crank, fine-mesh sifter is best. Triple-mesh sifters are very hard, sometimes impossible, to clean if anything gets stuck in the middle layer of mesh.

Vegetable Peeler: I prefer a peeler with a stainless steel blade. Make sure the blade is sharp and that the peeler fits comfortably in your hand. Besides peeling fruit, it's great for making chocolate curls.

Whisk: A balloon whisk is primarily for aerating eggs or cream, but if you have an electric mixer, you'll probably use a whisk mainly for stirring sauces. A 12-inch whisk is right for most people. Get one with a lot of heavy, somewhat stiff wires. They're more effective than sparser, more flexible whisks. Either a metal or a wooden handle is fine as long as it feels comfortable and you don't have to fight with it when you're using it. Look for a whisk that is sealed at the base of the wires; the seal helps to prevent bacteria buildup in an otherwise exposed and hard-to-clean area.

Wooden Spoons: It's important to have strong wooden spoons. Use them for stirring sauces, especially if you're using an aluminum pan or are making a sauce that's acidic and could react with a metal spoon to cause discoloration or off-flavors.

Yardstick: A yardstick will help you to cut uniform lengths of cookie dough and to roll tart and pie doughs to the right diameter. You can also use it as a guide for your pastry wheel when cutting large pieces of dough into strips.

Zester: A small hand-held zester allows you to cut long, decorative julienne strands of zest from oranges, grapefruits, lemons, and limes.

APPLIANCES

Blender: A blender will make excellent purees and pastes, but it won't chop evenly. It takes longer than a food processor to do the same job, and it requires more patience because you have to keep scraping it down.

Electric Mixer: If you're going to be making a lot of desserts and you're ready to buy a new mixer, by all means get one with a whisk attachment and either a "pastry knife" or a cake paddle. Use the whisk for beating eggs, creams, and meringues, and the paddle for creaming ingredients, mixing doughs, and other operations where you don't want to add a lot of air to the mixture. The problem with most beater-type mixers is that at high speed they whip too vigorously and incorporate very large, erratic air bubbles into batters and creams. If you have a mixer with just beaters, it's best to use it at medium-high speed when the recipe calls for high and at low speed when the recipe calls for medium, to get finer air bubbles.

Food Processor: The food processor is a wonderful machine for chopping and for making purees and pastes. It's important to buy a good one with durable blades. A high-quality machine is well worth the extra cost; it will work very efficiently and do a thorough job. It won't leave you with an ingredient three-quarters pureed and one-quarter in chunks.

Ice Cream Freezer: As long as a freezer has a stiff blade that works the ice cream against the outside of the bowl, it should do a good job. A flexible blade doesn't really whip enough air into the ice cream or work it smooth enough. Beyond the blade and the capacity you want (I suggest at least a quart), choosing a machine is largely a question of how involved you want to be with the process. If you don't mind dealing with salt and ice, buy an inexpensive machine; it will work just as well as the expensive models that freeze with Freon.

Juicer: An electric juicer is great if you love citrus and make lots of citrus desserts. It saves time and effort and is very efficient at extracting all the juice from the fruit. If you use just small quantities of citrus juice, a simple hand juicer is fine. I like the type that sits over a bowl. Choose a juicer that has sharply defined wedges on its head; if the head is too smooth, it takes too much effort to get the juice out.

KITCHEN EQUIPMENT

Aluminum Foil: Heavyweight aluminum foil is best for a pastry kitchen because it's stiff and holds its shape in a tart shell. You can reuse one piece several times. With lightweight foil you have to use twice as much, and it will not stand up to multiple use. When you line a tart shell, use a piece of foil at least one and one-half times the size of the tart. Fill it with beans or pie weights and bring the edges of the foil toward the center. The foil and beans will lift out easily, even when the shell is only partially baked.

Beans: When I prebake or blind bake a tart shell, I always line it with foil and fill it with beans. I prefer beans to metal or any other pie weights I've seen. Any kind of whole dry beans works well. About 4½ cups (2 pounds) will fill a 10-inch tart shell. Save the beans and use them over and over until they get black. But be aware that the darker your beans get, the faster your tart shells will brown.

Cake Racks: Most desserts should be cooled on cake racks so the air can circulate beneath as well as around them. This prevents moisture from forming on the bottom. (The exception is cookies, which I cool by sliding the parchment they have baked on onto a counter to cool.) When buying cake racks, make sure the wires are relatively close together so that the dessert stays above the rack and doesn't sink between the wires.

Cardboard Circles: When you remove a cake from its pan, set it on a cardboard cake circle. Then you can easily lift it to ice and decorate it, and you can transport it without the awkwardness or weight of a cake plate. Always use a cake circle white side up; the white side is cleaner and brighter looking than the brown side. The size of the circle should match the size of the cake, so you will need a supply of both 9-inch and 10-inch circles. Buy the ones that are stiff and not flexible. A flexible circle will bend under the weight of a moist cake, affecting the shape of the cake and limiting your ability to handle it. Since cake circles have to be very strong, it's not a good idea to try to make your own.

Double Boiler: A good stainless steel or Pyrex double boiler converts direct heat to a less direct, more gentle heat and helps prevent scorching of delicate ingredients. It also provides just the kind and amount of heat you need for melting chocolate. If you don't have a double boiler, you can do very well with a good saucepan and a heavy stainless steel bowl that fits snugly inside it.

Fruit Ripening Bowl: A fruit ripening bowl is a clear plastic, covered bowl with a circle of small air holes at the top. It creates an internal atmosphere in which fruits ripen faster and develop fuller flavor. If you live in an area where there's not a lot of ripe fruit available, a ripening bowl will help immensely. Of course, it will help only those fruits that continue to ripen after being picked. Many fruits, such as peaches and pineapples, will not ripen any further or become any sweeter once they have left the tree. If you can't find a fruit ripening bowl, you can get similar results by leaving unripe fruit at room temperature for a few days in a brown paper bag.

Marble Slab: You need a marble slab only if you're going to do a lot of work with chocolate or fondant. Marble is the perfect working surface for these because it is so smooth. Formica or any other smooth surface, though perhaps not quite as good, can certainly be substituted. Wood is not appropriate because it is too soft and porous.

Oven Thermometer: Most home ovens are inaccurate. A good oven thermometer is the only way to know you have the correct temperature. Even if you are one of the few lucky people with an accurate oven today, there's no guarantee it won't run hot or cold tomorrow. Every home oven should be equipped with an oven thermometer; it's a dependable and inexpensive way to avoid over- or underbaking your desserts.

Paper Baking Cups: These small (1¼-inch diameter) baking cups or candy cups simplify the process of prebaking tartlet shells. You simply set a cup inside each shell, fill it with beans, and bake. It's much easier than trying to bend pieces of foil to the purpose. Each cup can be reused three or four times. You should be able to find them in gift shops or specialty food shops. If not, you can certainly order them through kitchenware mail order catalogs.

Parchment: Parchment paper is far superior to wax paper for kitchen use because it doesn't smoke and cannot give off-flavors to foods. Because it is stiff, you can make cones from it for decorating or writing with chocolate. Because its surface is nonstick, you can use it for lining cake pans. I use it constantly in the kitchen for everything from catching spills to transporting measured ingredients from scale to mixing bowl. Parchment is available in specialty food stores, kitchenware stores, and large, well-stocked grocery stores (near the plastic wrap or foil). If you cannot get parchment, you can line cake pans with wax paper; instead of lining cookie sheets with parchment, you can grease them lightly with butter.

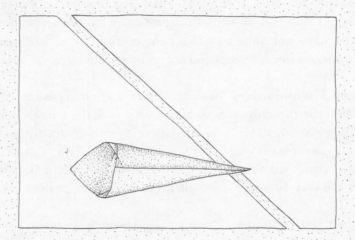

A parchment cone is the perfect implement for writing messages on cakes, making decorative Chocolate Butterflies (page 126), or doing any other job that requires drawing with a thin line of chocolate or frosting. The cone is easy to make, disposable, and inexpensive. Start with a rectangular piece of parchment, about 11 x 17 inches. Lay the sheet on a table with the long side near you. Measure in about 3 inches each from the lower right and upper left corners. Cut the sheet in half along the diagonal line between those two points. Each squared-off triangle will make one cone.

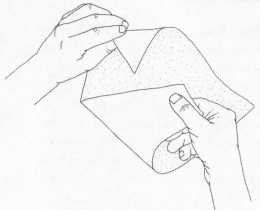

Position one triangle on the table with the long edge straight out in front of you on the left and the squared-off corner toward you. With your right hand, roll the squared-off corner toward the right-hand point of the triangle. With your left hand, bring the upper left point toward you until the paper begins to form a cone shape.

With the fingers of your right hand inside the cone for support, wrap the free corner around and around. When the cone is fully formed, tug the corner in your left hand toward the open top of the cone a few times to tighten the pointed tip. Test the tip by tapping it against your hand; it should feel sharp.

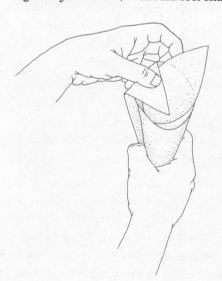

Holding the cone firmly to keep it from loosening, fold the outside corner in to secure the structure. Fill the cone halfway with melted chocolate or icing, and close the open top with a double fold. With scissors, cut off the tip of the cone high enough to give you the size opening you want for writing. Grasp the top of the cone with one hand, squeezing the icing out through the hole in a steady stream. Use the other hand to guide the writing tip.

Plastic Wrap: Everyone knows that plastic wrap keeps foods from drying out or picking up odors; many cooks don't realize that it also sometimes gives off its own unpleasant odor. I never wrap chocolate in plastic wrap for that reason. If something you need to store is particularly susceptible to odors, wrap it in parchment first and then in foil. In general, the plastic wraps available in supermarkets are not very strong, and they don't stick all that well. If there is a restaurant supply house in your area that sells to the public, buy a box of professional-quality plastic wrap, which is far superior. One box may last you a year and it will prove to be cheaper in the long run.

Saucepans: If you're going to buy new saucepans, buy heavy-bottomed ones. They conduct heat as well as thinner pans but provide a gentle buffer that prevents foods from burning or scalding on the bottom. I prefer stainless steel saucepans because they do not pick up food odors or flavors.

Scale: Professional pastry cooks do all their measuring by weight. For home cooks, working in much smaller quantities, measuring cups and spoons are more convenient. Still, some ingredients have to be weighed, and others (like butter) are easier to weigh than to smash into a measuring spoon (1 ounce of butter equals 2 tablespoons). If you don't already have a kitchen scale, buy one that has a decent capacity (5 pounds) and is easy to read. For best accuracy, check to see that the needle moves smoothly rather than jumps from point to point.

Stainless Steel Bowls: Stainless steel bowls are invaluable; every kitchen should have at least one set of various sizes. They perform better and last longer than plastic, pottery, or glass bowls, and they're more versatile. They can go over heat or into the refrigerator or even the freezer. They hold heat or cold longer than other bowls and will neither absorb odors (as plastic does) nor break.

Timer: If you buy a timer, make sure it's accurate. Personally, I never use one because once you start using it, you depend on it and no longer rely on your natural sense of time. Whether you use a timer or not, pay attention to the aromas of what you're baking. As soon as you start smelling something, go check it. The aroma means the baking process has reached an advanced stage and may need attention.

Tips for Using This Book

Read the entire recipe before you start.

Know exactly what you're going to do before you begin. Gather your ingredients and equipment so that once you start you can move along smoothly and not be slowed down looking for ingredients or reading unfamiliar technique instructions. In certain recipes, such as sponge cakes, a steady pace can make the difference between success and failure.

In timing recipes, use your common sense.

The baking times in these recipes are approximations. Every oven is different from every other, and many differ from one day to the next. If you know your oven tends to bake a little fast or a little slow, adjust the time in the recipe accordingly. Regardless of the dependability of your oven, never go by time alone. Always check a baking dessert before its suggested time is up. Judge its doneness by color, texture, aroma, or other indications suggested in individual recipes. Trust your own senses, not your oven.

The number of portions depends on the situation.

Most of the suggested number of servings in these recipes are based on my restaurant experience. They assume that dessert is being served at the end of a substantial meal. I get twelve servings from an average 10-inch tart, for instance. You may think my slices are too small or too large. By all means go by your own instincts and appetite and the rest of your menu.

What to do with leftovers.

Leftovers from any dessert made with cream, pastry cream, or butter cream should be refrigerated. Cover the leftover portions loosely with plastic wrap to keep them from absorbing other food odors. Poached fruits should also be covered and refrigerated. Plain cakes (Chiffon Cake, Fresh Fruit Pound Cake), fruit pies, cobblers, and crisps can be kept at room temperature for a day or two in cool weather, either wrapped or covered with a cake cover. In warm weather, wrap and refrigerate them. Cookies should be stored at room temperature, preferably in a box or cookie jar. Bread puddings, steamed puddings, sauces, and pastries should all be covered and refrigerated. The pastries won't really keep for more than a day, even in the refrigerator; their icings will begin to dissolve and their crusts will get soggy, so it's best to enjoy them on the day you make them.

Make the basics when you have time and keep them on hand.
     Many frequently used dessert components, including sponge cakes, glazes, some sauces, cookie doughs, pastry doughs, fondant, and candied fruit peels, can be made ahead and kept at the ready in the refrigerator or freezer. If you find you are using a particular component often, begin making it in bigger batches and store what you don't use. A supply of ready-to-use dough or glaze or sponge cakes will save you time and enable you to delight family and guests with spur-of-the-moment desserts.

4

Basic Doughs

Think of the best pies, tarts, and pastries you've ever eaten. Chances are the first thing you remember is the crust—crisp, light, melting in your mouth. Someone knew how to make a terrific dough. In terms of ingredients and technique, most doughs are basically alike. Combine fat with flour and perhaps some sugar, add liquid, and mix. The differences between doughs are subtle, but the subtleties make a world of difference. Pastry chefs spend years perfecting their doughs so that they emerge from the oven consistently light and flaky or buttery or crumbly or whatever that chef's ideal might be.

My own tastes run to crisp, light crusts with a minimum of sweetness. In keeping with these preferences and our changing eating habits, I've updated many classic recipes, making them lighter and less sweet than the originals. In developing new doughs for desserts of my own invention, I find myself leaning, especially in the last few years, toward flavored crusts. In an effort to put more excitement into some pies and tarts without overloading the fillings, I began adding such ingredients as coconut or cinnamon to the doughs and was delighted with the results. (I also like brushing an intriguing flavor onto the baked shell before filling it—such as unsweetened chocolate in my Chocolate Cream Pie— but more about that later.) Lately I've been experimenting with nut doughs for pastries. In Chapter 11 you'll find some of my favorites— lemon tartlets with pistachio-flavored shells and a variety of pastries made from Vienna doughs based on almonds or walnuts instead of the traditional hazelnuts.

In my hotel pastry shop and in this book, I've updated basic pastry-making techniques wherever possible to make the best use of contemporary kitchen equipment—electric mixers, food processors, and so forth. Some things, however, are best done in the traditional ways. Vienna Dough is one example. To understand how the ingredients combine, you need to work the dough with your hands, to see and feel it develop. The recipe for Vienna Dough in this chapter is the classical method, and I urge you to learn it. In fine pastry making, quick and easy is not always the best answer.

All my doughs (and all my cakes, for that matter) are made with butter. It simply tastes better than any other shortening. I've never had trouble producing light, delicate, flaky crusts with it, and you won't either if you learn to handle it properly. Always use cold butter to make your doughs, avoid overhandling or overmixing them, and refrigerate until firm before baking.

One of the most exciting things about the basic doughs explained in this chapter is the broad range of possibilities they will open for you as a pastry cook. If you can make an excellent tart shell, you can also make a light and crispy Chocolate Wafer and a mouthwatering Butter Wafer. You can shape them into circles as I do and slip them between the layers of a Chocolate Cassis Cake or a Strawberry Grand Marnier Cake to add contrast of both flavor and texture. If you can make a basic pie dough, you can make an endless variety of flavored doughs and use them to add new life to new or old-favorite desserts. I developed my Coconut Dough for Coconut Cream Pie. Then one day I thought I'd try it in a pineapple tart—delicious.

The doughs in this chapter are basic dessert building blocks. Each is not only a delicious end in itself but a step toward developing a vast and infinitely variable dessert repertoire.

Short Dough

The way you handle your dough makes all the difference in the texture and appearance of the finished shell. Even if you make only an occasional pie or tart, it pays to learn the proper technique. This recipe makes an exceptionally flaky, tender crust. I use it for most of my fruit pies and tarts.

For 1 pie or tart shell:

> 8 **tablespoons (¼ pound) unsalted butter (cold)**
> 1⅛ **cups all-purpose flour**
> 1½ **teaspoons sugar**
> ⅛ **teaspoon kosher salt (see page 42)**
> ¼ **cup cold water**

For 2 pie or tart shells or 1 double-crust pie:

> 16 **tablespoons (½ pound) unsalted butter (cold)**
> 2¼ **cups all-purpose flour**
> 1 **tablespoon sugar**
> ¼ **teaspoon kosher salt (see page 42)**
> ½ **cup cold water**

Cut the butter into 1-inch pieces. Using the paddle attachment on an electric mixer* blend the butter and flour at low speed until they resemble coarse meal. Mix the sugar, salt, and water, and add them to the flour mixture. Stop once, soon after you start mixing, to scrape the bowl and paddle. Blend only until the dough comes together. The dough will be moist, soft, and smooth. If you are making two shells or a double-crust pie, divide the dough in half. It's a good idea to weigh the halves to make sure they are even; each should be about 12 ounces.

For each pie or tart shell: Work on a well-floured table or board. Have a rolling pin, a flour brush (a clean dustpan brush works fine), and your baking pan close at hand. Put the dough down on the board and sprinkle a little flour on top. Shape the dough into a thick circle, about 6 inches

---

* See Equipment, page 58. If you prefer making pie and tart doughs by hand, you can, of course, do so. Use a pastry cutter or two French knives.

in diameter, like a big hamburger patty. Beginning in the middle and working to opposite sides, roll the dough into an elongated oval, about 13 inches long. Lift it carefully, with straight fingers under both ends to support it, and swirl it a little on the table to coat the bottom again with flour as you give it a quarter turn. Sprinkle a little more flour on top, then roll to opposite sides as you did before so that the dough begins to take on the shape of a circle. Continue rolling gently, from the center to the edges, until you have a smooth circle of uniform thickness. You can locate too-thick places by running your fingers gently over the dough. Work them out with a back and forth motion of the rolling pin. The finished circle should be 13 inches in diameter for a regular pie or tart shell, 15 inches for a deep-dish shell to be baked in a springform pan.

Brush the flour off the dough. Starting at the side farthest from you, lift the edge of the dough onto the rolling pin and begin rolling the pin gently toward you. As the dough rolls around the pin, brush away the flour clinging to the underside. Roll all of the dough except the last 2 inches around the pin, then hold the pin over the near edge of your tart or pie pan, about 1 inch above it, so that the dough is centered and its dangling end just touches the table. Slowly unroll the pin, letting the dough drape loosely over the pan, with at least 1 inch overlapping the

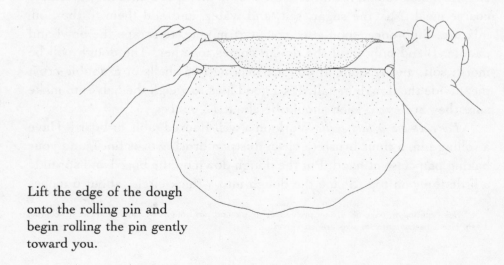

Lift the edge of the dough onto the rolling pin and begin rolling the pin gently toward you.

edge on all sides. Work your way around the pan, gently lifting the edges of the dough so that it settles to the bottom of the pan and against the sides without stretching. Gently press the dough against the sides of the pan and into the corners.

Shaping tart shells: Fold the overlapping dough into the pan just to where the sides and bottom meet, to form double-thick sides. Gently press the dough against the sides of the pan, being careful not to press against the bottom (if the dough is too thin at the juncture of sides and bottom, it will split during baking). Trim off extra dough at the top edge by running a cutting pin—a piece of dowel about 18 inches long—around the top edge.* (If you use your rolling pin for cutting, the edge of the pan

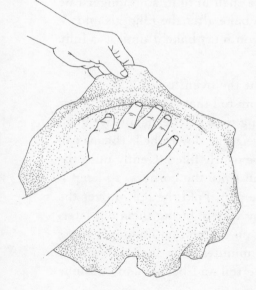

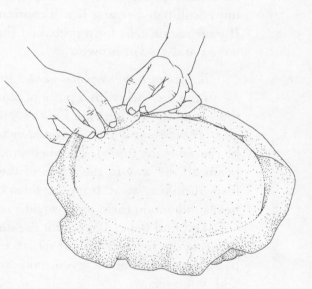

Gently lift the edges of the dough so that it settles into the pan without stretching.

Fold the overlapping dough into the pan, just to where the sides and bottom meet.

* Save the dough you trim off. You may need it for emergency patching later on. If after blind baking your shell has cracks or holes in it, moisten the area around each flaw and press on a thin piece of unbaked trimming.

will eventually chew it up.) Refrigerate until firm, about 20 minutes, before baking.

Shaping pies and deep-dish shells: Trim off the excess dough with a pair of scissors, leaving about a 1-inch overlap all the way around (see footnote, page 73). Refrigerate until firm, about 20 minutes. When firm, use a knife held vertically against the side of the pan to trim the inch of excess off the shell. Press the edge of the dough against the edge of the pan, hooking it slightly under the rim of the pan, to eliminate any chance of shrinkage during baking.

Blind baking and prebaking: If your recipe calls for an unbaked shell, your shell is ready to use when it is trimmed and firm. If the recipe calls for a blind-baked shell, you must bake the shell until it is no longer raw but is still pale because it will continue to bake after the filling is added. If your recipe calls for a prebaked shell, you must bake it until it is fully baked and golden brown.

Baking tart and deep-dish shells: Preheat the oven to 400°.

Line the shell with a piece of aluminum foil that is at least 1½ times the size of the baking pan. Fill the foil lining with dry beans, pie weights, clean pebbles, or whatever you have for weighing down shells (beans can be reused many times). The shell should be nearly filled. Gently push the beans all the way to the edges of the shell (into the corners) to keep it from shrinking away from the sides of the pan. Fold the foil in over the beans to contain them and provide an easy way of lifting them out later.

To blind bake: Bake until the dough on the bottom no longer looks raw (lift the foil and look at it), 15 to 20 minutes. The shell will still be pale. Remove from the oven, take out the foil and beans, and continue with your recipe.

To prebake: After baking 20 minutes, remove the foil and beans, and return to the oven. Bake until the shell is golden brown and has pulled away from the sides of the pan, about 15 minutes.

Baking pies: Preheat the oven to 400°.

To blind bake: Set another pie pan of the same size on top of the shell. Invert the two pans and bake upside down. After 10 minutes, press down on the top pan firmly but gently; otherwise, the shell may shrink away from the pan and not fit snugly against the bottom when you turn it right side up. Continue baking until the bottom of the shell no longer looks raw, about 10 minutes.

To prebake: After baking upside down for 20 minutes, turn the shell right side up, remove the top pie plate, and continue baking until golden brown, about 15 minutes.

Rich Short Dough

This recipe makes enough dough for one pie crust (top and bottom), two pie shells, or two tart shells. If you're making just one single-crust pie or one tart, wrap half the dough in plastic wrap and refrigerate until needed. It will keep for up to a week.*

      1   egg yolk
      1   teaspoon sugar
     ¼   teaspoon kosher salt (see page 42)
          Cold water
      1   tablespoon vegetable oil
      8   tablespoons (¼ pound) unsalted butter (cold)
    1¾ cups all-purpose flour

In a 1-cup measuring cup, blend together the yolk, sugar, and salt. Add enough cold water to reach the ⅓-cup mark. Add the oil and blend thoroughly.

Cut the butter into ½-inch cubes and put it in a bowl with the flour. Blend gently with your fingertips until all the butter is incorporated and the mixture has a coarse, mealy texture. Make a well in the center and pour the liquid into it. Mix gently with your fingers just until the dough forms a ball.

Roll out the dough and bake according to instructions in the recipe for Short Dough, page 71.

---

* Before using the dough you have stored in the refrigerator, unwrap it, cut it into small cubes so that it will warm up evenly, and let it come to room temperature. When the cubes feel soft on the outside but still firm inside, press the dough together into a ball and proceed to roll it out.

Sugar Dough

This is a slightly sweet, crumbly dough that makes tender, light tartlet shells. The number of shells you get depends in part on how thinly you roll out the dough.

MAKES 60 TARTLET SHELLS

- 2½ cups cake flour
- 1 cup powdered sugar
- 12 tablespoons unsalted butter (cold)
- 1 large egg
- 1 tablespoon milk

Using the paddle attachment on an electric mixer (see page 58) and low speed, mix the flour, sugar, and butter to a coarse meal. Add the egg and milk and mix just until the dough comes together.

Roll out the dough on a lightly floured surface, according to recipe directions. To prebake, place a small paper muffin cup in each tartlet shell and fill it with beans or pie weights. Bake on a cookie sheet at 375° until the edges are golden brown, 15 to 20 minutes.

Shortbread Dough

This is the sweet cookie dough I use in Currant Bars (page 289) and other pastries. This recipe will make a thin crust in a standard cookie sheet or a slightly thicker one in a 9 x 13-inch pan.

- 12 tablespoons unsalted butter (soft)
- ¾ cup powdered sugar
- 2 cups cake flour

Preheat the oven to 350°.

Using the paddle attachment on an electric mixer (see page 58), mix all the ingredients together until smooth. Roll out the dough on a lightly floured surface to approximately match the shape of your pan. Transfer it to the pan and even it out as much as possible with a rolling pin. Pierce the dough all over with a fork. Bake until lightly browned, about 15 minutes.

Cinnamon Dough

This is a cookie dough; that is, it produces a crumbly rather than a flaky crust. I use it for my Cinnamon Peach Tart (page 147) and Cinnamon Apple Tart (page 139). It also makes for a marvelous apple pie.

MAKES 1 TART OR SINGLE-CRUST PIE

- ¾ **cup all-purpose flour**
- ½ **cup cake flour**
- ¼ **cup plus 2 tablespoons sugar**
- 2 **tablespoons ground cinnamon**
- 6 **tablespoons unsalted butter (cold)**
- 3 **tablespoons cold water**

Lightly grease the bottom of a 10-inch tart pan or 9-inch pie plate. Set aside.

Using the paddle attachment on an electric mixer (see page 58), combine the flours, sugar, and cinnamon. Cut the butter into small pieces and add it to the flour. Blend at low speed until the mixture resembles coarse meal. Add the water, letting it dribble slowly down the side of the bowl, and mix just until the dough comes together.

For instructions on rolling out the dough, transferring it to the pan, and baking, see the recipe for Short Dough, page 71.

Coconut Dough

This is a crisp, golden shell that adds the aroma and tropical flavor of toasted coconut to a pie or tart. I use it for my Coconut Cream Pie (page 169) and Coconut-Pineapple Tart (page 134).

MAKES 1 PIE OR TART SHELL

1 **cup plus 2 tablespoons all-purpose flour**
½ **cup unsweetened coconut flakes**°
8 **tablespoons (¼ pound) unsalted butter (cold)**
1½ **teaspoons sugar**
⅛ **teaspoon kosher salt (see page 42)**
¼ **cup cold water**

Using the paddle attachment on an electric mixer (see page 58), and the lowest speed, blend the flour, coconut, and butter until the mixture resembles coarse meal. Dissolve the sugar and salt in the water and add it slowly, pouring down the side of the bowl. Mix just until the dough comes together. Gently press the dough into a ball. If it seems wet, knead it a few times.

On a well-floured board roll the dough into a circle 13 inches in diameter. Transfer the dough to a 9-inch pie plate or 10-inch tart pan by carefully lifting the edge of the circle farthest from you onto your rolling pin and rolling it toward you until all the dough is wrapped around the pin. (Brush off any flour clinging to the bottom of the dough as you roll it around the pin.) Hold the pin over the near side of the pie plate or tart pan and slowly roll it away from you, letting the dough fall lightly over the pan. Work your way around the edges of the dough, lifting gently so that the dough settles into the pan without stretching. For tarts, fold the overlapping dough into the pan to form double-thick sides. Trim the excess by rolling a cutting pin (see page 51) over the edges of the pan. Refrigerate for 20 minutes.

° Unsweetened coconut flakes are available in natural food stores and in most markets that sell ingredients in bulk. The flakes are more flavorful and not as dry as grated coconut. Smell the coconut before you buy it; old coconut smells stale. If you can't get flakes, use coarse- or medium-shredded coconut but not finely shredded. If you do get flakes and they are very broad (like noodles), chop them into pieces that are about the width of toothpicks. Always store coconut in a closed container.

Chocolate Wafer Dough

I use these flaky, unsweetened wafers to add texture and an intense chocolate flavor to cakes without adding sweetness. Try baking leftover dough into crisp, bitter-chocolate cookies. They are delicious with ice cream.

MAKES 2 (9- OR 10-INCH) WAFERS

> **2 ounces unsweetened chocolate**
> **¼ cup water**
> **8 tablespoons (¼ pound) unsalted butter (cold)**
> **1¼ cups bread flour**

Break the chocolate into small pieces. Melt it with the water in the top of a double boiler. Remove from the heat and set aside to cool.

Cut the butter into small pieces about 1 inch square. Place it in the bowl of an electric mixer, add the flour, and mix with the paddle attachment (see page 58) until the mixture resembles coarse meal. Add the melted, completely cooled chocolate and mix only until smooth and a little elastic. Cover and refrigerate for 30 minutes, until the outside of the dough is firm but still pliable.

Remove the dough from the refrigerator and work it a little with your hands. Lightly dust the dough, a rolling pin, and your work table with flour. Cut the dough in half and roll each half into a 9- or 10-inch circle. (To make a perfect circle, place a cake pan on the dough and cut around the edge with a sharp knife.)

Line two cookie sheets with parchment. Lift the far end of one of the circles onto your rolling pin and roll the pin gently toward you until the entire circle is wrapped around the pin. Unroll the dough onto one of the parchment-lined sheets. Repeat with the other circle. Refrigerate for 30 minutes, then bake in a preheated 400° oven for 10 to 15 minutes, until the center of each circle is firm to the touch. Set aside to cool.

Butter Wafer Dough

I use this flaky dough to make wafers that add crunch and a buttery flavor to cakes (see Strawberry Grand Marnier Cake, page 237).

MAKES 2 (10-INCH WAFERS)

- 1¼ **cups bread flour**
- 10 **tablespoons unsalted butter (cold), cut into pieces**
- ¼ **cup cold water**

Using the paddle attachment on an electric mixer (see page 58) and low speed, mix the flour and butter to a coarse meal. Add the water slowly and continue mixing until the dough comes together. Knead the dough a few times on a floured surface. As soon as the outside starts looking dry, stop kneading; working the dough too much will make it tough.

Divide the dough in half. Form each half into a patty, then roll each into a 10½-inch circle. Place the two circles on parchment-lined cookie sheets, pierce them all over with a fork, and refrigerate them until firm, about 20 minutes.

Preheat the oven to 375°. Bake the wafers until hard and golden brown, about 20 minutes. Cool to room temperature.

Vienna Dough

This is the way I was trained to make a classic nut dough—by hand. There are faster ways to do it, using machines, but by following the process step by step you will learn the principles behind important dessert-making techniques. And you will produce a light, delicately flavored shell, worthy of the most subtle hazelnut torte.

Note: You'll need a tabletop at least 20 inches square to work on.

- 1 **cup bread flour**
- ½ **cup plus 2 tablespoons cake flour**

⅓ cup sugar
⅓ cup filberts, lightly toasted
5 tablespoons unsalted butter (cold)
¼ teaspoon cream of tartar
⅛ teaspoon baking soda
⅛ teaspoon cornstarch
¼ cup water

Combine the two flours on the table, rubbing them gently between your hands to mix them thoroughly. With a scraper push the flour outward to form a ring with a 16-inch inside diameter. Place the sugar in a pile inside the ring. Finely grind the filberts in a coffee or spice grinder and place them inside the ring, too, in a pile near the sugar. Cut the butter into 3 or 4 pieces and place it inside the ring. Mix together the cream of tartar, baking soda, and cornstarch, and pour the mixture on top of the sugar pile. Now you're ready to begin mixing the dough. The trick is to work quickly and handle the butter as little as possible so that it won't melt. When working the dough, use the heel of your hand, which is cooler than your fingers. Use the scraper, not your hands, to move ingredients together.

Sprinkle about a third of the sugar over the butter and work it in with the heel of your hand, pressing down, folding the mixture over, and pressing again. When mixed, add more sugar until all the sugar is worked into the butter, then work in the filberts in the same way.

Using the scraper, bring the flour into the center of the ring, heaping about half on top of the butter mixture and using the rest to make a tight circle around it. Gently rub the flour and butter together with your fingertips, lifting it and dropping it back to the table as you work, to keep the butter from getting too warm. Continue until all the flour is worked into the butter and the mixture resembles coarse meal. Gather the mixture into a pile, make a shallow well in the center, and pour the water into it. Wait 2 minutes, then gently knead the dough until smooth (there should be no wet or dry spots). The dough will be moist and a little tacky.

Dust the outside of the dough with a little bread flour. Wrap it in plastic wrap and chill until firm, about 1 hour.

Take out the dough, cut it into 1-inch cubes so that it will warm

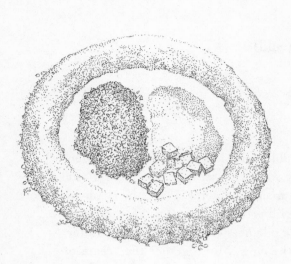

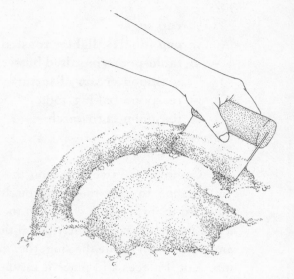

To mix Vienna Dough, form a ring with the flour and place the other ingredients inside.

Using the scraper, bring the flour into the center of the ring, heaping about half of it on top of the butter mixture.

evenly, and allow it to come to room temperature. Press the pieces of dough into a ball. Dust the dough and the table with flour. Roll the dough into a circle about 15 inches in diameter. Place a 10-inch tart pan next to the circle. Starting at the side farthest from you, lift the edge of the dough onto the rolling pin and wind the pin gently toward you until all but the last 2 inches of dough are rolled around the pin. Hold the pin over the near side of the tart pan, about 1 inch above it, with the edge of the dough just touching the table. Gently roll the pin away from you so that the dough is draped over the pan, overlapping about 2 inches all around. Now work your way around the pan, lifting the edges of the dough so that it settles into the bottom and against the sides of the pan without stretching. Fold the overhanging dough into the pan, pressing it against the sides of the pan to create a double-thick side crust. Roll a cutting pin (see page 51) around the rim of the pan to cut off any excess.

Prick all over the bottom of the shell with a fork. Chill until firm, about 30 minutes.

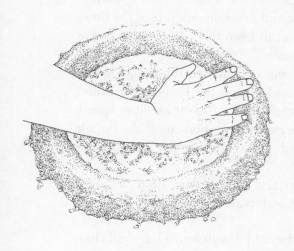

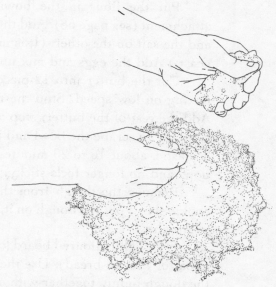

Work the dough with the heel of your hand, which is cooler than your fingers.

Lift the butter-flour mixture and drop it back onto the table as you work, to keep the butter from getting too warm.

Brioche

I use this fine-textured, butter-rich loaf to make Brioche Bread Pudding (page 244). It is also wonderful for sandwiches, toast, and just plain eating. The dough must sit in the refrigerator overnight, so start a day ahead.

MAKES 2 LOAVES

    3¼ **cups bread flour**
    3 **tablespoons sugar**
    ½ **ounce fresh active yeast**
    2 **teaspoons kosher salt (see page 42)**
    5 **large eggs**
   16 **tablespoons (½ pound) unsalted butter (soft)**

Put the flour in the bowl of an electric mixer with a paddle attachment (see page 58). Add the sugar and yeast on one side of the bowl and the salt on the other. (It is important to keep the salt away from the yeast.) Add the eggs and mix until smooth.

Cut the butter into 12 pieces. Slowly add half to the dough while mixing on low speed. Stop the mixer and scrape the bowl and paddle. Add the rest of the butter; stop and scrape again. Mix at medium speed, stopping to scrape the bowl and paddle every 2 minutes, until the dough is elastic, about 16 to 20 minutes. The dough is done when it cleans the bowl and no longer feels sticky.

Remove the dough from the bowl and dust it with flour. Flour a cookie sheet, put the dough on it, cover with plastic wrap, and refrigerate overnight.

On a lightly floured board knead the cold dough into a long roll (like a loaf of French bread). Use the heels of your hands to knead, pressing the dough tightly together with each movement to keep air pockets from forming. Flatten the roll and cut it in half crosswise. Put each half into a seasoned pan (see page 48), with the crease left from kneading on the bottom. (If you have covered bread pans, use those; if not, ordinary bread pans will work fine.) Press the dough evenly into the bottom of the pans. Cover with a damp cloth and put in a warm place to rise. (Instead of using a damp cloth on covered pans, slide the cover all but 2 inches closed.) Let the dough rise two-thirds of the way to the top of the pans.

Preheat the oven to 350°. Bake until the loaves are golden brown, about 55 minutes. Turn out immediately onto a wire rack.

Puff Pastry Dough

Of all the doughs you can make, this is the flakiest and most delicate. Alternating layers of butter and dough separate in baking to produce crisp, paper-thin leaves that crumble when you bite them. True traditionalists make the dough entirely by hand. I think it's fine to do the combining of ingredients with an electric mixer; the rolling and folding is a hand operation, however, unless you have a commercial kitchen with a 6-foot-long sheeter.

It's important to keep the butter cool during mixing and rolling. If at any time your dough feels warm, stop what you're doing, refrigerate it for 20 to 30 minutes, then pick up again where you left off. Obviously it's easier to make puff pastry on a cool day than a hot one, but if you're alert to how the dough feels beneath your hands, you'll do fine any day.

The finished dough can be baked in sheets for Napoleons (page 256) or cut into smaller pieces and made into turnovers (see Cranberry Turnovers, page 274) or other delicate pastries. Even if the dessert you are making calls for only a one-half or one-quarter recipe of puff pastry dough, I recommend making the full recipe. You can keep the unused portion in the refrigerator, wrapped in plastic, for up to a week or in the freezer for much longer.

3¼ cups plus 1 tablespoon bread flour
¾ cup cake flour
24 tablespoons (¾ pound) unsalted butter (cold)
1 rounded tablespoon kosher salt (see page 42)
1 cup water
1 tablespoon lemon juice

Be sure your work table and all your equipment are absolutely clean before you start. Combine 2 cups of bread flour and the cake flour in an electric mixer with a paddle attachment (see page 58). Add 3 tablespoons of butter cut into several pieces and mix on low speed until there are no more lumps of butter. Add the salt. Combine the water and lemon juice, and add them slowly while mixing on low speed. Mix until the dough comes together. Stop the mixer and scrape down the bowl and paddle. Turn the dough over with a spoon to bring any unincorporated dry ingredients to the top. Continue mixing on low, stopping to scrape the bowl and paddle a few times, until the dough is smooth. Add 1 tablespoon of bread flour and mix on medium-low speed until the dough is no longer sticky to the touch. It should be slightly elastic and cling to the paddle, cleaning the bowl as you mix. If it does not clean the bowl, keep mixing until it does. Remove the dough from the bowl, dust it with bread flour, wrap it in plastic wrap, and refrigerate it at least 1 hour.

Cut the remaining 21 tablespoons of butter into 1-inch cubes. Toss them lightly in bread flour and refrigerate for 30 minutes. Combine the butter with 1 cup of bread flour in an electric mixer with a bread hook (if you don't have a hook, use a paddle). Mix on low speed to a smooth paste. The butter should still feel cool and firm. Turn it out on a lightly floured table, sprinkle it with flour, and work it into a smooth ball, adding enough flour to keep it dry against your hands.

Form it into a 6-inch-round patty, wrap it in plastic wrap, and refrigerate until it is cold, about 20 minutes. (The butter should be cold but still pliable when you take it out. It will feel like a dough. Don't let it get too cold, or it will crack or crumble when you try to roll it out.)

Lay the dough on a lightly floured table and sprinkle it with flour. Using a heavy, ball bearing-type rolling pin, roll it into a 16 x 10-inch rectangle. Because the dough is so pliable, you can actually stretch its corners into right angles. Slip your flat fingers under the corners about 3 inches and pull them gently into shape. being careful not to tear the dough.

Sprinkle 3 tablespoons of bread flour on another section of the table. Place the chilled butter on it and sprinkle a tablespoon of flour over the butter. Roll the butter into a 10 x 9-inch rectangle.

Brush any remaining flour off both the dough and the butter. Lift the butter by winding it around your rolling pin, then unwind it on top of the dough, with the short side of the butter rectangle set 1 inch in from the short side of the dough. Fold in toward the center the portion of dough that is not covered with butter so that it covers half the butter. Brush off any flour clinging to the dough. Fold the dough in half from the opposite side, letting the 1-inch lip of unbuttered dough extend over the edge. Tuck the lip underneath. Seal the short ends by pressing down with the sides of your hands and tuck the lips underneath.

Flour the table and the top of the dough again. Have the short (5-inch) side closest to you. Roll the length of the dough out to 24 inches, rolling the middle first, then the near end. Give the dough a half turn and roll the other end. This helps distribute the butter evenly. Move the pin in a steady back and forth motion; don't lift it up and drop it back down on the dough.

Give the dough a quarter turn and roll out the width to 12 inches. The length will pull in to about 22 inches. Brush the flour off the dough.

Fold in the 2 short ends so they meet at the center, lining up all the edges as evenly as possible. Fold the dough in half as if you were closing a book. Sprinkle with flour. Roll out the dough to 24 x 12 inches, as you did before. Fold in the outside quarters and fold the dough in half like a book, as before. Wrap the dough in plastic wrap and refrigerate about 35 minutes, until it feels cold but not too firm (you don't want the butter to get brittle).

Flour the table and the top of the dough. Roll out the dough, as before, to 24 x 12 inches. Brush off the flour. This time, fold the long side of the dough in thirds to form a rectangle about 7½ x 12 inches. Sprinkle flour on top and roll out the dough to 24 x 12 inches again. Fold into thirds again. Brush away any remaining flour, wrap the dough, and refrigerate.

Cream Puff Pastry

This light, airy pastry is the traditional *pâte à chou*. When it bakes, it expands to three times its size and creates a hollow center, which can then be filled with pastry cream or whipped cream.

MAKES 80 (2¼-INCH) ECLAIRS OR (2-INCH) CREAM PUFFS

- **8 tablespoons (¼ pound) unsalted butter (cold)**
- **1 cup water**
- **1 cup bread flour**
- **6 large eggs**

If you are making eclairs, begin by cutting parchment to fit two cookie sheets. Draw pairs of guidelines the length of the parchment 2¼ inches apart, with ¾ inch between pairs. Turn the paper over on the sheet so that the marks are on the underside but still show through.

Preheat the oven to 400°.

Cut the butter into 8 pieces and put it in a heavy saucepan with the water. Bring to a boil. When the butter is completely melted, add the flour and stir over high heat until the dough pulls away from the sides of the pan and looks porous. Transfer the dough to an electric mixer with a paddle attachment (see page 58) and begin mixing at medium speed. Immediately add 2 eggs. Stop and scrape the bowl and paddle. Add 2 more eggs and scrape again. Add the final 2 eggs, scrape the bowl and paddle, and continue mixing until the dough is smooth and holds a crease. Spoon the dough into a pastry bag with a #5 plain tip.

To pipe out your eclairs, hold the bag at a 30-degree angle from the pan, with the tip ¼ inch above the lined parchment. Pipe out ½-inch-wide fingers of dough between the guidelines, 1½ inches apart. At the end of each eclair, stop squeezing the bag and pull the tip up and back over the shape you have piped out. This will make a small tail lying on top of the eclair.

Brush each eclair lightly with water, starting at the tail end and flattening the tail as you brush. (Scrape the brush against the side of the water dish each time you dip it to keep it from being too wet.)

To shape cream puffs, hold the tip of the pastry bag ¼ inch above a parchment-lined cookie sheet, pointing straight down, and pipe out 1½-inch-wide balls, 1½ inches apart. After piping each, stop squeezing and lift the tip up and off to one side. Brush with water, as for eclairs.

Bake until the eclairs or cream puffs are golden brown, about 40 minutes. They should have tripled in height and should sound hollow when tapped. Cool to room temperature.

Note: Wash the pastry bag as soon as you are done using it, or it will be very difficult to clean later.

5
Basic Sponge Cakes and Meringues

Sponge cakes and meringues provide the basic structure on which a whole range of cakes and pastries can be built.

A sponge cake, white or flavored, is like a blank sheet of paper waiting for you, the artist, to turn it into something special. It provides texture and form, yet it is infinitely adaptable. You can use a sponge whole or cut into two or three layers. You can stack the layers or mold them around another shape. You can use the sponge's subtle, light flavor to contrast with assertive fillings or change its character completely by drenching it with liqueurs, fruit juices, rum, or brandy, any of which it will drink up gladly.

Meringues, dry, light, and crisp, aren't meant to absorb other ingredients. I like to infuse them with tantalizing flavors of their own by baking toasted ground nuts into them. Circles of meringue create layers of feather-light crunchiness to contrast with rich cream fillings. Dacquoise, a traditional cake composed of hazelnut meringues and coffee butter cream, is always on the menu at The Stanford Court, and some people come just for that. It's just one of the ways to use meringues explored in this book.

Both sponge cakes and meringues can be tricky to make, but if you understand their basic principles, you won't have problems. Both depend for their texture on air—the air you beat into them during the mixing process, which then escapes during baking, leaving a light, porous structure behind. If you don't beat in enough air, your sponge or meringue will be heavy and flat. If you beat in too much air, your batter won't be able to contain it and will collapse. If you work the batter too much when folding in dry ingredients or let it stand too long before getting it into the oven, the air you've so carefully incorporated will find a way to escape. Again, your sponge or meringue will fall flat.

The answer to all of these problems is: Be bold. Assemble your ingredients before you begin mixing, then move through the process with courage and a steady pace. Hesitancy and caution will slow you down, make it more likely you'll overmix, and give your air a chance to get away. By following the recipes in this chapter step by step, boldly, you should be successful with sponges and meringues even if you've never made them before. And the more you make, the better they will become.

Because they keep so well, both sponges and meringues are very practical to make ahead. When you have a few free hours, gather your ingredients and practice. Your baked meringues will keep for days in a cool, dry place. Sponges freeze perfectly—and having one in the freezer opens all sorts of possibilities for marvelous, quick desserts.

Sponges defrost so quickly, you don't have to take them out of the freezer until just before you want to assemble a cake, so you're always ready for an impromptu dinner. Just pick up some cream and some fresh, ripe fruit on the way home, and you can put together a delicious cake in little more than the time it takes to whip the cream and slice the fruit.

When you have more time, you can turn your sponges and meringues into elaborate classical or distinctive modern desserts. In Chapter 9 you will find dozens of cakes that start with a simple sponge or meringue. Some are robed in swirls of butter cream. Some are decorated with truffles or candied citrus peels or berries or chocolate and nuts. One takes on the intriguing quality of sweet, ripe peaches; another the drama of rich, dark chocolate; a third the bite of bittersweet caramel. It's sometimes hard for people to believe that such a variety of tastes and textures could develop from the very same beginnings.

Not all cakes start out as a sponge or meringue, but so many do that I encourage anyone who loves cakes and wants to make good ones to start by mastering the basic techniques in this chapter.

White Sponge Cake (Génoise)

The most important thing to remember when mixing the batter for a sponge is to work quickly and steadily, so read the recipe thoroughly before you begin. Lay out your ingredients within easy reach, and once you start working, do not stop until the cake is in the oven.

For a 2-layer cake, bake in a 9-inch (2-inch-deep) cake pan:

4 tablespoons unsalted butter
⅔ cup cake flour
½ cup plus 2 tablespoons sugar
4 large egg yolks
4 large whole eggs

For a 3-layer cake, bake in a 10-inch springform pan:

5 tablespoons unsalted butter
1 cup cake flour
¾ cup plus 3 tablespoons sugar
5 large egg yolks
5 large whole eggs

Preheat the oven to 300°.

Cut a circle of parchment to fit the bottom of the cake pan. Butter the bottom and sides of the pan. Line the bottom with the parchment (be sure it lies flat), then flour the sides.

Melt the butter and keep it warm (body temperature is ideal).

Sift together the flour and 2 tablespoons of the sugar. Toss them a little with your hands to make sure they are thoroughly mixed. Set aside.

Bring some water to a boil in a large saucepan or the bottom of a double boiler. In a large stainless steel bowl, stir together the egg yolks, whole eggs, and the rest of the sugar. Whisk continuously over the boiling water just until hot (not long enough to cook the eggs). Transfer to the bowl of an electric mixer and whip at high speed until double in volume. The batter will be pale and thick. Beat at medium-high speed a

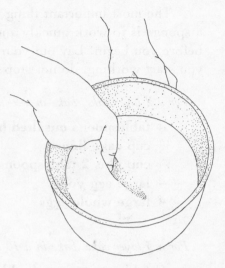

The batter should form a ribbon on the surface as it drips from the beater and hold that shape for about 30 seconds.

The batter should hold a deep crease for about 30 seconds after you have drawn a finger through it.

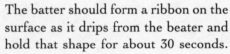

few minutes more, until the batter forms a ribbon and holds a deep crease.

Sprinkle the flour mixture over the batter and gently but briskly fold it in. Transfer one-quarter of the batter to a smaller bowl; stir the melted butter and fold it in. Fold this mixture back into the rest of the batter, working quickly so that the butter does not thicken.

Pour immediately into the prepared pan. Bake for about 1 hour and 10 minutes, until the center springs back when touched lightly. The top will be lightly browned, and when you press down gently on the cake, you should hear the whisper of breaking air bubbles. Remember, this is a delicate cake. It can fall 1 inch or more if you slam the oven door or open it too many times or too wide during baking.

Let the cake rest a full 10 minutes in the pan before turning it out onto a wire rack. If you are not going to use the sponge immediately, let it cool completely, then wrap it in plastic wrap and refrigerate (leave the parchment attached). You may also freeze the sponge for several days. Remove from the freezer and unwrap just before assembling the cake.

Trimming the sponge: The hard outer skin that develops on the top and bottom of a sponge cake during baking should always be trimmed off before assembling the final cake. Use a long-bladed slicer or serrated knife (you can't do the job right with a short blade). Cut off any raised area on the top of the sponge to make the surface completely level. Then go back and trim away any skin that remains. Turn the cake over and trim the bottom.

Splitting the sponge into layers: Many of the cake recipes in this book require a sponge to be split into two or three layers. It is very important to keep the knife level as you cut. Most people have a tendency to draw the knife downward.

Use a long-bladed slicer or serrated knife. Lay one hand flat on top of the cake to steady it. Position the knife against the edge of the cake at the level you want to cut, making sure it is flat. Draw the knife through the cake in one long cut (with a sawing motion if using a serrated knife). Watch where the knife cuts the edges to be sure it stays level.

Chocolate Sponge Cake (Génoise)

This extremely light chocolate cake is the foundation of many classic desserts. As with White Sponge Cake, the secret of making it right is to work quickly and steadily from the time you start combining ingredients until the cake is in the oven.

For a 2-layer cake, bake in a 9-inch (2-inch-deep) cake pan:

   4 tablespoons unsalted butter
   ½ cup cake flour
   3 tablespoons cocoa powder
   ½ cup plus 3 tablespoons sugar
   4 large egg yolks
   4 large whole eggs

(continued)

For a 3-layer cake, bake in a 10-inch springform pan:

> 5 **tablespoons unsalted butter**
> ⅔ **cup cake flour**
> 4 **tablespoons cocoa powder**
> ¾ **cup plus 3 tablespoons sugar**
> 5 **large egg yolks**
> 5 **large whole eggs**

Preheat the oven to 300°.

Cut a circle of parchment to fit the bottom of the cake pan. Butter the bottom and sides of the pan. Line the bottom with the parchment (be sure it lies flat), then flour the sides.

Melt the butter and keep it warm (body temperature is ideal). Sift together *twice* the flour, cocoa, and 2 tablespoons of sugar. Set aside.

Bring some water to a boil in a large saucepan or the bottom of a double boiler. In a large stainless steel bowl, stir together the egg yolks, whole eggs, and the rest of the sugar. Whisk continuously over the boiling water until hot (not long enough to cook the eggs). Transfer to a mixing bowl and beat at high speed until double in volume. The batter will be pale and thick. Beat at medium-high speed a few minutes more, until the batter forms a ribbon and holds a deep crease. Be sure you don't overbeat at this stage. If you do, the batter will collapse when you fold in other ingredients later.

Sprinkle the flour mixture over the batter and gently fold it in until it is almost but not entirely incorporated. Transfer one-quarter of the batter into a smaller bowl; stir the melted butter and fold it in. Fold this mixture back into the rest of the batter, working quickly so the butter does not thicken. Pour immediately into the prepared pan and bake about 1 hour and 10 minutes, until the center springs back when touched lightly. Be gentle. This is a delicate cake that can fall 1 inch or more if you slam the oven door or open it too many times during baking.

Let the cake rest a full 10 minutes in the pan before turning it out onto a wire rack.

Note: You can bake the sponge a day or two before making the rest of a cake. When cool, wrap it in plastic wrap (leave the parchment attached) and freeze. Remove from the freezer and unwrap just before assembling the cake.

Jelly Roll Sponge Cake

I use this sponge cake for the small filled "jelly roll" slices offered on our miniature pastry trays. Each sponge makes two rolls, for a total of thirty pieces, each about 1 inch thick and 2 inches across. Make your sponge the day before you plan to make the jelly rolls.

MAKES 1 (11 X 17-INCH) SPONGE

> 6 **large eggs**
> 1 **cup sugar**
> 1 **cup cake flour**
> ½ **teaspoon lemon zest (if you are making Lemon Roll)**

Preheat the oven to 350°. Grease an 11 x 17-inch cookie sheet or jelly roll pan. Cut a piece of parchment to fit the bottom of the pan. Line the bottom of the pan with the parchment and lightly flour the sides.

Combine the eggs and ¾ cup of sugar in the top of a double boiler. Heat, whisking constantly, until hot and frothy. Transfer to an electric mixer and beat with the whisk attachment (see page 58) at high speed until thick, about 3 minutes. Lower the speed to medium and continue beating until the mixture forms soft peaks and holds a crease.

Sift the flour and the remaining sugar together. Sprinkle the flour mixture and lemon zest over the egg mixture and gently fold them in. Pour the batter into the prepared pan. Spread evenly and smooth the surface with a rubber scraper.

Bake until the surface springs back when touched lightly, about 18 minutes. Cool in the pan for 5 minutes, then cover the sponge with a piece of parchment and turn it out onto a table. Tap the pan sharply on the table to loosen the sponge if it does not come out easily. Carefully peel off the baking parchment and lay it loosely back in place. With the long (17-inch) edge toward you, roll the sponge into a fairly tight 17-inch-long log, rolling both sheets of parchment in with the cake as you go. (You must roll the sponge while it is still warm; later it will be too brittle.) Secure the roll with tape or a rubber band (the outer layer should be parchment) and refrigerate it overnight.

Chocolate Jelly Roll Sponge Cake

The Chocolate Jelly Roll Sponge Cake is made like the plain Jelly Roll Sponge Cake above, except that it uses one less egg and substitutes unsweetened cocoa for part of the flour.

MAKES 1 (11 x 17-INCH) SPONGE

> 5 large eggs
> 1 cup sugar
> ¾ cup cake flour
> ¼ cup unsweetened cocoa powder

Follow the procedures for Jelly Roll Sponge Cake (page 97), sifting the cocoa with the flour and sugar. Sift *twice* rather than once.

Hazelnut Meringue

These circles are filled with Mocha Butter Cream to make a sumptuous, rich Dacquoise (page 194). The meringues have to be thoroughly dried out after baking. If possible, bake them in the evening and leave them in the turned-off oven overnight.

MAKES 2 (10-INCH) CIRCLES

> ¾ cup hazelnuts, toasted
> 3 tablespoons cornstarch
> 1 cup plus 3 tablespoons sugar
> 6 large egg whites

Preheat the oven to 225°. Line two cookie sheets with parchment. Draw a 10-inch circle on each parchment sheet (trace a cardboard cake circle or a 10-inch plate). Then turn over the sheets of parchment.

Finely grind the nuts in a food processor. With your hands, rub together the ground nuts, cornstarch, and 3 tablespoons of sugar. Set aside.

Combine the egg whites and 1 cup of sugar. Heat over slowly boiling water just to body temperature, then whip at high speed to soft peaks. Fold in the nut mixture. Spoon the meringue into a pastry bag with a #4 plain tip.

Pipe two 10-inch circles of meringue on the parchment-lined cookie sheets as follows: Hold the tip about 1 inch above the center of one of the circles. Starting with a dot of meringue, pipe out a continuous spiral, with each circle touching but not overlapping the one before, until you have filled the entire 10-inch circle. If there are large gaps, go back when the

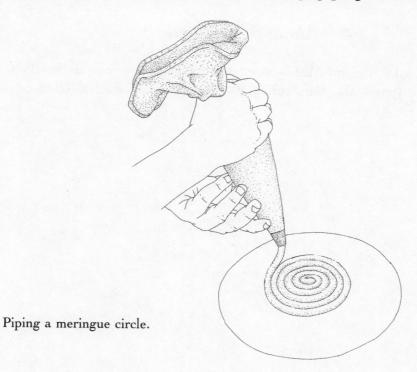

Piping a meringue circle.

circle is finished and fill them in. Small gaps can usually be closed by simply lifting one edge of the parchment. If there are lumps, smooth them with a fingertip. Repeat with the second circle. (Meringues vary in volume. If you have some left over, pipe out little cookies on the unused segments of the sheet and bake them with the circles.)

Bake for 1 hour, then turn off the oven and leave the meringues to dry out overnight. (If that is not possible, put them in a warm, dry place.) When done, the circles will feel like very light pie crusts and should be golden brown. Slide the parchment onto a counter and let the circles stand until completely cool, then turn them over on the counter and very carefully pull off the parchment. Trim the meringue circles by putting each between two 10-inch cardboard circles and trimming off any meringue that sticks out.

Almond Meringue

To make Almond Meringue circles, follow the recipe for Hazelnut Meringue (page 98), substituting ¾ cup of toasted natural (skin on) almonds for hazelnuts.

6
Creams, Sauces, Glazes, and Decorations

A beautiful dessert is a source of pride for the baker and a joy to everyone who gets to see and partake of it. But somewhere in the history of dessert making a terrible thing happened: Pastry cooks—not all, but many—began paying more attention to the appearance, the "presentation," of desserts than to their taste. Many pastry kitchens even today turn out beautiful desserts that just don't taste very good. It is as easy to produce great-tasting creams, sauces, glazes, and decorations as bland or overly sweet ones, provided you use the best ingredients and combine them with a light touch. The recipes in this chapter offer you a full palette with which to finish and decorate gorgeous desserts that taste equally gorgeous.

The creams that decorate and give substance to cakes, tarts, and pastries should be rich, light, and flavorful—never cloyingly sweet. The simplest is unsweetened whipped cream. I use it often as an icing for cakes or as a topping for pies, tarts, and other desserts. If your cream is fresh and unadulterated with preservatives, there is no reason to mask its wonderful flavor with sugar or vanilla. Buy the best cream you can find, whip it to soft peaks, and enjoy one of the world's great treats.

Butter creams are by nature thicker and richer than plain whipped cream because the water content of cream is reduced in the butter-making process. But butter creams should still be light and fresh tasting. Mine are less sweet than most and, I think, cleaner in taste. Although sugar is an important ingredient for its contribution to texture, I always use as little as is reasonable, to keep from masking other flavors. The same is true of cooked creams, such as the Pastry Cream and Lemon Cream in this chapter.

Fruit sauces should taste like fruit, not sugar. Never use old or inferior-tasting fruits in a sauce, on the theory that their flavor will be improved by sugar or other flavorings. Nothing can bring a tired or flavorless fruit back to life. Your sauces will taste only as fresh and delicious as the fruits you make them from, so use the best and ripest (but not overripe) you can find. Try to use fruits at the peak of their season; they always taste best. The fruit sauces in this chapter were developed to show off, not alter the sparkling flavors of fresh fruit.

The nonfruit sauces are also sweetened sparingly. I like my chocolate sauces slightly bitter so that they dance on the tongue rather than weigh it down. When using bittersweet rather than unsweetened chocolate in creams and sauces, I often sift unsweetened cocoa powder over the finished cake or pastry to add just a hint of the bitterness that makes chocolate exciting. My caramel sauces, in which all or most of the flavor comes from sugar, are lively rather than cloying because the sugar is cooked until it turns slightly bitter. In any dessert sauce or cream if your first and most dominant taste sensation is sweet, something is wrong.

I don't like fussy decorations on desserts any more than I like overly sweet flavors. If a dessert is fresh, well balanced, and bursting with wonderful flavors, it deserves to be presented simply and elegantly. The outside should celebrate, not disguise, what is within. I finish most fruit tarts with a simple glaze to make them sleek and gleaming—apricot glaze for light-colored fruits, currant for dark. When a more decorative presentation is appropriate, I add rosettes of unsweetened whipped cream; chopped, toasted nuts; or grated chocolate.

Cake decorating needs to be a bit more elaborate. I frequently cover the sides of a cake with crushed, toasted nuts or coarsely grated chocolate. On top I like to create simple, balanced designs with small pieces of fruit, candied citrus peel or ginger, or sometimes chocolate rosettes or truffles. My one hard-and-fast rule is that the ingredient used on top for decoration must reflect a flavor inside the cake. I wouldn't decorate with strawberries, for instance, if none were used inside the cake. The outside of a cake creates anticipation and expectation in those who are going to eat it. Failure to fulfill those expectations brings disappointment, even if the cake is very good.

By the same token, I wouldn't hide a major unexpected ingredient inside a dessert. A friend once ordered a mango mousse in a restaurant because it promised a light and fruity ending to a rather large lunch. On the third bite her spoon hit something hard: A whole chocolate truffle was hidden inside—sweet, rich, chocolaty, no doubt delicious, but not what she wanted right then or had been led to expect.

Creams, sauces, glazes, and decorations are the finishing touches to many desserts, but they are also an integral part of those desserts. Their role is to complete a carefully thought out combination of flavors and textures, to heighten the pleasurable impact of the dessert, not only visually but in every way.

Pastry Cream

MAKES 1½ CUPS

¼ **cup sugar**
1 **tablespoon all-purpose flour**
2 **teaspoons cornstarch**
1 **large egg**
1 **cup milk**
3 **tablespoons unsalted butter (soft)**
¼ **teaspoon vanilla extract**

Sift the sugar, flour, and cornstarch together into a mixing bowl. Add the egg and beat until light. Bring the milk to a boil in a heavy-bottomed saucepan. Stir half the milk into the egg mixture, then pour the whole mixture back into the pan. Cook over high heat, stirring continuously with a wire whisk, until the center bubbles and the mixture is very thick. Stir vigorously to keep the mixture from sticking and the egg from scrambling. The best way is to move your whisk back and forth, scraping the bottom of the pan, then rapidly circle the edge and repeat.

Remove from the heat and stir in the butter and vanilla. Pour into a bowl, cover with plastic wrap, and chill.

Chocolate Pastry Cream

MAKES 2 CUPS

    1 large egg
    2 teaspoons cornstarch
   ¼ cup sugar
    1 tablespoon all-purpose flour
 1½ cups milk
    2 ounces unsweetened chocolate, melted

Beat the egg using the whisk attachment on an electric mixer (see page 58). Combine the cornstarch, sugar, and flour, and add them to the egg. Beat at medium speed until light in color. Stop at least once to scrape the sides and bottom of the bowl.

Bring the milk to a boil in a 2½-quart (or larger) saucepan. Stir about ¼ cup of the milk into the egg mixture, then pour all of the egg mixture into the milk. Cook, stirring constantly with a whisk, to boiling. Remove from the heat, add the chocolate, and continue stirring until smooth. Cool.

English Custard (Crème Anglaise)

This light custard sauce has many uses. I serve it most often with unfrosted cakes (see Chiffon Cake, page 216) and with puddings. It's also delicious as a topping for fresh berries.

MAKES 4 CUPS

   6 large egg yolks
 ½ cup sugar
   2 teaspoons vanilla extract
   2 cups milk

Combine the egg yolks, sugar, and vanilla in the bowl of an electric mixer. Using the wire whisk attachment (see page 58), beat at high speed until thick and light in color.

Bring the milk to a boil in a heavy-bottomed saucepan. Remove from the heat. With the mixer on low speed, stir ½ cup of the hot milk into the beaten eggs, then add all of the egg mixture to the pot of milk. Turn the heat to high and whisk vigorously until the mixture begins to bubble in the middle and thicken around the edges, about 30 seconds. Whisk energetically or the eggs will curdle. Move the whisk back and forth, scraping the bottom of the pan, then briskly around the edge. Be sure you don't miss any spots—the milk will stick and burn if you do. Turn off the heat and stir 1 minute more. The custard should look like cream, with some body but not really thick. Pour it through a fine sieve into a bowl. Let stand at room temperature. Whisk every 5 minutes until completely cool. It will thicken as it cools.

Lemon Cream

By itself, Lemon Cream is a refreshingly tart, creamy topping. (Try it on Fresh Fruit Pound Cake, page 225.) Combined with softly whipped cream and bourbon, it becomes a satin smooth Bourbon Sauce (page 120). Once you've mastered the recipe, use it as a base upon which to improvise your own distinctive sauces.

MAKES ABOUT 1 CUP

  2 **large eggs**
  ½ **cup sugar**
  ⅓ **cup lemon juice (about 2 small lemons)**
    Zest of 1 lemon, grated
  4 **tablespoons unsalted butter**

Whip the eggs and sugar at high speed until double in volume and very light in color. Mix in the lemon juice and zest. Transfer to the top of a double boiler and cook over high heat until very thick, 20 to 30 minutes.

Once the mixture has begun to thicken, stir occasionally with a wire whisk to help the eggs cook evenly (they cook around the edges first).

Remove from the heat. Cut the butter into small pieces, add it to the egg mixture, and stir until melted. Strain through a fine sieve and set aside to cool. If you don't use it right away, Lemon Cream can become too thick. If so, thin it with about 1 tablespoon of half-and-half.

Chocolate Cream

  8 ounces bittersweet chocolate
¾ cup milk
  2 cups whipping cream

Cut the chocolate into small chunks. Bring the milk to a boil in a saucepan. Turn off the heat. Add the chocolate and stir until melted. Transfer to a bowl and refrigerate until the mixture is cool and coats a spoon.

Whip the cream until thick. Add the chocolate mixture and continue whipping to soft peaks.

Chocolate Butter Cream

20 tablespoons unsalted butter
1⅔ cups sugar
½ cup egg yolks (about 6 large eggs)
 1 cup whipping cream
 4 ounces unsweetened chocolate

Allow the butter to stand at room temperature for 1 hour to soften.

Whip ⅔ cup of sugar with the egg yolks until pale yellow. Stir 1 cup of sugar into the cream and bring to a boil. Stir the hot cream into the egg yolks. Pour into a heavy 2-quart pot. Stir continuously with a wire whisk over medium-high heat until the center bubbles. Remove from the heat, transfer to a mixing bowl, and whip until cool. Melt the chocolate over hot water and set aside to cool. Whip the soft butter into the cooled cream. Add the chocolate and mix until smooth.

Custard Butter Cream

24 tablespoons (¾ pound) unsalted butter (soft)
1 cup powdered sugar
1 cup Pastry Cream (page 105)

Using the paddle attachment on an electric mixer (see page 58), beat the butter and sugar until light. Add the pastry cream and mix until smooth.

Egg White Butter Cream

This is a very light and smooth butter cream. It is a bit sweet for my taste by itself. I prefer it mixed with unsweetened chocolate (see Chocolate Fondant Cake, page 201) or another tart or bitter flavor, such as lemon or coffee.

½ cup egg whites (about 4 large eggs)
1 cup sugar
1 pound unsalted butter (soft)

Beat the egg whites and sugar to stiff peaks. Cut the butter into pieces and mix it in. Beat at medium-high speed until very smooth.

Swiss Butter Cream

This is the butter cream that gets sandwiched between hazelnut meringues to create the lush richness and tantalizing coffee aroma of Dacquoise. The recipe makes enough for one Dacquoise (page 194).

   6 **large egg yolks**
1½ **cups sugar**
   1 **cup whipping cream**
   3 **tablespoons instant coffee powder**
28 **tablespoons unsalted butter (soft)**

Whip the egg yolks and ¾ cup of sugar until light. Meanwhile, bring the whipping cream and the rest of the sugar to a full boil. Add the whipped yolks to the cream and continue cooking, stirring constantly with a wire whisk, until thick. Be sure you scrape the bottom and sides of the pan often when stirring. If brown spots begin to appear, stir up the bottom quickly. Don't stop stirring. Remove from the heat and add the coffee, stirring until it is completely dissolved.

Transfer the mixture to a mixing bowl and whip at low speed until cold. Add the butter in 3 segments, then whip at medium speed until very thick and smooth.

Fondant

Making fondant—that silky smooth icing that crowns napoleons and other fine pastries—is a precise art. You can't do it "by eye" or by feel. You will need an accurate thermometer that goes to at least 240° and a quick hand when the thermometer tells you it's time to act. You will also need a marble (or Formica) surface that's at least 14 x 25 inches and a good heavy saucepan. You can work fondant either by hand, with the aid of a metal dough scraper, or in an electric mixer with a paddle attachment.* You may find the mixer slightly easier.

Don't get discouraged if your fondant doesn't come out the first time you try. The ingredients are simple and inexpensive and the process doesn't take long, so if at first you don't succeed, throw out that batch and start again. Since you have to make fondant at least a day ahead of using it, you don't have to worry about guests waiting at the table for you to get it right. When you do get the technique down—which won't take more than a couple of tries—the feeling of accomplishment and your incredibly smooth and glistening fondant will be more than ample reward for your efforts.

MAKES 1 PINT

> 2½ **cups sugar**
> ½ **teaspoon cream of tartar**
> 1 **cup water**
> ¼ **cup simple syrup**†

Rub your marble or Formica work surface with vegetable oil. Have a clean pastry brush in a glass of water next to the stove. Have a plastic container (to receive your finished fondant) and the simple syrup close by.

Combine the sugar, cream of tartar, and water in a heavy saucepan. Stir with a spoon over medium heat to dissolve the sugar. Stop stirring and bring to a boil. Brush the sides of the pan with the pastry brush and water to wash any sugar crystals down into the boiling liquid. Even a few crystals left inside the pan can cause the entire mixture to crystallize. Watch the temperature of the boiling liquid carefully (for an accurate reading, don't let the thermometer touch the bottom of the pan). The magic number is 238: If you let the liquid get hotter than 238°, your fondant will be gummy and unworkable. If you don't get it up to 238°, it will be runny. Now, I know some fondant recipes say you should go to

---

* This is one time when only a mixer with a paddle attachment will do because you do not want to incorporate air into the fondant. If your mixer has just beaters, work the fondant by hand.

† Simple syrup is equal parts sugar and water. Combine and bring to a boil and cook only until the sugar dissolves. Cool to room temperature. Although you need only ¼ cup for this recipe, it's a good idea to make more and keep some on hand.

240°, and in fact you can achieve a good fondant anywhere from 238° to 240°. But if you wait until the temperature reaches 240°, by the time you can get the mixture out of the pan and onto the marble, it will have gone even higher, and it will turn into a gummy mass.

When the temperature reaches 220°, start watching it like a hawk. If it's rising fast, turn down the heat so you'll be able to act at precisely 238°.

When the temperature is 238°, quickly pour the liquid out onto the marble, forming a large puddle (about 10 x 20 inches) with a back and forth motion of the pan. The puddle should be transparent and hold its edge, and it should not spread after you've poured it. Bury the tip of your thermometer in the puddle (push some fondant over it if necessary) and let it cool to 120°. Test for doneness by touching the surface of the puddle with your finger. It should form a skin where you touch it.

At this point you can work the fondant either by hand or electric mixer.

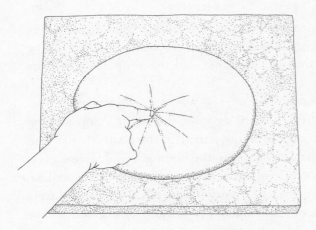

Test for doneness by touching the surface of the puddle with your finger. It should form a skin where you touch it.

By hand: The purpose of this step is to work air through the fondant by repeatedly folding it over on itself and then flattening it against the marble. Slip the blade of your scraper under one end of the fondant puddle, then move it in a sweeping motion under the edge furthest from you, lifting about half of the fondant mass. When you get to the opposite end, fold the raised fondant toward you. Now move the scraper over the fondant, back to your starting position, pressing the fondant against the

Many cooks prefer to work fondant
with two scrapers, one in each hand.
Alternate hands, working first in one
direction, then in the other.

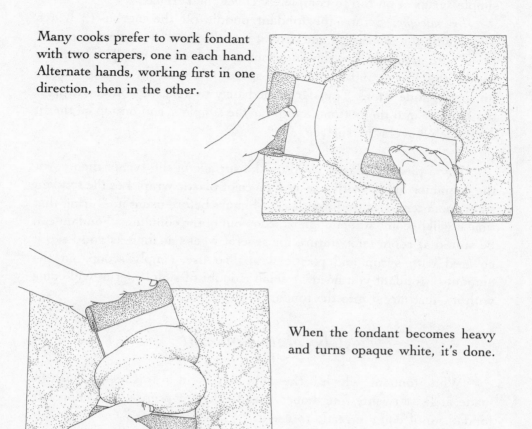

When the fondant becomes heavy
and turns opaque white, it's done.

marble as you go. Repeat this circular movement several times, making
sure the entire mass of fondant is being manipulated. Work quickly and
steadily. Be sure you don't lose bits of fondant as you move it around.
With each sweep of the scraper bring into the mass of fondant any bits
you dropped on the previous round. When the fondant starts turning
opaque white, it's done. Transfer it immediately to a plastic container and
press it into the bottom. (It will harden fast, so work quickly.) Pour the

simple syrup in on top to completely cover the surface.

By machine: Scrape the fondant puddle off the marble (2 bench scrapers do the job easily) and drop it into the bowl of an electric mixer. Make sure none sticks to the sides, out of reach of the paddle. Using the paddle attachment and medium-low speed, mix until the fondant begins turning opaque white. Transfer immediately to a plastic container, press the fondant into the bottom, and pour the simple syrup on top so that it completely covers the surface.

Lay a piece of plastic wrap on the surface of the syrup, then cover the container tightly with a second piece of plastic wrap. Let the fondant sit at room temperature for at least 24 hours before using it. During that time it will become soft enough to scoop out of the container. Fondant can be stored at room temperature for several weeks as long as you keep it covered with syrup and plastic wrap. To use, simply scoop out the amount of fondant you need. A small amount of simple syrup will come with it—just mix it into the fondant.

Chocolate Fondant

White fondant, which is the main ingredient in this recipe, must be made at least twenty-four hours ahead. Do not prepare the chocolate fondant until you are ready to use it.

- ¾ **cup sugar**
- ¾ **cup water**
- 1 **recipe Fondant (page 110)**
- 6 **ounces unsweetened chocolate, melted and cooled**

Prepare a simple syrup by combining the sugar and water in a saucepan. Bring to a boil and cook only until the sugar dissolves. Cool to room temperature.

Transfer the fondant from its storage container into a stainless steel bowl or the top of a stainless double boiler. Add the melted chocolate and ¾ cup of the cooled simple syrup. Mix well with your hand—utensils won't do here, so roll up your sleeves and dive right in. Once the mixture is smooth, test its consistency by dipping your hand in, then holding it over the bowl with fingers spread. The excess fondant should run off, leaving your fingers smoothly and thickly coated (about 1/16 inch thick). If all the coating runs off, your fondant was too thin, and there's really no way to fix it, short of running out to buy a container of commercial fondant (not as good but all right in such an emergency). If the fondant clings to your fingers and doesn't run off at all, it's too thick. Thin it by adding simple syrup, 1 tablespoon at a time, until you get the right consistency.

Heat the fondant over simmering water, stirring constantly with a rubber spatula. As it accepts the heat, it will become thinner, easier to stir, glossy, and streaked. Keep stirring until all the streaks have disappeared, but don't get the fondant warmer than body temperature (test it with your finger).

Chocolate Sauce

I don't like overly sweet sauces. This one is rich and very chocolaty without being sweet. Use it as a topping for ice cream, profiteroles (miniature cream puffs, see page 87), or anything else you like with chocolate sauce.

MAKES 1½ CUPS

1 cup milk
8 ounces bittersweet chocolate

Bring the milk to a boil in a heavy-bottomed saucepan. Remove from the heat. Cut the chocolate into pieces and add it to the hot milk; stir until melted. Cool to room temperature.

Lemon Sauce

This is a thick, tart, very lemony sauce. Use it warm or at room temperature on cakes, ice cream, puddings, or whatever you like.

MAKES 1½ PINTS

> 3 large eggs
> 1 cup sugar
> 4 lemons (or enough to yield ½ cup of juice)
> 1 cup water

Using the whisk attachment of an electric mixer (see page 58), beat the eggs at medium speed until foamy. Add the sugar and beat at high speed until thick and white.

Meanwhile, zest one lemon, then squeeze ½ cup of lemon juice. Combine the zest, lemon juice, and water in the top of a double boiler. Add the beaten eggs and cook over boiling water, whisking occasionally, until the sauce starts to thicken around the edges, about 10 minutes. Transfer to a bowl and allow to cool.

Strawberry Sauce

This is a slightly sweet, very fresh-tasting sauce I use on cheesecake and ice cream.

MAKES 1 PINT

> 1 pint strawberries
> ½ cup strawberry jam

Wash the strawberries, cut off their tops, and cut them in half. Combine with the jam in a bowl. Stir and let stand about 1 hour. The sugar in the jam will draw the juice from the berries and thin the sauce. Use immediately or store in the refrigerator up to two days.

Cranberry Sauce

I've used this slightly tart, deep red sauce to add sparkle to ice cream, poached pears, and simple cakes. I especially like it on Cranberry

Turnovers (page 274) topped with Caramel Ice Cream (page 304).

MAKES 2½ CUPS

1 package (12 ounces) cranberries
4 cups water
1½ cups sugar

Combine all the ingredients in a large saucepan and bring to a boil. Turn down the heat and simmer until all the berries have popped and the volume is reduced to 3 cups, about 15 minutes. Pour into a food processor and process until liquid. Pour back into the pan through a fine strainer. Return to a boil. Turn off the heat and skim off any white foam on the surface. Transfer to a bowl and cool. Serve at room temperature or refrigerate and serve cold.

Apricot Sauce

This is a thick, fruity sauce with lots of apricot chunks to give it texture. There is very little sugar, so be sure your apricots are ripe and sweet.

MAKES 1½ CUPS

8 medium-size apricots, ripe and firm
1 cup water
¼ cup sugar

Wash and towel-dry the apricots. Cut them in half and discard the pits. Cut 6 of the halves lengthwise into quarters and then in half crosswise. Set aside. Put the other 10 halves into a heavy-bottomed saucepan with the water and sugar. Bring to a boil. Lower the heat and cook gently until the apricots are soft, about 5 minutes. Pour the fruit and liquid into a food processor and puree until smooth.

Return the puree to the saucepan, add the reserved apricots, and bring to a boil. Turn down the heat and simmer until the apricot pieces are tender and glossy, about 5 minutes. The idea is to cook the apricot chunks long enough for them to become integrated into the sauce but not so long that they disappear.

Transfer the sauce to a bowl and allow it to cool before using. If you are not going to use it immediately, you may store it, covered, in the refrigerator up to three days.

Raspberry Sauce

The tart, fruity taste of fresh raspberries comes through loud and clear in this versatile, deep red sauce. Serve it chilled or at room temperature with ice cream, puddings, cakes, or whatever you like.

MAKES 1 CUP

1 pint fresh raspberries
1 cup water
½ cup sugar

Puree the raspberries. Combine the puree with the water and sugar, and bring to a boil. Reduce to a simmer and cook gently until reduced to 1½ cups, about 30 minutes. Pour through a fine strainer, working it through with a rubber scraper to get all the juice. Cool to room temperature. Chill if desired.

Caramel Sauce

This richly flavorful sauce is slightly bitter, not sweet. I use it as an ice cream topping and as the base for Caramel Ice Cream (page 304), as well as for various icings. Always be careful when working with caramel; melting sugar is very hot.

MAKES 1 CUP

1½ cups sugar
¼ cup water

For safety, always pour liquids into hot caramel through a colander or large strainer. Caramel is very hot and sometimes bubbles up when liquids are added to it.

Heat the sugar in a heavy-bottomed saucepan over medium heat. Do not stir but shake the pan occasionally to ensure even browning. When most of the sugar has dissolved and turned a rich caramel color, turn off the heat. Continue shaking the pan in long movements until all the sugar is dissolved and evenly colored.

Cover the pan with a colander or large strainer to prevent splashing and carefully pour the water through it into the sugar. When the bubbling stops, stir, transfer the sauce to a stainless steel bowl, and allow it to cool.

Rum Caramel Sauce

This is a nice variation on plain Caramel Sauce. Be extra careful when making it—not only is the sugar hot, the rum is flammable.

MAKES 1 CUP

1½ **cups sugar**
¼ **cup rum**

Follow the instructions for Caramel Sauce (page 118), substituting the rum for the water. Pour the rum through a large, fine-mesh strainer rather than a colander.

Butterscotch Sauce

I like to use this rich, pungent sauce over ice cream and my Apple and Walnut Tart (page 141). Note that this recipe calls for apple cider vinegar; never use any other kind of vinegar in pastry making.

MAKES 2 CUPS

1½ **cups dark brown sugar**
¼ **cup water**
4 **tablespoons unsalted butter**
1 **cup whipping cream**
1 **tablespoon apple cider vinegar**

Combine the sugar and water in a heavy-bottomed saucepan that holds at least 2½ quarts. Stir over low heat until the sugar dissolves, then raise the heat to medium and bring to a boil. Let the mixture boil until it begins to smoke and thicken. It will rise up in the pan, become very foamy, and start emitting puffs of smoke. Drop in the butter and stir until it dissolves. Stir in the cream. Return to a boil, then turn off the heat and stir in the vinegar. Cool to lukewarm. Use immediately or refrigerate and warm in a double boiler when ready to use.

Bourbon Sauce

I always serve a dollop of Bourbon Sauce on my Apple Crisp (page 187). If you like the taste of bourbon, you'll probably want to use it with other desserts as well. Be sure you use a smooth-tasting, well-aged bourbon. I use Maker's Mark.

MAKES 3 CUPS

    2 **cups whipping cream**
    1 **recipe Lemon Cream (page 107)**
    ¾ **cup good bourbon**

Whip the cream to soft peaks. Fold in the cooled lemon cream and the bourbon. Refrigerate until ready to use. Store leftover bourbon sauce for 2 to 3 days in a covered container in the refrigerator.

Rum Sauce

I make this sauce to go with Praline Ice Cream Pie (page 174). You can also use it on your favorite ice cream.

MAKES 2 CUPS

    1⅓ **cups sugar**
    ½ **cup water**
    1 **cup whipping cream**
    4 **tablespoons unsalted butter**
    2 **tablespoons dark or refined rum (I use Mt. Gay Eclipse)**

Combine the sugar and water in a large (at least 2½-quart), heavy saucepan. Bring to a boil over medium-high heat and cook without stirring to a rich mahogany color. If the caramel starts to color unevenly, swirl the pan to distribute the color. Remove from the heat and carefully pour in the cream. Swirl the pan to combine the ingredients. When the mixture stops bubbling, put it back over medium-high heat and bring to a boil, stirring with a metal spoon. Add the butter. Remove from the heat and stir until the butter is dissolved. Stir in the rum. Cool to room temperature.

Apricot Glaze

This is the glaze I use on light-colored fruit tarts. It should be made ahead and kept, covered, in the refrigerator. You can keep it for up to a week. Depending on how heavily you glaze, this recipe makes enough for two to four tarts.

MAKES 1½ CUPS

  1 **cup apricot preserves**
⅓ **cup sugar**
⅓ **cup water**

Combine all the ingredients in a heavy-bottomed saucepan and bring to a boil. Stir with a rubber spatula, pressing out any lumps. Let the mixture boil for 3 minutes, then set it aside to cool a little. Pour the glaze through a fine strainer, working it through with a rubber spatula. Allow to cool, then transfer to a bowl or jar and refrigerate until needed.

To use: Heat the glaze over a low flame, stirring occasionally, just until it liquefies. Dab it on with a pastry brush while warm.

Note: Always heat glazes over a low flame just enough to soften for "painting" with a pastry brush. If you let a glaze get too hot, it won't coat the fruit. What's more, it will draw out the natural juices from the fruit; they in turn will thin the glaze, and your tart will be swimming in a pool of liquid.

Currant Glaze

When I make tarts with dark-colored fruit, I use this purple glaze. I also use it on my Chocolate Cassis Cake (page 202) and on some pastries. Make the glaze ahead and keep it in the refrigerator. Heat it slowly to liquefy before using (see *Note* above).

MAKES 1 CUP

1 cup currant jelly
¼ cup sugar

Bring the jelly and sugar to a boil in a heavy-bottomed saucepan. Lower the heat and simmer, stirring occasionally to help dissolve the lumps. The mixture will be cloudy at first. When the lumps are gone, let the mixture simmer until it turns glossy. Skim any foam off the top. Strain through a fine sieve and set aside to cool. When cool, transfer to a jar or covered container and refrigerate.

Chocolate Glaze

When melting chocolate, make sure all your pans and utensils are absolutely dry. Even a little bit of water will cause chocolate to "break."

MAKES 1 CUP

6 ounces semisweet or bittersweet chocolate
6 tablespoons unsalted butter

Cut the chocolate into ½-inch chunks. Melt the butter and chocolate together in the top of a double boiler over boiled (not boiling) water. Remove from the heat and stir until the mixture is completely smooth, with no streaks.

If you get the glaze too hot, it will break. If that happens, let it cool until thick and gently melt it again.

Candied Ginger

This is a sweet yet pungent confection much like Chinese ginger in syrup. I use it to add punch to tarts and cakes. Remember, mature ginger can be very strong flavored. If you prefer a milder taste, do what the

Chinese do—use thin-skinned young ginger, also known as stem ginger (available from early summer into the fall in Asian markets and some supermarkets).

> 8 ounces fresh ginger
> 1 cup sugar
> 2 cups water

Peel the ginger and cut it into ¼-inch-thick slices. Bring the sugar and water to a boil in a saucepan. Lower to a simmer and add the ginger. Cook until the ginger slices turn golden and are pierced easily with the tip of a knife, about 45 minutes. Cool to room temperature.

When cool, spoon the ginger into an 8-ounce jar and pour in enough of the syrup to cover all the pieces. Cover the jar tightly and store at room temperature.

To make chocolate-dipped candied ginger: Remove the ginger slices from the syrup and pat them dry with a towel. Cut the slices in half or, if you prefer, into strips. Dip about one-third of each piece in Chocolate Glaze (page 123). Let the pieces dry on a sheet of parchment or wax paper. You can also make chocolate-dipped ginger with store-bought crystallized ginger.

Candied Orange Peel

These tasty and colorful confections can be eaten out of hand, but they are really meant for decorating cakes. For obvious reasons you should look for oranges with unbruised bright orange skins.

> 4 medium-size eating oranges
> 1½ cups sugar
> 2 cups water

Remove the peel from the oranges with a sharp knife: First cut off the top and bottom. Then stand the orange on one cut end and cut off a strip of peel about 2 inches wide from top to bottom, following the curve of the fruit. Looking at the cut section, you can see where the orange peel ends and the white pith begins. Following that line, cut the peel away in 2-inch strips all around the orange. Cut the strips of peel in half lengthwise to make them easier to work with, then cut or scrape away as much as you can of the white pith that is left clinging to the peel. Cut the strips in half again, to ½ inch wide, then cut each diagonally from corner to corner, making a long, slim triangle.

Combine the sugar and water in a heavy-bottomed saucepan. Stir to dissolve the sugar. Bring to a boil. Add the strips of orange peel and swirl the pan a little to keep them from clumping together. Simmer gently for 10 minutes. Remove from the heat and let the peels cool in the syrup. When cool, store peels and syrup in a tightly covered jar.

Variation: For Candied Lemon Peel, follow the instructions above, substituting lemons for oranges.

To make chocolate-dipped candied orange (or lemon) peel: Remove peels from the syrup and pat them dry with a towel. Dip about one-third of each piece in Chocolate Glaze (page 123). Let the pieces dry on a sheet of parchment or wax paper.

Chocolate Ganache Shells

These graceful decorative shells dress up cakes and add an extra hit of almost pure chocolate. You can make them ahead and store them at room temperature, as you would store cookies.

MAKES 14

4 ounces bittersweet or semisweet chocolate
⅓ cup sour cream (room temperature)

Melt the chocolate over boiled (not boiling) water. Stir in the sour cream. Put the mixture in a pastry bag with a #3 star tip. Lay down a half sheet of parchment. Hold the pastry bag with the tip pointing straight down, about ¼ inch above the parchment. To form the shell shape, squeeze out a 1-inch star, then pull the bag toward you. When the tip is over the edge of the rosette, stop squeezing. Bring the bag toward you another ½ inch, pushing the tip down toward the table to cut off the flow of ganache. Each shell should be about 1 inch across and 1½ inches long.

Allow the shells to dry at room temperature.

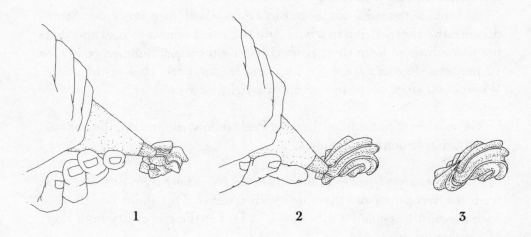

Piping ganache shells: 1. Squeeze out a 1-inch star. 2. Bring the bag toward you, pushing the tip down to cut off the flow of ganache. 3. The finished shell.

Chocolate Butterflies

These lacy chocolate butterfly wings will add a touch of whimsy to cakes, ice cream dishes, puddings, and pies. They will keep in the freezer, covered, for up to three months.

MAKES 26 TO 28 PAIRS

4 ounces bittersweet or semisweet chocolate

Melt the chocolate over boiled (not boiling) water. Cool until the chocolate thickens and begins to hold its shape. Line a cookie sheet with parchment and make a parchment cone (see directions on pages 61–63). Spoon the chocolate into the cone and cut a ⅛-inch opening in the tip.

Holding the tip of the cone about ¼ inch above the parchment-lined sheet, pipe out a 2-inch elongated figure 8. Starting from the center of the 8, pipe out three overlapping loops, all on the same side (see illustration below). Now make another figure 8 and repeat the process, this time putting the loops on the opposite side. The two together form a pair of butterfly wings. Pipe out the rest of the chocolate into pairs of wings. Freeze, uncovered, until the chocolate is hard. Cover with plastic wrap and keep frozen until needed.

To use, carefully peel off the parchment. There will be some broken wings but most should come out fine. To decorate an individual dessert, insert the plain edges of a pair of wings into the whipped cream or other topping. Use several pairs to decorate a cake, pie, or other large dessert.

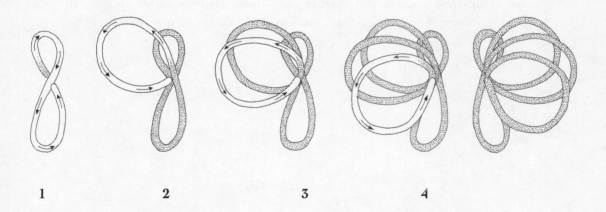

1   2   3   4

To make chocolate butterfly wings: Pipe out an elongated figure 8. Starting from the center of the 8, pipe out three overlapping loops. Use two wings with loops on opposite sides together to form a butterfly.

Chocolate Truffles

Over the last few years truffles have become extraordinarily popular as the chocolate lover's ultimate treat. In their basic form they are simple to make. I use these small ones for decorating cakes and my Chocolate Cream Pie (page 171). You can, of course, just eat them out of hand.

MAKES 16

¼ cup whipping cream
3 ounces bittersweet chocolate
¼ cup unsweetened cocoa powder

First make a ganache: Bring the cream to a boil in a very small saucepan over medium-low heat. Remove from the heat and add the chocolate. Stir with a spoon until smooth and glossy. Transfer to a bowl and allow to cool. Refrigerate until the ganache is dense, about the texture of soft fudge.

Scoop out a heaping ½ teaspoon of ganache and roll it in your hands to form a ball. (Your hands will get thoroughly coated with chocolate.) Repeat until you have made all the ganache into tight balls. Sift the cocoa into a shallow bowl and roll the ganache balls in it, one by one, until they are completely coated. Refrigerate until firm. Truffles soften quickly in heat, so keep them refrigerated until you are ready to use them.

Rhubarb Tart with Fresh Strawberries (page 157)

Fig and Lemon Tart (page 161)

Peach and Pistachio Ice Cream (page 302)

Top to bottom: Pink Grapefruit Ice (page 307), Fresh Mango Ice Cream (page 302), Watermelon Ice (page 309)

7
Tarts

Tarts, the European equivalent of American pies, have become very popular in the U.S. over the last few decades, and with good reason. Besides tasting great, they are usually quite beautiful, topped with colorful fruit arranged in geometric patterns and glazed to a high shine. The tart has an air of elegance. It is an arena in which the pastry cook can show off his artistic flair. Plump, ripe fruits are so beautiful in themselves, it's hard to go wrong as long as you obey the basic rules of simplicity and complementary flavors.

I seldom combine more than two dominant flavors in a single tart. I think an array of five or six different fruits just makes for confusion on the palate. Instead, I look for two flavors that will complement each other, each bringing the other excitingly to life. Some "right" combinations are obvious, like cinnamon and apple, or coconut and pineapple, but many of my favorite and most successful tarts are based on less predictable combinations—plum and vanilla, mango and lime, figs and lemon. I knew that strawberries and apricots would work well together, but when I combined baked apricots in a tart with plump, raw strawberries, even I was amazed at what they did for each other. They created a new flavor on the tongue, different from both and absolutely delicious (see Strawberry-Apricot Tart, page 145).

I usually begin my flavor explorations by tasting a ripe fruit in season. I try to imagine another flavor that would add depth or contrast

131

or some new dimension. Usually something comes to mind. I test the combination by tasting the raw ingredients together—a bit of papaya, for instance, and then a blueberry. If they combine in a pleasant and interesting way on my tongue, I take the next step and begin to plan the tart.

In thinking about each new tart, I carefully consider each element and how it will set off the others. A crisp, buttery crust contributes lightness and a dry, pleasant crunch. It contrasts well in both flavor and texture with a rich, creamy filling such as Pastry Cream or Lemon Cream; I frequently use one or the other. The fruit tops it all with a texture between crisp and creamy and a flavor that is bright and distinctive. If the three work together well, offering both contrast and harmony, the tart will be a success.

I prefer not to bake soft, lush fruits such as ripe peaches or even very ripe pears at all. I simply prebake a tart shell and arrange the fruit in it, with or without a layer of pastry cream underneath. I do bake firmer fruits, such as apples and plums, because baking improves their texture, making them softer and easier to eat. Be careful not to overbake the fruit in your tarts, or you'll lose the texture and flavor that makes that particular fruit—and your tart—special.

If fruits are very juicy, I slip a layer of sponge cake (génoise) underneath to absorb the excess liquid. Or I extract some of the juice, reduce it with sugar, and reintroduce it in the form of a glaze (see Rum Plum Tart, page 136).

The less the filling needs to be baked, the longer I prebake the shell.

And I finish almost every tart with glaze. Tarts are meant to gleam and sparkle, to dazzle the eye as well as the palate.

Field-Ripened Pineapple Tart

A field-ripened pineapple is a treasure—sweet and succulent, with just the slightest hint of tartness. When I was given a beautiful specimen as a gift, I knew I had to create a special dessert to do it justice. Here the sliced pineapple rests on a light tart sponge so that not a single drop of its delicious juice is lost. Apricot glaze adds an exotic finish. Field-ripened pineapples are expensive and hard to come by. If you can't get one, buy the sweetest, juiciest pineapple you can find.

SERVES 12

1 **field-ripened or very sweet pineapple**
8 **tablespoons (¼ pound) unsalted butter (soft)**
⅓ **cup sugar plus ¼ cup sugar if not using field-ripened pineapple**
2 **large eggs (room temperature)**
½ **cup cake flour, sifted**
1 **10-inch Rich Short Dough tart shell, blind baked (page 75)**
½ **recipe Apricot Glaze (page 122)**

If you are not using a field-ripened pineapple, peel the pineapple (see page 32). Cut it vertically into quarters and remove the woody core. Cut each quarter crosswise into ½-inch slices. Put the slices in a bowl, sprinkle them with ¼ cup of sugar, and let them stand until you are ready to assemble the tart. The sugar will sweeten the fruit and draw liquid from it, making it almost as sweet and juicy as its tree-ripened cousin. Brush all the liquid from the pineapple slices over the baked sponge before arranging the slices on the tart.

If you are using a field-ripened pineapple, peel and slice it as directed while the baked tart is cooling.

Preheat the oven to 375°.

Cream together the butter and ⅓ sugar until light. Add in order 1 egg, half the flour, the second egg, and the rest of the flour, beating until smooth after each addition. Pour the batter into the cooled, blind-baked tart shell. Bake until the top is golden brown, about 30 minutes.

Remove from the oven and prick with a fork every ½ inch over the entire top of the filling. Allow the tart to cool.

Arrange the pineapple slices on top of the tart, overlapping them in concentric circles.

Heat the apricot glaze over a low flame to liquefy. Brush a very thin coating over the pineapple slices.

Coconut-Pineapple Tart

The coconut is in the crust, making it fragrant and toasty. Inside is a layer of pastry cream, topped with fresh, sweet pineapple and glazed with apricot.

SERVES 12

> 1 **10-inch Coconut Dough tart shell, unbaked (page 77)**
> 1 **recipe Pastry Cream (page 105)**
> ½ **large pineapple, ripe and sweet**
> ½ **recipe Apricot Glaze (page 122)**

Preheat the oven to 400°.

Line the tart shell with foil that is at least 1½ times the size of the pan and fill it with dry beans or pie weights. Gently push the beans all the way to the edges of the shell to keep it from shrinking during baking. Fold the foil over the beans to contain them and make them easier to remove later. Bake for 20 minutes. Remove the foil and beans and continue baking until the shell is golden brown and has pulled away from the sides of the pan, about 15 minutes. Set aside to cool on a rack.

When the shell is cool, spread the pastry cream evenly in the bottom (I like to pipe it in with a pastry bag). Since it is awkward to deal with half a pineapple, I suggest you peel the whole pineapple (see pages 32–33), cut it in half vertically, and use one half for something else. Cut the other half in half again vertically and remove the core from the two quarters. Using a slicer or a long, slender knife with a thin blade, cut the quarters crosswise into slices as thin as possible. Arrange the slices on the tart in concentric circles, with the wider side outward and the pieces overlapping slightly. Overlap the circles a little as you work from the edges to the center of the tart.

Heat the apricot glaze gently to liquefy. Brush a thin layer of glaze over the pineapple, being careful not to get it on the shell. Serve at room temperature. This tart should be served within 2 hours of being assembled.

Vanilla Plum Tart

This is a deep-dish tart, baked in a springform pan. The vanilla and plum flavors merge during baking, and the smooth richness of the vanilla softens the tartness of the plums. Purple plums will stain the pastry cream a vibrant color. I like to heighten the effect with currant glaze.

SERVES 12

24 medium-size tart plums
1 recipe (1½ cups) Pastry Cream (page 105)
1 Short Dough tart shell, unbaked, in a 10-inch springform pan (page 71)
1 tablespoon sugar
1 tablespoon cornstarch
1 vanilla bean
½ recipe Currant Glaze (page 122)

Preheat the oven to 400°.

Wash and towel-dry the plums. Cut them in half and discard the pits. Cut each half into a fan by making three parallel cuts from one end to about ½ inch from the other end. The result will look something like a 4-fingered glove.

Spread the pastry cream evenly over the bottom of the tart shell. Arrange the plums on top of the pastry cream in concentric circles, skin side down. Begin at the outer edge and partially lean the plums, "fingers" up, against the side of the shell. Overlap each new circle so that you have a deep, almost solid layer of plums covering all of the pastry cream. Place the last plum half flat in the very center, skin side down. Press the plums gently into the pastry cream, making sure the top of the tart is level.

Combine the sugar and cornstarch on a piece of parchment or wax paper. Split the vanilla bean lengthwise and scrape out the soft pulp with a knife. Rub the vanilla pulp into the sugar with your fingertips until well mixed. Sprinkle the sugar over the fruit. Using a pastry wheel, trim the shell to about ½ inch above the plum line. Bake until the crust is golden brown and the sides have pulled away from the pan, about 1½ hours. Cool on a wire rack. When cool, transfer to a plate. Heat the currant glaze over a low flame until it liquefies and brush it over the plums with a pastry brush. Serve at room temperature.

Rum Plum Tart

This is a deep-dish tart fragrant with the aromas of dark rum and fresh plums. Be sure to use tart plums, to contrast with the smooth richness of the pastry cream. The plums need to marinate in the rum overnight, so begin the day before you want to serve the tart.

SERVES 12

- **16 tart plums**
- **1 cup dark or refined rum (I use Mt. Gay Eclipse)**
- **½ cup sugar**
- **1 recipe Pastry Cream (page 105)**
- **1 Short Dough tart shell, unbaked, in a 10-inch springform pan (page 71)**

Wash and quarter the plums and discard the pits. Place the plums in a bowl and pour the rum over them. Sprinkle on the sugar and stir with a spoon. Cover the bowl with plastic wrap and refrigerate overnight. The rum will draw out the excess liquid from the plums, and the plums will absorb the flavor of the rum.

Preheat the oven to 400°.

Spread the pastry cream evenly in the unbaked tart shell. Remove the plums from their liquid with a slotted spoon and pat them dry in a towel. Save the liquid to make a glaze. Arrange the plum quarters, skin side down, on the pastry cream in concentric circles, with the outer circle half-leaning against the sides of the pan, points toward the center. Overlap the circles a little as you work toward the center. The final arrangement will look something like a flower.

With a pastry wheel trim the sides of the tart shell to ½ inch above the fruit. Place a circle of parchment over the plums and bake. When the shell has begun to brown and the plums have given off some moisture (after about 30 minutes), remove the parchment. Continue baking until the shell is golden brown and has pulled away from the sides of the pan, and the filling is bubbling around the edges, about 30 minutes. Let the tart cool for 1 hour before glazing it.

Make a glaze by cooking the marinating liquid down to one-quarter its volume. Cool slightly, then brush over the plums.

Almond Apple Puff

This is a covered puff pastry tart based on the classic French *pithiviers*. The filling is a rich almond *frangipane* (pastry filling) topped with apple wedges.

SERVES 12

> 8 **ounces Puff Pastry Dough, divided in half (page 84)**
> 4 **ounces almond paste**
> 4 **tablespoons unsalted butter (cold)**
> ⅓ **cup bread flour**
> 1 **large egg**
> 2 **medium-size tart apples**

Roll out the pieces of puff pastry into two circles, one 12 inches in diameter, the other 10 inches. (Roll the 10-inch piece a bit larger and, using a pastry wheel and a cardboard circle or cake pan as a guide, trim it to a perfect 10-inch circle.) Line a cookie sheet with parchment and place the 10-inch circle on it. Refrigerate until needed.

Using the paddle attachment on an electric mixer (see page 58), mix the almond paste, butter, and flour at low speed until smooth. (Rub a bit between your fingers to make sure there are no lumps.) Add the egg and mix at medium speed until smooth.

Preheat the oven to 400°.

Remove the 10-inch pastry circle from the refrigerator. Spread the almond filling on it; leave about 1 inch around the edge and pile the filling slightly higher in the center, making a dome.

Peel, quarter, and core the apples. Cut each quarter lengthwise into four slices. Arrange the apple slices in two concentric circles on the almond filling—points toward the center in the outer circle, point to point in the inner circle, and one slice in the center.

Cover the filling with the 12-inch pastry circle, molding it gently to the fruit with your hands. Press the edges of the two circles together and trim, making 1½-inch-long scallops with a pastry cutter all the way around. With a sharp knife cut steam holes: a 2-inch slit along the curve of every second apple slice in the outer circle and five 1-inch slits in a circle around the center.

Bake until golden brown, about 1 hour.

Cranberry and Almond Puff

This light, covered puff pastry tart is filled with almond *frangipane* (pastry filling) and fresh cranberries. The overall effect is rich and buttery, with a lively spark of tartness from the cranberries.

SERVES 12

>   8 ounces Puff Pastry Dough, divided in half (page 84)
>   4 ounces almond paste
>   4 tablespoons unsalted butter (cold)
>   ⅓ cup bread flour
>   ⅓ cup sugar
>   1 large egg
>   6 ounces (½ bag) cranberries
>   ¼ cup sliced, blanched almonds

Roll out the pieces of puff pastry into two circles, one 12 inches in diameter, the other 10 inches. (Roll the 10-inch piece a bit larger and, using a pastry wheel and a cardboard circle or cake pan as a guide, trim it to a perfect 10-inch circle.) Line a cookie sheet with parchment and place the 10-inch circle on it. Refrigerate until needed.

Using the paddle attachment on an electric mixer (see page 58), mix the almond paste, butter, flour, and sugar at low speed until smooth. (Rub a bit between your fingers to make sure there are no lumps.) Add the egg and mix at medium speed until smooth.

Preheat the oven to 425°.

Remove the 10-inch pastry circle from the refrigerator. Spread the almond filling on it; leave about 1 inch around the edge and pile the filling slightly higher in the center, making a dome. Top with the cranberries.

Cover the filling with the 12-inch pastry circle, molding it gently to the fruit with your hands. Press the edges of the two circles together and trim. If you wish, make 1½-inch-long scallops with a pastry cutter all the way around. With a sharp knife cut 8 slits for steam holes. Brush the puff with water and spread the sliced almonds over the top.

Bake for 15 minutes, then lower the oven temperature to 350°. Continue baking until golden brown, about 20 minutes. Cool to room temperature before serving.

Cinnamon Apple Tart

This is a simple apple tart in a spicy cinnamon shell. The effect is two separate tastes—cinnamon and apple—mingling on the palate instead of in the oven.

SERVES 12

5 medium-size tart apples (I use Gravenstein or Pippin)
1 tablespoon lemon juice
1 10-inch Cinnamon Dough tart shell, blind baked (page 77)
1 tablespoon sugar
½ recipe Apricot Glaze (page 122)

Preheat the oven to 400°.

Peel, quarter, and core the apples. Cut each quarter into four or five wedges (depending on the size of the apple). As you cut them, toss the wedges in a bowl with the lemon juice.

Arrange the apple wedges in the blind-baked tart shell. Start at the edge and place the wedges close together in concentric circles until the entire tart is covered. Place the last wedge right in the center of the tart. Sprinkle the sugar over the apples to keep them moist during baking. Bake until the apples give when you touch them but are still slightly firm, about 40 minutes. Cool to room temperature.

Heat the glaze gently to liquefy. With a pastry brush dab a coating of glaze over the fruit. Serve at room temperature.

Gingered Dutch Apple Tart

The trouble with most Dutch apple tarts is that there's too much topping and not enough fruit. This version is similar to a deep-dish apple pie, chock-full of tart, juicy apples. The topping is crunchy, buttery, and studded with chewy nuggets of candied ginger.

SERVES 12

    8 medium-size tart green apples
    1 Short Dough tart shell, unbaked, in a 10-inch springform
        pan (page 71)
    ⅓ cup Candied Ginger (page 123)
    1¼ cups bread flour
    ¾ cup sugar
    ¾ cup dark brown sugar
    12 tablespoons unsalted butter (cold)

Preheat the oven to 425°.

Peel the apples, cut them in quarters, and remove the cores. Cut each quarter in half lengthwise and then in half crosswise. Put the apples into the unbaked tart shell.

Drain the candied ginger and dice it into ⅛-inch cubes.

Using the paddle attachment on an electric mixer (see page 58) and low speed, combine the flour and sugars. Add the diced ginger. Cut the butter into 18 pieces and add it while mixing. Once the mixture gets to the coarse meal stage, watch it closely. As soon as you see it start to form clumps, stop mixing. Sprinkle the topping evenly over the apples. Tap the pan a few times on the table to settle the fruit.

Bake for 15 minutes, then lower the oven to 400° and continue baking until the topping is brown and hard and the shell is golden, about 45 minutes. Cool. When the tart has cooled to room temperature, carefully transfer it to a serving plate. Serve warm or at room temperature.

Apple and Walnut Tart with Butterscotch Glaze

This deep-dish tart is a wintertime favorite. The unsweetened fruit and rich butterscotch glaze create a happy interplay on the tongue. The walnut pieces add crunch and a pleasant toastiness.

SERVES 12

> 6 medium-size tart green apples
> 2 cups toasted walnuts, coarsely chopped
> 1 Short Dough tart shell, unbaked, in a 10-inch springform pan (page 71)
> 1⅓ cups brown sugar
> ½ cup water
> ¼ cup corn syrup
> 1 cup whipping cream
> 4 tablespoons unsalted butter
> ⅛ cup apple cider vinegar

Preheat the oven to 375°.

Peel and core the apples. Cut them into 2-inch chunks. Toss the apples and walnuts together and put them in the unbaked tart shell. Bake until the shell is golden and the apples are tender, about 1 hour and 20 minutes. Set aside to cool.

To make the glaze, combine all the remaining ingredients in a

heavy-bottomed saucepan and bring to a boil. Continue boiling until the
mixture smokes. Remove from the heat and cool until the glaze begins to
thicken, 5 to 10 minutes. Spoon the glaze over the fruit. Serve warm or
at room temperature.

Almond Apricot Tart

This tart has a light, cakelike almond filling that puffs up during
baking to surround the fresh apricots. It's topped with golden almond
slices and a homemade apricot glaze.

SERVES 12

> ¾ cup whole natural (skin on) almonds
> ¼ cup sugar
> 7 tablespoons unsalted butter (soft)
> ⅓ cup sugar
> ⅓ cup cake flour (packed)
> 2 large eggs
> 12 medium-size apricots, ripe and firm
> 1 10-inch Short Dough tart shell, blind baked (page 71)
> ½ cup sliced almonds
> ½ recipe Apricot Glaze (page 122)

Preheat the oven to 375°. Toast the whole almonds in the oven for 10
minutes, then set aside to cool.

When the almonds are cool, grind them to a fine powder in a food
processor, about 1 minute. Add ¼ cup of sugar and process about 1
minute more, until the mixture looks crumbly. Add 1 tablespoon of water
and process just until the almond paste comes together.

Using the paddle attachment on an electric mixer (see page 58),
cream the butter and ⅓ cup of sugar until very light in both color and
texture. Stop the mixer at least once and scrape down the sides and
bottom of the bowl. Mix in the almond paste. Sift the flour. With the
mixer on low speed, add one egg, half the flour, then the other egg, and

the rest of the flour, mixing after each addition until completely smooth. Stop to scrape down the sides of the bowl if necessary. Continue mixing on low speed for 5 minutes more, until the mixture is very fluffy.

Meanwhile, wash the apricots, cut them in half, and remove the pits. Cut each half into a fan: Cut as if you were dividing the apricot half into vertical quarters but stop about ¼ inch from the top of the piece so that the quarters remain attached.

Spread the almond batter evenly in the blind-baked shell. Arrange the apricots skin side down on top of the batter. I start at the outer edge and work in concentric circles toward the center. The size of your apricots will determine how many you need to cover the tart. Do not overlap them. Press the apricots gently into the batter. They must all be below the top edge of the shell, or they may burn during baking. Sprinkle the sliced almonds over the tart.

Bake until golden brown, about 55 minutes. Cool to room temperature. Gently heat the apricot glaze to liquefy. Brush on a thick layer, being careful not to get any on the crust.

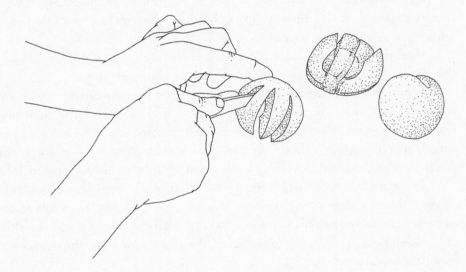

To cut an apricot fan, cut each apricot half as if you were dividing it into vertical quarters but stop about ¼ inch from the top.

Ginger Crumb Apricot Tart

This deep-dish tart is packed with ripe, fresh apricots and topped with a buttery crumb topping. Nuggets of fresh ginger in the topping add zing and play off the smooth richness of the fruit.

SERVES 12

> 2¼ pounds fresh apricots (about 22), ripe and firm
> 1 Short Dough tart shell, unbaked, in a 10-inch springform pan (page 71)
> 1½ ounces fresh ginger (a piece about 2½ x 1 inch)
> 1¼ cups bread flour
> 10 tablespoons unsalted butter (cold)
> 1¼ cups dark brown sugar

Preheat the oven to 400°.

Wash and quarter the apricots and discard the pits. Arrange the quarters skin side down in two layers in the unbaked tart shell. (If the skin is exposed, it will blister during baking.) Refrigerate the filled shell while you prepare the topping.

Peel the ginger and cut it into ¹⁄₁₆-inch-thick slices. Coarsely chop the slices. You should have about ¼ cup of chopped ginger.

When you measure out the bread flour, tap the measuring cup on the table to pack the flour slightly. Add enough flour to fill the measure. Using the paddle attachment on an electric mixer (see page 58) and low speed, mix the ginger, flour, butter, and sugar. Stop mixing when the mixture is coarse and crumbly, with small chunks of butter still visible.

Trim the tart shell with a pastry wheel about ¾ inch above the fruit. Spread the crumb topping on top. Bake for 30 minutes, then lower the oven temperature to 375°. Continue baking until the topping and the shell are golden brown, about 1 hour. Serve slightly warm from the oven or at room temperature.

Strawberry-Apricot Tart

When used together, ripe strawberries and apricots produce an amazingly bright and luscious flavor that resembles them both yet is also different from either. An unusual technique—baking the apricots but not the strawberries—gives this tart its special character. The apricots, smooth and rich, contrast with the sweet juiciness of the fresh strawberries. An apricot glaze makes the strawberries sparkle.

SERVES 12

   16 **medium-size apricots***
    1 **10-inch Short Dough tart shell, unbaked (page 71)**
    1 **tablespoon sugar**
    2 **pints strawberries, ripe and firm**
  ½ **recipe Apricot Glaze (page 122)**

Preheat the oven to 400°.

Wash and towel-dry the apricots. Cut them into quarters lengthwise and discard the pits. Arrange the quarters in the tart shell in four concentric circles, skin side down. I start at the outer edge and work to the center. The wedges should be very close together, points toward the center of the tart. Place the last piece right in the center, skin side down. Sprinkle the sugar over the apricots. Bake until the fruit is soft and the crust is golden brown and has pulled away from the sides of the pan, about 1 hour. Cool on a wire rack.

When cool, remove the sides of the tart pan and slide the tart off the pan bottom onto a plate or cardboard circle. Wash and towel-dry the strawberries. Cut off the tops and split the berries in half, leaving one whole. Place the whole berry, stem end down, in the middle of the tart. Arrange strawberry halves in a circle around the whole berry, points toward the center, cut side down. Arrange the rest of the berry halves in

---

* The apricots I use run 10 or 11 to a pound. If you can't find sweet, ripe ones that size, use 1½ pounds of whatever size you can get.

slightly overlapping concentric circles until the entire top of the tart is covered with strawberries.

Heat the apricot glaze over low heat until liquid. Using a pastry brush, coat the strawberries with glaze. Serve at room temperature.

Strawberry Goat Cheese Tart

Goat cheeses range in flavor from mild to quite assertive. By choosing the kind you like best, you can suit this tart to your own taste. Personally, I prefer a full-flavored cheese such as Montrachet.

SERVES 12

- 20 ounces soft goat cheese
- 4 tablespoons unsalted butter
- ⅔ cup sugar
- 1 tablespoon all-purpose flour
- 4 large eggs
- 1 10-inch Short Dough tart shell, blind baked (page 71)
- 2 pints strawberries
- ½ recipe Apricot Glaze (page 122)

Let all your ingredients sit out at room temperature for about 45 minutes before you start. When the goat cheese and butter are just starting to get soft, begin mixing the filling.

Preheat the oven to 300°.

Using the paddle attachment on an electric mixer (see page 58), cream the goat cheese, butter, and sugar together. Add the flour. Add the eggs one at a time, stopping to scrape the sides and bottom of the bowl after the first two. Mix only until all the ingredients are combined; do not overbeat.

Pour the filling into the blind-baked tart shell. Bake until the filling is lightly firm and the shell is golden brown and has pulled away from the sides of the pan, about 40 minutes. Cool to room temperature. The filling may crack as it cools; it will not affect the final look of the tart.

Wash the strawberries, cut off the tops, and cut the berries in half. Transfer the cooled tart from the pan to a serving plate. Arrange the berries on the tart in slightly overlapping concentric circles, points toward the center. Gently heat the glaze to liquefy. Brush a thin coating of glaze over the berries, being careful not to get any on the shell.

Serve at room temperature.

Cinnamon Peach Tart

The cinnamon is in the tart shell, making it deep brown and fragrant. A teaspoon of orange zest in the pastry cream brings out the rich smoothness of the peaches and helps link the cinnamon and peach flavors together.

SERVES 12

- 1 **teaspoon grated orange zest**
- 1 **cup Pastry Cream (page 105)**
- 1 **10-inch Cinnamon Dough tart shell, prebaked (page 77)**
- 6 **large ripe peaches**
- ½ **recipe Apricot Glaze (page 122)**

Stir the orange zest into the cooled pastry cream. Spread the pastry cream evenly in the prebaked, cooled tart shell.

Wash the peaches, cut them in half, and discard the pits. Cut each half into thin slices, about ¼ inch thick. Arrange the slices on top of the pastry cream: Make a circle of slices around the edge, with each slice cupped inside the last, points toward the center. Arrange the remaining slices in three semicircles in the center of the tart. Refrigerate.

Just before serving gently heat the apricot glaze to liquefy. Brush a layer of glaze over the fruit.

Deep Peach Almond Tart

A layer of coarsely chopped roasted almonds adds crunch and a toasty flavor to this deep-dish tart full of ripe, fresh peaches. It's a succulent summer dessert, served plain or with a dollop of unsweetened whipped cream.

SERVES 12

   9 medium-size peaches, ripe and firm
1½ cups whole natural (skin on) almonds
   1 Short Dough tart shell, unbaked, in a 10-inch springform pan (page 71)
   ¼ cup cornstarch
   ¼ cup sugar

Preheat the oven to 425°.

Wash the peaches, cut them into quarters, and discard the pits. Cut each quarter in half crosswise. Set aside.

Toast the almonds for 10 minutes in the preheated oven, then coarsely chop them, to about the size of raisins.

Spread the nuts in the bottom of the unbaked tart shell. Rub the cornstarch and sugar together between your fingertips until well blended. Sprinkle over the peaches and toss with your hands to coat the fruit. The cornstarch will help thicken the peach juice as the tart bakes. Dump the peach pieces into the tart shell, then go over them carefully, making sure they are evenly spread out and that all the pieces are skin side down. Bake for 15 minutes, then lower the oven to 400° and continue baking until the shell is golden brown and has pulled away from the sides of the pan, about 45 minutes. Cool to room temperature before serving. Serve plain or with unsweetened, lightly whipped cream.

Blueberry-Lemon Tart

This is a very simple tart. The fresh blueberries are unbaked, unarranged, and unglazed. When a blueberry is ripe and bursting with spicy flavor, you can't do much to improve on it. Except, of course, put it against a background that shows it off. Part of the fun of this tart is the way the blueberries tumble onto the plates when you serve it.

SERVES 12

   1 **recipe Lemon Cream (page 107)**
   1 **10-inch Short Dough tart shell, prebaked (page 71)**
   1½ **pints blueberries**

Spread the lemon cream in the cooled shell, working some of it up onto the sides (to help hold the berries). Wash and towel-dry the blueberries. Remove any stems. Pour the berries into the shell. Press them gently with your hands to pack them a little. Serve at room temperature.

Blueberry-Papaya Tart

This is a festive tart. Its pinwheel pattern makes it look as if the blueberries are whirling around on a bed of papaya. Look for firm, spicy blueberries. Medium or medium-large, not extra-large, berries are your best bet for the spiciness you need to balance the delicately sweet papaya and tangy apricot glaze.

SERVES 12

   1 **10-inch Short Dough tart shell, prebaked (page 71)**
   1 **recipe Pastry Cream (page 105)**
   1 **medium-size papaya, ripe and firm**
   ½ **recipe Apricot Glaze (page 122)**
   1 **pint blueberries**

Cool both the tart shell and the pastry cream before assembling the tart. Spread the pastry cream evenly in the tart shell. Peel the papaya, cut it in half, and discard the seeds. Cut each half lengthwise into ½-inch-thick wedges. Arrange the wedges like slightly curved spokes of a wheel on the pastry cream. Set the wedges close to the edge of the tart, as close together as you can and still have enough to go all the way around. You will have a circular space in the center, the size of which will depend on the size of your papaya.

Gently heat the apricot glaze to liquefy. Using a pastry brush, coat the papaya wedges with glaze (you will probably have some left over). The glaze protects the delicate papaya wedges and will help the blueberries to stick.

Wash and towel-dry the blueberries. Heap them in the center of the tart and in the spaces between the papaya wedges. Some of the blueberries will tumble off when you serve—it is part of what makes this tart so appealing.

Lemon and Bitter Chocolate Tart

Sometimes I think the world is divided into chocolate lovers and lemon lovers; this tart will delight both. A ribbon of dark, unsweetened chocolate beneath the lemon filling adds contrast, richness, and an element of surprise.

SERVES 12

1 cup (4 ounces) grated unsweetened chocolate
1 10-inch Short Dough tart shell, prebaked (page 71)
Double recipe Lemon Cream (page 107)

Preheat the oven to 400°.

Spread the grated chocolate in the bottom of the prebaked shell. Smooth it with a knife or scraper. Pour the lemon cream over the chocolate and smooth the surface. Bake until the filling has darkened a little and is set (lightly firm), about 15 minutes. Cool to room temperature before serving.

Lemon-Pear Tart

A rich, tart lemon cream is not only beneath the slices of fresh pear, where you'd expect it to be, it's also on top. As the tart bakes, the lemon cream melts into the fruit and turns a golden brown.

SERVES 12

   1 **teaspoon vanilla extract**
   1 **recipe Lemon Cream (page 107)**
   1 **10-inch Short Dough tart shell, unbaked (page 71)**
   5 **medium-size pears, ripe and firm**

Preheat the oven to 400°.

Stir the vanilla into the lemon cream. Spread half of the cream evenly in the unbaked tart shell. Peel, quarter, and core the pears. Cut each quarter lengthwise into four slices. Arrange the pear wedges in concentric circles on the cream, close together with points toward the center. Place the last piece right in the middle.

Using a rubber scraper, spread the rest of the lemon cream over the pears. Be careful not to get any cream on the shell—it will burn during baking.

Bake until the shell is brown and has pulled away from the sides of the pan, and the top of the tart is golden, about 1 hour and 5 minutes. Cool to room temperature before serving.

Pear Tart

Vanilla mingles with the subtle flavor of ripe pears to make this tart special. A layer of pastry cream beneath the fruit adds substance and a smooth richness, and apricot glaze a touch of brightness.

SERVES 12

1 10-inch Short Dough tart shell, blind baked (page 71)
1 recipe Pastry Cream (page 105)
5 pears, ripe and firm
1 vanilla bean
1 tablespoon sugar
½ recipe Apricot Glaze (page 122)

Once the tart shell is blind baked, lower the oven temperature to 350°. Allow the shell to cool, then spread the pastry cream evenly in it. Peel, halve, and core the pears. Cut each half vertically into 8 wedges. Arrange the wedges on the pastry cream in concentric circles, working from the edges to the center.

Split the vanilla bean in half lengthwise and scrape out the seeds (you should get about ¼ teaspoon). With your fingertips, rub the vanilla seeds and sugar together. Sprinkle the mixture over the pears. Cover the top of the tart with a circle of parchment. Bake for 1 hour. Remove the parchment and continue baking until the shell is brown and has pulled away from the sides of the pan, and the liquid on the surface of the tart has been absorbed, about 25 minutes. Cool.

Prepare the apricot glaze and allow it to cool. When the tart has cooled to room temperature, gently heat the glaze to liquefy. Brush a thin layer over the pears.

Arrange the pear wedges in concentric circles, working from the edges to the center.

Walnut Caramel Tart

Slightly bitter caramel coats the walnuts in this crunchy tart, and it brings out their flavor without making them sweet. Serve with a dollop of unsweetened, softly whipped cream.

SERVES 12

2 cups sugar
½ cup water
1½ cups whipping cream
3 cups walnut pieces
2 large eggs
1 10-inch Short Dough tart shell, prebaked (page 71)

Preheat the oven to 350°.

Combine the sugar and water in a heavy-bottomed saucepan. Bring to a boil over medium heat and cook without stirring until all the sugar has dissolved and the syrup is a light mahogany color (350° on a candy thermometer). You can swirl the pan during cooking if the syrup is not darkening evenly. Remove from the heat and very carefully pour in the cream (the hot syrup may splatter). When the bubbling stops, stir and set aside to cool at least 15 minutes. This is important because if the syrup is too hot when you add it to the eggs, it will cook them and ruin your filling.

Toast the walnuts for about 5 minutes in the oven. Chop them into ½-inch pieces.

Using the paddle attachment on an electric mixer (see page 58), beat the eggs for about 1 minute at medium-high speed. Mix in the caramel. Stir in the walnut pieces. Spoon the mixture into the prebaked tart shell with a slotted spoon. Pour any remaining caramel over the top and smooth the surface of the tart with the back of the spoon. Bake for 20 minutes. The filling will feel soft when it comes out of the oven but will set as it cools.

Cranberry Caramel Tart

This is a wonderful winter tart. The slight bitterness of the caramel brings out the fruity flavor of the cranberries without masking them in sweetness. Serve with a scoop of Vanilla Ice Cream (page 305).

SERVES 12

1 10-inch Short Dough tart shell, blind baked (page 71)
2 cups sugar
½ cup water
24 ounces (2 packages) cranberries (room temperature)

Make sure there are no holes in your tart shell. If any appear during the blind baking, press the dough back together while it is still soft or patch the spots with leftover raw dough. If the cranberry filling leaks through the crust, you will have real problems getting it off the pan bottom.

Lower the oven to 375°.

Stir the sugar and water together in a saucepan. Bring to a boil and cook without stirring until the mixture is a mahogany color. Put one package of cranberries in a warm stainless steel bowl. *Carefully* pour in the caramel and stir with a long spoon to coat the fruit. Let the berries sit for 10 minutes. If the caramel begins to harden, put the bowl over hot water and stir occasionally until the caramel dissolves. Stir in the second bag of cranberries.

Pour the berries into the blind-baked tart shell. Smooth the surface with the back of a spoon. Bake until the shell is golden brown and has pulled away from the sides of the pan, about 20 minutes. Let cool in the pan at least 2 hours before cutting.

Orange and Brandy Tart

Here's one of the benefits of keeping an extra sponge cake in your freezer. This tart uses one white sponge layer to add texture and to absorb both the brandy and the sweet juices of the orange slices. (If you make a sponge cake for this tart, you can freeze the other half and use it later to make a Strawberry Grand Marnier Cake, page 237.)

SERVES 12

- 1 **Short Dough tart shell, prebaked, in a 10-inch springform pan (page 71)**
- 1 **recipe Pastry Cream (page 105)**
- 1 **layer White Sponge Cake (page 93)**
- 3 **tablespoons good brandy**
- 8 **eating oranges**
- ½ **recipe Apricot Glaze (page 122)**

Be sure the tart shell has cooled to room temperature, then spread the pastry cream evenly in the bottom. Lay the white sponge layer over the pastry cream and sprinkle the brandy on it.

Peel the oranges (see page 321) and cut them into ¼-inch slices. Arrange the slices on the sponge layer in concentric circles starting at the outer edge and working toward the center. Overlap the slices by about half their width; overlap the circles slightly (it will probably take 3 circles to completely cover the tart).

Gently heat the apricot glaze to liquefy; brush a layer of glaze over the oranges. If you are not going to serve the tart within 1 hour of finishing it, it is better to refrigerate it unglazed and glaze the top just before serving.

Cheese Tart

This very popular tart strikes a perfect balance between light texture and rich cheese taste. It can be topped with almost any ripe fruit that is tender without being cooked. I use berries when they're in season and pineapple most of the rest of the year.

SERVES 12

>   8 ounces cream cheese
>   8 tablespoons (¼ pound) unsalted butter (soft)
>   ¾ cup plus 2 tablespoons sugar
>   2 large eggs
>   ½ teaspoon grated lemon zest
>   1 10-inch Short Dough tart shell, blind baked (page 71)
>   1 pint berries (any kind) *or* 1 medium-size pineapple
>   ½ recipe Apricot Glaze (page 122)

Preheat the oven to 375°.

Cream the cream cheese, butter, and sugar together until light and smooth. Add the eggs one at a time and mix well. Stop after each addition to scrape the sides and bottom of the bowl. Stir in the lemon zest. Pour the batter into the tart shell. Watch for lumps as you pour; if you see any, smooth them out with a rubber scraper. Bake until the filling is golden brown, about 35 minutes. Cool to room temperature.

If you are using berries, gently wash and towel-dry them (there's no need to wash raspberries). If you are using a pineapple, peel it, cut it into vertical quarters, remove the core, and cut each quarter crosswise into ½-inch slices (see pages 32–33). Gently heat the apricot glaze to liquefy; brush a thin layer over the top of the cheese filling (this will help the fruit to stick). Arrange the fruit on the tart. Dab a thin coating of glaze on the fruit. Serve at room temperature.

Red Banana and Raspberry Tart

Red bananas taste like yellow bananas, only much more so. If you've seen them in the markets and wondered what to do with them, wonder no more. Their smooth richness goes wonderfully well with the fresh, bright flavor of raspberries.

SERVES 12

    3 **large, ripe, red bananas**
   ¼ **cup fresh orange juice**
    1 **recipe Pastry Cream (page 105)**
    1 **10-inch Short Dough tart shell, prebaked (page 71)**
    1 **pint raspberries**

Peel the bananas. Cut them in quarters lengthwise, then across into 1-inch chunks. Toss them in the orange juice (to keep them from turning color), then drain them and pat with a towel to remove the excess liquid. Stir them into the pastry cream.

Spread the banana cream in the prebaked (cooled) tart shell. Cover the top with the raspberries. It's a good idea to arrange the raspberries somewhat, for instance by making sure all those along the crust are pointing in the same direction. There is a limit, however, to how much raspberries will allow themselves to be arranged, and anyway they look best more or less free-form. Refrigerate the tart until ready to serve.

Rhubarb Tart with Fresh Strawberries

Here's a new twist on an American classic combination. Inside this bright and fresh-tasting tart is a generous layer of tangy rhubarb, baked until it is tender and thick. On top are fresh, juicy strawberries, lightly glazed to make them shine.

SERVES 12

1½ pounds trimmed rhubarb (to yield 5 cups)
½ cup sugar
2 tablespoons cornstarch
1 10-inch Short Dough tart shell, blind baked (page 71)
2 pints strawberries
½ recipe Currant Glaze (page 122)

Preheat the oven to 350°.

Wash the rhubarb. Cut off the top and bottom of each stalk, including any green. Cut the stalks into ¾-inch pieces. You should have 5 cups. Sift together the sugar and cornstarch. Toss the rhubarb in the sugar mixture to coat it well, then spread it in an even layer in the blind-baked tart shell. Sprinkle on any sugar left in the bowl. Bake until the shell is brown and has pulled away from the sides of the pan, and the rhubarb is soft and thick, about 1 hour and 10 minutes. Cool to room temperature.

Wash the strawberries, cut off their tops, and cut them in half vertically. Starting at the center of the tart, arrange the berry halves in concentric circles, points toward the center. Try to put berries of the same size in the same circle, saving the largest ones for the last circle, touching the shell. Warm the currant glaze gently to liquefy. Brush a thin layer of glaze over the strawberries, being careful not to get any on the shell. Serve at room temperature.

Mango and Lime Tart

Ripe mangoes are messy to deal with and impossible to cut into neat, uniform slices. But they taste so wonderful, they're well worth getting juice all over your hands and the table. Here lime juice and zest add zing to the lush, tropical mango flavor. For some reason, when the two fruits bake together they produce a bold day-glo yellow color that surprised me at first and now delights me.

SERVES 12

>   3 limes (or enough to yield ½ cup of juice)
>   2 large eggs
>   ½ cup sugar
>   4 tablespoons unsalted butter
>   2 large, ripe mangoes
>   1 10-inch Short Dough tart shell, blind baked (page 71)

Preheat the oven to 375°.

Grate the zest of one lime, then juice all three. Whip the eggs and sugar together until white. Add ½ cup of lime juice. Transfer to the top of a double boiler and cook over medium heat, stirring constantly with a whisk, until thick and glossy. Remove from the heat. Stir in the butter until completely incorporated. You've just made lime curd.

Wash the mangoes well. (Then wash your hands; some mangoes still have pesticide clinging to them.) Peel the mangoes and cut away as much of the flesh as you can from the big, hairy pit. Be careful not to get any of those hairs into the tart—they will end up in your teeth. Cut the mango into cubes and fold it into the lime curd. Add the lime zest. Pour the mixture into the blind-baked shell. Smooth the top with a rubber scraper or the back of a spoon.

Bake until the shell is brown and has pulled away from the sides of the pan, about 20 minutes. The filling will be bright yellow and will have the semifirm consistency of custard. It will get firmer as it cools. Serve at room temperature.

Fig and Vanilla Tart

Almost all of the great taste in this tart comes from the figs, so make sure the ones you get are ripe and delicious. The vanilla will bring out their flavor even more. I developed the pastry cream variation in this recipe, which has no assertive flavor of its own, to provide a subtle background for the figs. Do not substitute the pastry cream recipe in Chapter 6; you will end up with too strong a vanilla flavor that will overwhelm the figs.

SERVES 12

      1 **10-inch Short Dough tart shell, unbaked (page 71)**
      1 **cup milk**
     ¼ **cup plus 1 tablespoon sugar**
      1 **tablespoon all-purpose flour**
      2 **teaspoons cornstarch**
      1 **egg, lightly beaten**
      2 **tablespoons unsalted butter**
      1 **vanilla bean**
18–20 Black Mission figs

Prepare the tart shell. While it is chilling, make the pastry cream, as follows:

Bring the milk to a boil in a heavy-bottomed saucepan. Meanwhile, sift ¼ cup of sugar with the flour and cornstarch and whisk them into the egg. When the milk starts to boil, whisk in the egg mixture and the butter. Continue stirring vigorously over medium heat until the pastry cream is very thick. Transfer to a bowl and chill.

Preheat the oven to 400°.

Split the vanilla bean lengthwise and scrape out the pulp with the tip of a knife. Rub the vanilla pulp and the remaining tablespoon of sugar together with your fingertips until well combined. Set aside.

Wash the figs and cut off the stems. Cut the figs into quarters. Spread the cooled pastry cream evenly in the bottom of the chilled, unbaked tart shell. Arrange the figs on top of the pastry cream in concentric circles, starting at the outer edge and working to the center. The quarters should be close together, with their stem ends toward the center and the flat, cut side up. Sprinkle the vanilla sugar over the figs. Bake until the shell is brown and has pulled away from the sides of the pan, about 1 hour and 30 minutes. Cool to room temperature before serving.

Fig and Lemon Tart

The first time I made this tart I was amazed at how beautiful it was. The purple figs turn an even deeper shade during baking, and they gleam when glazed. The lemon and fig flavors enhance each other beautifully, making this one of my favorite inventions.

SERVES 12

    1 recipe Lemon Cream (page 107)
    1 10-inch Short Dough tart shell, unbaked (page 71)
18–20 Black Mission figs (be sure they are fully ripe)
    ½ recipe Currant Glaze (page 122)

Preheat the oven to 400°.

Spread the lemon cream evenly over the bottom of the unbaked tart shell. Wash the figs and cut off the stems. Cut each fig lengthwise into quarters. Arrange on top of the lemon cream: Starting at the outside edge, make a ring by placing the quarters close together, with one flat, cut side up. The pieces will sort of nest inside one another. Make a second ring inside the first, and continue making concentric circles until the tart is entirely covered. Press the fruit gently into the lemon cream. Bake until the shell is brown and has pulled away from the sides of the pan, about 50 minutes. If you see the filling puff up during baking, pierce it with the tip of a knife to let the air inside escape. Cool to room temperature.

Gently heat the glaze to liquefy. Using a pastry brush, dab a thin coating of glaze on the figs. Serve at room temperature.

Double Fig Tart

Ripe purple figs have such marvelous deep flavor and color, they can carry a tart all by themselves. Here baked and unbaked figs provide an interesting contrast in color and texture. If you're lucky enough to own a fig tree, it's a great way to show off your crop.

SERVES 12

30 purple figs, ripe and firm
 2 teaspoons lemon juice
 1 10-inch Short Dough tart shell, prebaked (page 71)
 ½ recipe Currant Glaze (page 122)

Preheat the oven to 400°.

Wash the figs and cut off and discard the stems. In a food processor puree 20 of the figs with the lemon juice. Pour the puree into the prebaked tart shell and bake for 10 minutes. Remove from the oven and cool about 10 minutes.

Cut each remaining whole fig in half vertically. Lay the halves cut side down on the table and cut each horizontally into three slices (from each half you will get a small, medium, and large slice). Arrange the slices on top of the tart with the large slices around the rim; the medium slices in an inner circle, overlapping the large slices; and the small slices, also overlapping, closest to the center. There will be an opening in the middle where the baked fig layer shows through.

Heat the currant glaze over low heat to liquefy. Brush a layer of glaze over the fruit.

8
Pies, Cobblers, and Crisps

Pies have always been American favorites, especially in New England where I grew up, and over the years I have developed my own versions of many old standards. Most I have modified to emphasize the natural flavors of the fillings, which, after all, is the point. For instance, my Banana Cream Pie is made with six bananas rather than the usual two or three, my Chocolate Cream Pie has a thin layer of melted chocolate brushed inside the shell to deepen the flavor of the chocolate filling, and my Coconut Cream Pie has coconut not only in the filling but in the crust as well.

I don't use large amounts of sugar in my fruit pies, and I use thickeners sparingly. The more starch or flour you add to thicken the fruit juice in a pie, the less its natural flavors will come through. I prefer to thicken the juices just slightly so that they still flow a little when you cut the pie. A pie with light fluidness in its filling is more appetizing than one that is set very firm and looks dry. I like the slight tartness of apples and berries, and I don't want to mask those flavors. In my cobblers I use no thickeners at all, nor in my Apple Crisp. Rhubarb Crisp, however, gives off so much liquid in baking it needs a little thickening; a few tablespoons of cornstarch do the trick. My rule is always to alter the taste and texture of fruits as little as possible. The filling of a fruit pie, cobbler, or crisp should run a little when you cut it. It's the nature of cooked fruit. And individual pieces of fruit should be as identifiable as when they went in. Homogenized is fine for milk; fruit fillings should maintain the texture and taste of fruit.

Cobblers and crisps are as much a part of the American food tradition as pies. Deeper than most pies, with a good 2 inches of filling, the cobbler or crisp is an exuberant celebration of the abundance of the season's ripe fruit. Neither has a bottom crust. Strictly traditional cobblers have a biscuitlike topping; mine are topped with a light buttermilk cake that is springy and tender, and blends perfectly with the fruit underneath. One reason I avoid using thickeners and leave my cobblers a little liquidy is that the cake tends to dry out a little bit after it's baked, and the juice provides a nice contrast to the slightly dry topping. My fruit fillings vary with the seasons, from apples and cranberries in fall and winter to rhubarb in spring to nectarines, peaches, strawberries, apricots, and blackberries in summer.

Crisps can also be made with a variety of seasonal fruits. Apple is the most common filling, but rhubarb and peaches are at least as good, perhaps better for the element of surprise. My crisp toppings are light and crunchy, made with white or brown sugar depending on the fruit being used. Because of the high proportion of sugar in the topping, I use less sugar in the filling than I otherwise might, to assure that it will have enough tartness to balance the topping.

When making pies, cobblers, or crisps, it's always important to think in terms of balance, considering texture as well as taste. A good pie, for instance, contrasts its predominant flavor and texture, which is in the filling, with a dry, crisp, flavorful crust and, if it's a cream pie, with its whipped cream topping. Even though the crust is a very thin layer, it's very important to bake it properly. People notice a well-made golden brown crust. It stands out and makes the pie more appetizing because it promises a delicious crispness. There's nothing more disappointing than putting your fork through the lush filling of a fruit or cream pie and hitting a soggy or tough crust.

In cobblers, the cakelike topping is there only to complement the depth of fruit. It does that best when you have a balance of two-thirds fruit and one-third topping. A crisp is different. The topping is more assertive than a cobbler topping, so it has to be in a thinner layer to keep from overwhelming the fruit.

Both cobblers and crisps (and most pies for that matter) go well with cream or ice cream or a special sauce. They carry with them a feeling of hominess and comfort that few other desserts can match; I love their simplicity and straightforwardness, and the unembellished goodness of native fruit at the peak of ripeness.

Lemon-Orange Meringue Pie

Orange zest in the lemon cream gives that perennial favorite, lemon meringue pie, a new twist. Piled high with lightly browned meringue, this dessert always makes a dramatic entrance.

I recommend that you use a small propane torch to brown the meringue. They're available at hardware stores, are not very expensive, and are extremely handy in any pastry kitchen. If you can't get or don't want to use a torch, see the alternative browning method in the footnote (page 168).

SERVES 12

> **Triple recipe Lemon Cream (page 107), with changes noted below**
> **Grated zest of 3 oranges**
> 1 **10-inch Short Dough pie shell, prebaked (page 71)**
> 6 **large egg whites**
> 1½ **cups sugar**

Make the lemon cream, substituting the grated zest of 3 oranges for the lemon zest, and using half the amount of butter. You'll need about 8 lemons for juicing. Make the cream in a 5-quart stainless steel bowl, set on a saucepan large enough to support it steadily, or in a large double boiler.

Prebake the pie shell as directed. When it is brown, pour in the lemon cream. Lower the oven temperature to 375° and bake until the filling springs back when touched lightly, about 15 minutes. The cream will feel like set custard. Cool to room temperature.

Beat the egg whites and sugar to stiff peaks. Spoon into a pastry bag with a *#7* star tip. Decorate the top of the pie with meringue as illustrated below. Light your propane torch and moving it over the pie, lightly brown the meringue as illustrated on page 175.* Refrigerate until 15 minutes before serving.

One of my favorite ways to decorate with meringue is to create a herringbone pattern. Pipe out zigzag lines, the first from left to right, the next from right to left. Repeat until the pie is completely covered.

* If you don't want to use a propane torch for browning, chill the filled shell in the freezer until very cold, then top with meringue as directed. Put the pie in a 425° oven until the meringue is lightly browned.

Banana Cream Pie

This is the best banana cream pie there is because it's almost all bananas, with just enough pastry cream to hold them together.

SERVES 12

6 medium-size bananas, ripe and firm
1 cup fresh orange juice
1 recipe Pastry Cream (page 105)
1 10-inch Rich Short Dough pie shell, prebaked (page 71)
2 cups whipping cream

Peel the bananas and cut them into ½-inch slices. Toss them in a bowl with the orange juice to keep them from turning brown. Drain them well and pat dry with a paper towel. Fold the bananas into the chilled pastry cream. Pour into the cooled pie shell. Smooth the top of the filling.

Whip the cream to soft peaks. Cover the top of the pie with ½ inch of cream. Put the rest of the cream in a pastry bag with a #7 star tip. Pipe out a border of 12 large rosettes close together around the perimeter of the pie. (Before you begin decorating, see pastry bag techniques, pages 53–55.) Fill in the middle with 12 elongated shells, as follows: Start each shell about 1 inch from a rosette. Hold the pastry bag with the tip 1 inch above the pie, pointing straight down. Squeeze the bag to pipe out a mound of cream. Keep squeezing until the mound expands to about the size of a half dollar, then pull the pastry bag toward the center of the pie, gradually decreasing the pressure as you come to the center. End each shell at the center of the pie so that the tails of all the shells overlap and form a peak. Chill until 10 minutes before serving.

Coconut Cream Pie

The grated white chocolate that crowns this pie not only looks like coconut, it brings out the flavor of coconut. In fact, all three tropical ingredients here—coconut, vanilla, and cocoa butter—highlight one another and combine beautifully to create a rich and luscious all-American dessert. To add some crunch and intensify the flavor, I've added coconut to the crust too.

SERVES 10

1 Coconut Dough shell in a 9-inch pie plate (page 77)
2 cups milk
2 cups unsweetened coconut flakes (see footnote, page 78)
2 vanilla beans, split
½ cup sugar
2 tablespoons all-purpose flour
2 large eggs
4 tablespoons unsalted butter
1 cup whipping cream
2 ounces white chocolate

Preheat the oven to 400°.

With a sharp knife trim the edges of the shell even with the edge of the pie plate. Set another 9-inch pie plate on top. Invert the two plates and bake upside down for 20 minutes. Turn right side up, remove the top plate, and bake until the shell is golden brown, about 5 minutes. Cool on a wire rack to room temperature before filling.

Bring the milk to a boil in a heavy-bottomed saucepan. Add the coconut. Scrape the pulp from the vanilla beans and add both the pulp and the scraped beans to the milk. Simmer together for 5 minutes.

Meanwhile, sift the sugar and flour together. Add the eggs and beat until light. Stir ¼ cup of the hot milk into the egg mixture, then pour the egg mixture into the saucepan of milk and cook over high heat, stirring vigorously with a wire whisk, until the center bubbles and the mixture is very thick. Remove from the heat and stir in the butter. Set aside to cool.

When both the pie shell and filling are cool, remove the vanilla beans and pour the filling into the shell. Smooth the top with a spatula or the back of a spoon. Whip the cream to soft peaks and spoon it into a pastry bag with a #7 star tip. Make a circle of whipped cream rosettes around the edge of the pie. Rake the chocolate (see page 37) or grate it with a vegetable peeler into long, thin curls. Arrange the chocolate in the center of the pie, with all the pieces pointing toward the edge, creating a kind of sunburst pattern. (If your chocolate is not in graceful, long, fingerlike pieces, just heap it in the center of the pie.)

Serve immediately or refrigerate until ready to serve.

Chocolate Cream Pie

This is an update of a traditional American favorite, even more chocolaty than you remember because the shell is painted with chocolate before the filling goes in.

SERVES 10

    ¾ cup sugar
    3 tablespoons all-purpose flour
    2 tablespoons cornstarch
    3 large eggs
    3 cups milk
    9 tablespoons unsalted butter (soft)
  5½ ounces bittersweet chocolate
    1 9-inch Short Dough pie shell, prebaked (page 71)
  2½ cups whipping cream
   12 Chocolate Truffles (page 128)

Sift the sugar, flour, and cornstarch together into a mixing bowl. Add the eggs and beat with the whisk attachment of an electric mixer (see page 58) at high speed until light. Bring the milk to a boil in a large heavy-bottomed saucepan. Stir half of the milk into the egg mixture, then pour all the egg mixture into the milk. Cook over high heat, stirring vigorously with a whisk to keep the eggs from scrambling, until the mixture thickens and bubbles in the middle. Remove from the heat. Cut the butter and 3½ ounces of the chocolate into pieces and stir them in a little at a time. Cool to room temperature.

Melt the remaining chocolate over boiled (not boiling) water. Using a pastry brush, paint the inside of the prebaked pie shell with the melted chocolate. Pour in the cooled chocolate filling and smooth the top. Refrigerate until firm.

Whip the cream to soft peaks. Put it in a pastry bag with a #7 plain tip. Pipe the cream onto the pie in rows of snowball-like mounds. Start at one edge, and with a single up-and-down motion, make a round mound of cream about 1 inch across. (Practice on a sheet of parchment before you start on the pie.) Make 5 mounds side by side, then begin a new row, lining up 8 or 9 mounds in a straight line across the pie. Continue, row after row, until the entire pie is covered. Refrigerate until just before serving.

When ready to serve, decorate the top of the pie with the chocolate truffles, evenly spaced around the edge of the pie.

Strawberry Cream Pie

Strawberries and cream were meant for each other; however you serve them—alone, in shortcake, or in this richly flavorful pie—they are always a special treat. Try this recipe when strawberries are at their peak—plump and fragrant, and locally grown if possible.

SERVES 12

1 10-inch Short Dough pie shell, prebaked (page 71)
1 recipe Pastry Cream (page 105)
2 pints large strawberries
1 cup whipping cream

Prepare the pie shell and the pastry cream far enough ahead so that they have both cooled to room temperature before you begin assembling the pie.

Wash the strawberries. Set aside 3 beautiful ones. Cut the tops off the rest and cut them vertically into thirds (into quarters if they are very big). Cut off and discard any green areas, especially at the tips. Fold the

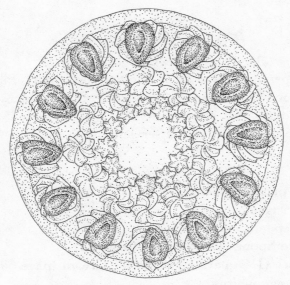

Finished Strawberry Cream Pie

cut berries into the pastry cream. Continue folding until the pastry cream is an even, pink color without streaks. Spread the mixture evenly in the prebaked pie shell.

Whip the cream to soft peaks and put it into a pastry bag with a #4 star tip. Starting at the edge of the pie, pipe out a triple rosette (3 rosettes in a row, so close they touch) pointing toward the middle of the pie. Make another triple rosette at the opposite edge. Make 12 triple rosettes all together, evenly spaced around the pie, creating sort of a spoked-wheel effect with a hub of strawberry pastry cream in the center.

Now cut the tops off the 3 strawberries you set aside. Cut each in half vertically, then cut each half vertically in half again. Place a quarter on each triple rosette, close to the edge of the pie, with the point toward the shell. Refrigerate until ready to serve.

Praline Ice Cream Pie

This is a perennial favorite at The Stanford Court. Piled high with meringue, smoothly rich and at the same time crunchy, it delights children and adults alike. It's best to make it ahead since it needs a good 4 to 6 hours in the freezer before serving.

SERVES 12

- 1¼ **cups pecans, toasted**
- 2 **cups sugar**
- 3 **tablespoons water**
- 1 **White Sponge Cake layer** (page 93)
- 1½ **recipes (1½ quarts) Vanilla Ice Cream (page 305)**
- 6 **large egg whites**
- ⅛ **teaspoon cream of tartar**
- 1 **recipe Rum Sauce (page 12)**

To make the praline, line a cookie sheet with greased parchment and lay the pecans in the center in a tight single layer. Stir together ⅔ cup of sugar and the water in a saucepan and bring them to a boil. Cook over medium-high heat, without stirring, until the mixture turns a rich mahogany color. If the liquid colors unevenly, swirl the pan to distribute the color. Pour the hot caramel over the nuts on the parchment paper and set aside to cool.

Press the sponge layer into a 9-inch pie plate. Flatten the cake with your hands against the sides and bottom of the pan. Wrap in plastic wrap and freeze.

Prepare the vanilla ice cream according to directions. While it is freezing, check to see if the praline is hard—it should look and feel like brown glass. If it is, pull it off the parchment and flip it over. Using a big spoon, a hammer, a wooden mallet, or some other pounding tool, smash it into ½-inch chunks. Don't crush it any finer; smaller pieces have a

---

 To make this pie you need just one ½-inch-thick layer of white sponge. If you have a sponge conveniently in the freezer, just cut a ½-inch layer from it (for technique, see page 95). If you don't have one, make a sponge, cut off one layer, and wrap and freeze the rest.

tendency to dissolve when you fold them into the ice cream. When the ice cream is frozen, fold in the chunks of praline—the paddle attachment on your electric mixer can be used for this (see page 58). Do not overmix. Spoon the ice cream into the frozen cake shell. Smooth the top, shaping it into a dome. Freeze until hard.

Beat the egg whites, cream of tartar, and the remaining 1⅓ cups of sugar to stiff peaks. Spread a ½-inch layer of meringue over the ice cream, smoothing it with an icing spatula. Spoon the rest of the meringue into a pastry bag with a *#7* star tip. Decorate the pie by piping out 16 large rosettes around the outer edge (see page 55). Then pipe 8 large shells inside the circle of rosettes, points toward the center, and a smaller shell between each two large shells.

Light a propane torch and adjust the flame to medium. Move the tip of the flame quickly over the surface of the meringue until it is golden (see illustration below). Freeze the pie, covered loosely with plastic wrap, for 4 to 6 hours before serving; it will keep in the freezer for 4 or 5 days. Serve with the rum sauce.

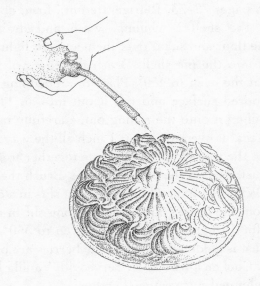

To brown meringue, adjust the propane torch to a medium flame. Hold the torch with the tip of the flame just touching the meringue. Keep the flame moving in circles until the top of the pie is lightly browned.

Huckleberry Pie

Huckleberries grow wild in many areas and can be found in produce markets in summer, but usually only where they grow. They are similar to blueberries but smaller and with more noticeable seeds. Baked in a pie they are smooth and bright tasting.

SERVES 10

1 **Short Dough recipe for pie crust, top and bottom, for 9-inch (page 71)**
3 **pints huckleberries**
¼ **cup all-purpose flour**
1 **cup sugar**
1 **tablespoon milk**

Divide the Short Dough in half. Wrap one half in plastic wrap and refrigerate. Roll out the other half and line a 9-inch pie plate with it, as directed on pages 72–73. Refrigerate until firm, about 20 minutes.

While the shell is chilling, wash and drain the huckleberries. Sprinkle the flour and sugar over them and stir lightly with a spoon. Pour the berries into the pie shell. Brush the edges of the shell with water.

Preheat the oven to 450°. Place the remaining half of the dough on a lightly floured surface and roll it out into an 11-inch circle. Lift the circle by rolling it onto the rolling pin. Carefully unroll it over the filled pie shell so that it overlaps about 1 inch all the way around. Gently press the edges of the top and bottom crusts together to fuse them. Crimp the edges as illustrated on the opposite page. Brush the top of the pie lightly with milk. With the tip of a knife cut eight slits in a circular pattern about 2 inches from the center of the pie and one slit in the middle.

Bake for 15 minutes. Lower the oven to 350° and continue baking until the crust is golden brown and the berries are bubbling inside, about 30 minutes. Cool on a wire rack. Serve with Vanilla Ice Cream (page 305) or lightly whipped unsweetened cream.

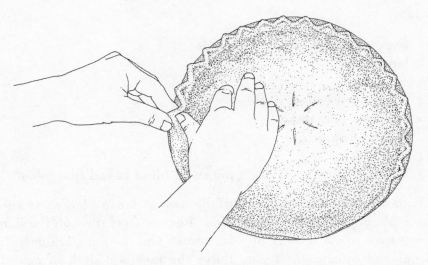

To crimp the edges of a double-crusted pie, first lift and fold under the fused edges of the top and bottom crusts to form a border that stands up about ½ inch from the edge of the pan all the way around. Place the tips of the thumb and first finger of one hand against the outside of the border, about 1 inch apart. With the thumb of the other hand, gently push the dough out into a point between your fingers. Move the outer hand so that the finger rests where the thumb was before. Make another point. Continue moving around the rim of the pie until the entire edge is crimped.

Pumpkin Pie

Any pumpkin can make a great jack-o'-lantern, but only a sugar pumpkin will make a first-rate pumpkin pie. A 3-pound sugar pumpkin (approximately 7 inches in diameter and 4½ inches high) will give you enough puree for two pies. Excess puree freezes very well. Serve the pie at room temperature, topped with unsweetened, softly whipped cream.

SERVES 10

    1 **sugar pumpkin, about 3 pounds**
    2 **large eggs**
  ⅓ **cup sugar**
  ⅓ **cup golden brown sugar**
  ⅛ **teaspoon cinnamon**
      Pinch of nutmeg
    1 **cup milk**
    1 **9-inch Rich Short Dough pie shell, blind baked (page 75)**

Wash the pumpkin and break off the stem. Place in a large pan and bake at 375° until soft to the touch, about 2 hours. Cool. Peel off the skin (you may have to cut it away in some spots). Cut the pumpkin in half; scoop out and discard the seeds. Puree the pumpkin flesh in a food processor or blender, or mash it with a potato masher. Pass the puree through a fine sieve or China cap (Chinoise strainer).

Preheat the oven to 375°.

In a bowl, mix together the eggs and sugars. Add 1¼ cups of pumpkin puree, the cinnamon, and nutmeg. Add the milk and mix until all the ingredients are well blended. Pour into the partially baked shell and bake until the filling puffs up and is firm at the edges, about 35 minutes. Cool on a rack.

Mincemeat Pie

To make the best-tasting mincemeat, start with excellent lean beef and good veal suet. The spices, fruit juices, and rum combine to preserve the meat and impart a rich, deeply satisfying flavor. By cooking my mincemeat for the shortest possible time and aging it for two full months, I have found I can achieve a smooth, complex flavor without sacrificing the texture of the fruit. This recipe makes two 9-inch pies. Serve at room temperature, topped with unsweetened softly whipped cream.

MAKES 2 PIES. SERVES 20

1 pound lean beef (preferably inside round)
8 ounces veal suet (flaky, firm, and pinkish white, not yellow)
3 medium-size tart green apples
2⅓ cups dark brown sugar
2 cups raisins
2 cups golden raisins
2 cups currants
Grated zest and juice of 1 medium-size lemon
1 cup dark rum (preferably Mt. Gay Eclipse, from Barbados, for its rich caramel flavor)
2 teaspoons cinnamon
2 teaspoons mace
2 teaspoons ground cloves
2 teaspoons chopped fresh ginger *or* 1 teaspoon powdered ginger
½ teaspoon nutmeg
1 recipe Rich Short Dough (page 75)

Cut the beef and suet into several chunks. Place in a heavy saucepan, cover with water, and cook until tender. Remove from the heat and allow to cool. When cool, remove the meat and suet from the liquid and grind in a grinder or food processor. Bring the liquid to a boil, lower the heat, and simmer until reduced to half its volume.

Peel and core the apples. Chop them into pieces about the size of peas. In a large saucepan, combine the meat, suet, cooking liquid, and apples with all the remaining ingredients except the Rich Short Dough. Bring the mixture to a boil, remove from the heat, and allow to cool. Pack into clean glass jars, cover tightly, and refrigerate for two months.

Preheat the oven to 350°.

Roll out the Rich Short Dough, line two 9-inch pie pans with it, and refrigerate as directed.* Divide the mincemeat evenly between the two unbaked shells. Smooth the top of the filling. Bake until the crust is golden brown, about 40 minutes. Cool to room temperature before serving.

---

* Of course, you can make the two pies separately, on two different days. Refrigerate the unused half of the dough and bring it to room temperature before rolling out the second pie.

COBBLERS

Cobblers are one of the simplest and most delicious ways to take advantage of the abundance of luscious summer (or even winter) fruits. They are like deep-dish pies except that they have no bottom crust. I find them exciting; I love to plunge a spoon through the cakelike topping into a generous helping of warm, pungent fruit below. It must remind me of my New England childhood. I also love the contrasts of texture and flavor you can achieve in cobblers. I'm forever coming up with new fruit combinations for them, just because it's so much fun.

Traditionally cobblers have been topped with biscuit dough. Mine are topped with light, delicately flavored buttermilk cake; I think it makes for a better balanced dessert. And I'm adamant about using no butter and very little sugar in the filling so there's nothing to mask the taste of the fruit.

The trick to making cobblers is keeping the batter on top of the fruit. If it seeps down and bakes around the fruit, you'll have a tasty cake but you won't have a cobbler. So make sure you cream the butter and sugar until very light, and beat the rest of the ingredients in thoroughly. Most important, don't spread the cake batter over the fruit. Let it drop lightly in place from your rubber scraper, and once it's settled, don't try to smooth or move it. Leave a 1-inch border around the batter so that it can expand as it bakes without spreading down the sides of the dish.

The cobblers in this chapter are good just as they are, still warm from the oven. If you want to dress them up, you can serve them with ice cream or lightly whipped, unsweetened cream.

Cobbler Batter

8　tablespoons (¼ pound) unsalted butter (soft)
¾　cup sugar
1½　cups cake flour
2　teaspoons baking soda

1 **teaspoon cream of tartar**
1 **teaspoon kosher salt (see page 42)**
½ **cup buttermilk**
1 **large egg, lightly beaten**

Have the fruit filling ready in a 2½-quart baking dish. Using the paddle attachment on an electric mixer (see page 58), beat the butter and sugar at medium-high speed until very light in color and texture, about 10 minutes. (The butter will turn from yellow to off-white.) Meanwhile, combine the rest of the dry ingredients and set aside. Warm the buttermilk just enough to remove the chill.

When the butter is light, add the egg and mix well. Turn the mixer down to low speed and slowly pour in ⅓ of the flour mixture. Mix until smooth. Stop the mixer and scrape the sides and bottom of the bowl. Add ½ the buttermilk, another ⅓ of the flour, the rest of the buttermilk, and the rest of the flour, mixing well after each addition and stopping several times to scrape the sides and bottom of the bowl. The mixture should be smooth and unbroken. Mix a few minutes longer, until it is very smooth and light (it will resemble butter cream).

Topping the fruit with batter: Pick up a dollop of batter on a large rubber scraper. Using a slow, sweeping motion, move the scraper about 1 inch above the baking dish, letting the batter slide off in a broad ribbon. Continue dropping the batter gently onto the fruit until you have covered the whole surface except for a 1-inch strip around the edges (to give the topping room to expand during baking). Do not spread the batter.

Blackberry-Lime Cobbler

This recipe is my gift to everyone who has blackberries taking over the yard. If you're not so blessed, this cobbler just might be delicious enough to merit a trip to the country—or wherever blackberries grow in your area. Store-bought berries are fine too, of course, but they tend to be expensive, and you need a lot.

SERVES 12

> 3 **pints (6 baskets) blackberries**
> 2 **limes**
> ¼ **cup sugar**
> 1 **recipe Cobbler Batter (page 180)**

Preheat the oven to 375°.

Rinse the berries, let them drain, and put them in a 2½-quart shallow earthenware baking dish. Zest the limes and then juice them. Add both the zest and the juice to the berries, and toss lightly. Sprinkle the sugar over the fruit and toss gently to coat the berries.

Prepare the cobbler batter and top the fruit as directed on page 181.

Bake until the topping is golden brown and springs back when touched lightly, about 45 minutes. If you're not absolutely sure the topping is done, pierce it with a knife and look to see that no wet batter is left.

Apricot-Strawberry Cobbler

Apricots and strawberries bring out the best in each other. They make an especially bright and inviting summer cobbler.

SERVES 12

> 24 **medium-size apricots**
> 2 **pints strawberries**
> 1 **recipe Cobbler Batter (page 180)**

Preheat the oven to 375°.

Wash and towel-dry the apricots and strawberries. Cut the apricots into quarters, discarding the pits. Cut the tops off the strawberries, then split them in half. Mix the apricots and strawberries together and pack them gently into a 2½-quart shallow earthenware baking dish.

Prepare the cobbler batter and top the fruit as directed on page 181.

Bake until the topping is golden brown and springs back when touched lightly, about 45 minutes. To be absolutely sure the topping is done, pierce it with a knife and look to see that there is no wet batter left.

Peach and Ginger Cobbler

Ginger has a way of gently infusing everything it touches with its wonderfully nippy flavor. The effect here is subtle. If you're crazy about the taste of ginger, go ahead and add some more.

SERVES 12

    8 medium-size peaches
½ cup (about 3 ounces) crystallized ginger slices
    1 recipe Cobbler Batter (page 180)

Preheat the oven to 375°.

Wash and towel-dry the peaches. Cut them into eighths. Discard the pits and cut each eighth in half. Coarsely chop the ginger. Toss the peaches and ginger together in a 2½-quart shallow earthenware baking dish. Press the fruit down gently with your hands to pack it in the dish.

Prepare the cobbler batter and top the fruit as directed on page 181.

Bake until the topping is golden brown and springs back when touched lightly, about 45 minutes. To be absolutely sure the topping is done, pierce it with a knife and look to see that no wet batter is left.

Apple-Cranberry Cobbler

Apples and cranberries are a well-loved combination, but if you add lime juice and zest, you get a lot more sparkle out of them. This is a great cold weather dessert, perfect for the holiday table.

SERVES 12

1 **package (12 ounces) cranberries**
4 **medium-size tart apples**
½ **cup sugar**
4 **limes**
1 **recipe Cobbler Batter (page 180)**
1 **teaspoon cream of tartar**

Preheat the oven to 350°.

Spread the cranberries in a 2½-quart shallow earthenware baking dish. Peel, quarter, and core the apples. Cut each quarter in half lengthwise, then in quarters crosswise (each piece should be about twice the size of a cranberry). Toss the apples with the cranberries. Sprinkle on the sugar and toss to coat the fruit.

Zest the limes and set the zest aside. Squeeze the juice of all four limes over the fruit in the baking dish.

Prepare the cobbler batter, adding the additional teaspoon of cream of tartar and the lime zest. Top the fruit with batter as directed on page 181. Bake until the top is golden brown and springs back when touched lightly, about 50 minutes. To be absolutely sure the topping is done, pierce it with a knife and look to see that all the wet batter is gone.

Orange-Zested Nectarine Cobbler

Orange zest in the topping provides a lively counterpoint to the lushness of ripe nectarines.

SERVES 12

9 **medium-size nectarines**
2 **tablespoons sugar**
1 **recipe Cobbler Batter (page 180)**
   Zest of 2 medium-size oranges

Preheat the oven to 375°.
Wash the nectarines, cut them into quarters, and discard the pits.

Cut each quarter crosswise into quarters. Place the fruit in a 2½-quart shallow earthenware baking dish. Sprinkle the sugar over the fruit and toss lightly to distribute it. Press the fruit down gently with your hands to pack it in the dish.

Prepare the cobbler batter and top the fruit with batter as directed on page 181, stirring in the orange zest just before you top the fruit.

Bake until the topping is golden brown and springs back when touched lightly, about 55 minutes. To be sure the topping is done, pierce it with a knife and look to see that no wet batter is left.

Gingered Rhubarb Crisp

People keep telling me they didn't think they liked rhubarb until they tasted this crisp. For some reason most cooks either oversweeten this delicious vegetable-fruit or leave it too tart. Here the rhubarb is flavorful without being sweet. A hint of honey rounds off any sharpness in the rhubarb or the ginger, which I've added to the topping to give it chewiness and zing.

SERVES 12

> 3 **pounds rhubarb (try to get slender stalks, less than 1 inch wide)**
> ¼ **cup honey**
> 2 **ounces (about ⅜ cup) crystallized ginger**
> 1 **cup sugar**
> 1 **cup bread flour**
> 10 **tablespoons unsalted butter (cold)**

Preheat the oven to 375°.

Wash and towel-dry the rhubarb. Using a very sharp knife (so it will cut cleanly through the skin), trim off the top and bottom of each stalk, including any green. If any stalks are more than 1 inch wide, split them in half. Cut the stalks into 1-inch pieces. Run hot water over a 2½-quart shallow earthenware baking dish to heat it; dry it and put in the rhubarb. Add the honey and toss with your hands to coat all the pieces. Set aside.

Coarsely chop the ginger (I use a cleaver) and put it in the bowl of an electric mixer. Add the sugar and flour. Cut the butter into pieces and add it to the dry ingredients. Mix with the paddle attachment (see page 58) at low speed until the mixture is crumbly. Stop mixing as soon as you see the color begin to turn yellowish. Cover the rhubarb with the topping and bake until the topping is golden and the rhubarb is bubbling, about 1 hour.

Serve warm from the oven or at room temperature, plain or topped with Vanilla Ice Cream (page 305) or unsweetened softly whipped cream.

Note: If you serve your crisp soon after baking, be sure each serving gets some of the juice—it carries much of the rhubarb's tartness. As the crisp cools, the rhubarb reabsorbs the liquid.

Rhubarb Crisp with Strawberry Sauce

During rhubarb season this crisp is always on the menu at The Stanford Court. It's slightly tart, juicy, and satisfying. Vanilla ice cream and a pool of fresh strawberry sauce make it both elegant and comfortingly old-fashioned.

SERVES 12

> 3 pounds red rhubarb (try to get slender stalks, less than 1 inch wide)
> 2¼ cups sugar
> 3 tablespoons cornstarch
> 1 cup bread flour
> 10 tablespoons unsalted butter (cold)
> 2 pints strawberries

Preheat the oven to 375°.

Wash and towel-dry the rhubarb. Using a very sharp knife (so it will cut cleanly through the skin), trim off the top and bottom of each stalk, including any green. If any stalks are more than 1 inch wide, split them in half. Cut the stalks into 1-inch pieces. Run hot water over a 2½-quart shallow earthenware baking dish to heat it; dry it and put in the rhubarb. Sift 1 cup of sugar and the cornstarch together. Sprinkle over the rhubarb and toss with your hands to coat all the pieces. Set aside.

Combine 1 cup of sugar, the flour, and the butter, cut into pieces, in the bowl of an electric mixer. Mix with the paddle attachment (see page 58) at low speed until the mixture is crumbly. Stop mixing as soon as you see the color begin to turn yellowish. Cover the rhubarb with the topping and bake until the topping is golden and the rhubarb is bubbling, about 1 hour.

Wash the strawberries and cut off the tops. Puree the strawberries with the remaining ¼ cup of sugar in a food processor or blender until liquid.

Serve the crisp warm from the oven or at room temperature, accompanied by a scoop of Vanilla Ice Cream (page 305) and the strawberry sauce.

Note: If you serve your crisp soon after baking, be sure each serving gets some of the juice—it carries much of the rhubarb's tartness. As the crisp cools, the rhubarb reabsorbs the liquid.

Apple Crisp

This is one of the "regulars" on The Stanford Court menu and a great favorite. The apples are plentiful, juicy, and slightly tart. The topping is crunchy and fragrant. We serve it warm, with Bourbon Sauce (page 120).

SERVES 12

    10 large tart green apples
     2 tablespoons fresh lemon juice
  1¼ cups bread flour
   ¾ cup sugar
   ¾ cup dark brown sugar
    12 tablespoons unsalted butter (cold)

Preheat the oven to 375°.

Peel the apples, cut them in half, and remove the cores (a melon baller works great as a corer). Cut each apple half in thirds across the core and then in quarters the other way. Toss the pieces in the lemon juice to keep them from turning brown, then put them in a 2½-quart shallow earthenware baking dish. Lightly press them into the dish, making a fairly even surface.

Using the paddle attachment on an electric mixer (see page 58) and low speed, combine the flour and sugars. Cut the butter into 18 pieces and add it while mixing. Once the mixture gets to the coarse meal stage, watch it closely. As soon as you see it start to form clumps, stop mixing. Sprinkle the topping evenly over the apples.

Bake until the topping is lightly browned and the apples are tender, about 40 minutes. Serve warm from the oven or at room temperature, plain or with unsweetened whipped cream or Bourbon Sauce (page 120).

Peach Crisp with White Chocolate and Brandy Sauce

A crunchy, buttery crumb topping makes the peaches in this dish seem even more lush, ripe, and delicious. The sauce is light enough to tie the flavors together and distinctive enough to add its own excitement.

SERVES 12

- 10 medium-size peaches, ripe and firm
- 2 tablespoons cornstarch
- 1 cup plus 3 tablespoons sugar
- 10 tablespoons unsalted butter (cold)
- 1 cup bread flour
- 6 ounces good white chocolate
- ½ cup brandy

Preheat the oven to 375°.

Wash the peaches; cut them in quarters vertically and then crosswise in half. Rub the cornstarch and 3 tablespoons of sugar together with your fingers. Toss with the fruit in a bowl. Run hot water over a 2½-quart shallow earthenware baking dish to warm it. Dry it and put in the peaches. Scrape any residue left clinging to the bowl over the fruit.

Cut the butter into 1-inch pieces. Put it in a mixing bowl with the remaining sugar and the flour. Mix with the paddle attachment (see page 58) at low speed until the mixture is crumbly. Stop mixing as soon as you see the color begin to turn yellowish. Spread the topping over the fruit and bake until the topping is golden brown and the fruit is bubbling around the edges, about 1 hour and 10 minutes. Set aside to cool.

To make the sauce, slowly melt the white chocolate over simmering water. Be careful not to raise the heat too high; too much heat will curdle the chocolate. Stir in the brandy until completely incorporated.

Serve the crisp still warm from the oven or at room temperature. To serve, spoon a portion of crisp onto a dessert plate and top with sauce.

9
Cakes

Cakes have a special meaning for most of us. They're part of almost every major celebration in our lives—birthdays, weddings, graduations. A beautiful cake can practically create an occasion just by being there.

I like all kinds of cakes, from simple pound cakes to complicated classical multilayer extravagances. But I don't like them overdecorated, and I don't like them overly sweet. Like pies and tarts, a cake should taste of the fresh, first-quality ingredients that went into it. Although sugar is essential to the texture of fine cakes, too much sugar will mask other flavors, so I keep it to a minimum.

I like to introduce contrasting flavors into my cakes (chocolate and lemon, peach and pistachio) as well as contrasting textures (crisp wafers interspersed with light sponges and lush butter creams). I also like to explore and extend the possibilities of favorite ingredients. My Chocolate Beret Cake, for instance, contains chocolate in five different forms—a light chocolate sponge cake; crisp, unsweetened chocolate wafers; chocolate whipped cream; coarsely grated bittersweet chocolate; and unsweetened cocoa. Sometimes, for variety, I sprinkle crème de cacao over the sponge.

For finishing cakes, I tend toward whipped cream or butter cream decorated with toasted nuts, fresh fruit, or grated chocolate. There are many cakes, however, that I prefer to leave without either cream or decoration. A simple, straightforward chiffon cake or apple walnut cake, for instance, is much better left unadorned and served with a sauce— English custard and boysenberry sauce for the chiffon cake, a whipped cream-based bourbon sauce for the apple walnut.

When you do decorate, remember that understatement is the key to elegant cakes. Clean lines and simple, symmetrical decoration are far more striking than elaborate scrolls and curlicues, and natural flavors and colors are always more appetizing than anything artificial. If you want to be an impressive cake decorator, begin by becoming skillful with a pastry bag, then fill it with only unsweetened whipped cream or richly flavorful butter creams. Decorate your cakes generously with fresh fruit at the peak of ripeness or with good-quality chocolate or fresh, toasted nuts, whichever is in keeping with the ingredients inside the cake. Your cakes will not only look inviting but also smell tantalizing and taste terrific. Your guests will marvel at your artistry and leave your table delighted— not weighted down.

Dacquoise

Some people order dacquoise for dessert every time they come to The Stanford Court. Dacquoise lovers are staunchly loyal; for them it's the only dessert rich enough or exciting enough to merit the name. For the rest of us, it's an elegant indulgence reserved for special occasions. You won't find many desserts as rich or as tantalizingly fragrant with the mixed aromas of hazelnuts and coffee.

SERVES 12

½ cup hazelnuts
1 recipe Swiss Butter Cream (page 110)
2 10-inch Hazelnut Meringue circles (page 98)
2 teaspoons powdered sugar

Toast the hazelnuts in a 350° oven until fragrant, about 5 minutes. Coarsely chop and set aside.

Make the butter cream and spoon it into a pastry bag with a #9 plain tip. Place one hazelnut meringue circle on a cardboard cake circle or a cake plate. Using the same spiralling motion with which you piped out the meringues, pipe all the butter cream onto the meringue. Let it extend over the edge just a little. Smooth the surface with a knife or spatula and lay the second meringue circle on top, bottom side up. Smooth the sides of the dacquoise with a spatula or knife, then cover them with the chopped hazelnuts, pressing them into the butter cream with your open palm. Sprinkle the powdered sugar over the top meringue. Refrigerate at least 2 hours. Remove from the refrigerator 30 minutes before serving.

California Almond Cake

This is my version of the classic Dutch Almond Torte. It has a tart shell bottom and a latticed top. The cakelike almond filling is moist and light. A tangy apricot glaze sets off the richness of the almonds and adds an elegant finish.

SERVES 12

    Double recipe Short Dough (page 71)
1⅓ cups natural (skin on) almonds
 ½ cup sugar
 ½ teaspoon almond extract
  3 tablespoons water
14 tablespoons unsalted butter (soft)
⅔ cup sugar
  4 large eggs
¾ cup cake flour
  1 recipe Apricot Glaze (page 122)
24 blanched almond slices

Preheat the oven to 400°.

Line a 10-inch tart pan with half the short dough as directed starting on page 72. Prebake according to directions. Roll the other half of the dough into a circle about 13 inches in diameter. Cut ten strips about ½ inch wide (start from the center and work outward in both directions). Transfer the strips to a parchment-lined cookie sheet and refrigerate until needed.

Toast the almonds in the oven for about 5 minutes, then finely grind them in a food processor. Add ½ cup of sugar and the almond extract. Process. Add the water and process until the ingredients come together in a firm paste.

Using the paddle attachment on an electric mixer (see page 58), beat the butter and ⅔ cup of sugar at high speed until light. Lower the speed to medium and add the almond paste in four batches, mixing well after each addition. Add 2 eggs and mix well. Add half the flour, the other 2 eggs, and the rest of the flour, mixing well after each addition. Mix until very smooth.

Heat the apricot glaze over a low flame until liquid. As soon as you remove the tart shell from the oven, brush the bottom (not the sides) with a thin layer of glaze. Allow the shell to cool before filling.

Lower the oven temperature to 375°.

Spread the almond filling in the shell. Lay the short dough strips over the filling in a lattice pattern (lay five strips in one direction, give the cake a quarter turn, and lay the other five strips). Press down the ends of the strips to seal them to the crust and cut off the excess dough by

Lay the dough strips over the filling in a lattice pattern.

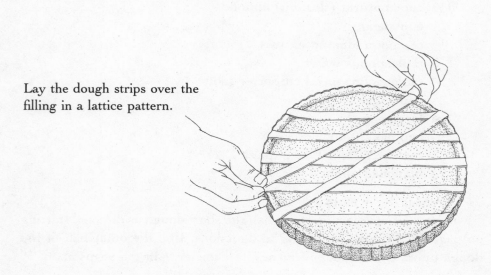

pressing it against the pan. Place an almond slice in each open section of the latticework. Bake until the latticing is golden brown and the almond filling is firm, about 35 minutes.

Brush a thin layer of apricot glaze over the top of the cake as soon as it comes out of the oven. Cool 10 minutes. The glaze will begin to wrinkle or get splotchy as the cake absorbs it; brush on a second layer of glaze to smooth it. Serve warm from the oven or at room temperature.

Valencia Orange Cake

This is a light, moist cake that uses almost every part of the orange — chunks between the layers, zest in the butter cream, and juice to moisten the sponge. I recommend Valencias because they are meaty and sweet. If you cannot get good Valencias, substitute the best eating oranges you can find.

SERVES 12

  1 **9-inch White Sponge Cake (page 93)**
  4 **medium-size Valencia or eating oranges (preferably seedless)**
 24 **tablespoons (¾ pound) unsalted butter (soft)**
 ¾ **cup powdered sugar**
  1 **recipe Pastry Cream (page 105)**

Trim the top and bottom of the sponge and split it into two equal layers (see page 95). Wash and dry the oranges. Remove the zest and chop it fine. Peel all the oranges (see page 321) and cut them into ¼-inch-thick slices. Cut half the slices into ½-inch chunks. Discard any seeds. Set aside.

Using the whisk attachment on an electric mixer (see page 58), beat the butter and sugar until white. Add the orange zest and pastry cream. Beat until thick.

Center one sponge layer on a cake plate. Spread the orange chunks evenly on top of the layer. Drizzle on any orange juice you can reclaim from the counter. Spread 1 cup of butter cream over the orange chunks. Smooth the surface with a knife or icing spatula. Add the second sponge layer and press it gently into the butter cream.

Cut the orange slices in half and arrange the pieces in a circle on top of the cake, about 1 inch from the edge. Cover the sides of the cake with butter cream. Put the remaining butter cream in a pastry bag with a *#7* plain tip. Holding the tip about 1 inch above the edge of the cake make a curl of butter cream (shaped like an apostrophe). Repeat around the entire border of the cake. Starting at the center of the cake, pipe out a tight spiral of butter cream ending at the circle of oranges.

Note: If you don't beat the butter cream enough, you may not get the volume required.

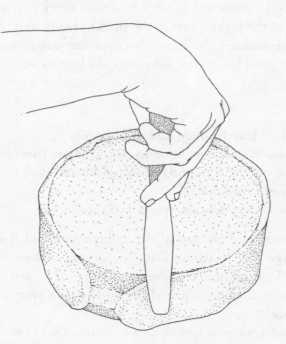

When spreading whipped cream or butter cream on the sides of a cake, hold the icing spatula with the tip down, the edge against the cream, and the flat side of the blade forming a 30-degree angle with the side of the cake. Move the spatula around the cake in a smooth motion to spread the cream evenly.

Dark Chocolate Cake with Brown Sugar Caramel

This cake is a celebration of intense flavors. Alternate layers of moist chocolate cake and crisp bitter chocolate wafers are fused together with caramel and unsweetened chocolate. If you're not a chocolate fanatic, perhaps you should skip this one.

Note: This is a relatively short cake—intentionally so. We tried it with more layers, but it was far too rich.

SERVES 12

> 1 **10-inch Chocolate Sponge Cake (page 95)**
> 1 **cup (8 ounces) plus 2 tablespoons dark brown sugar**
> ¼ **cup water**
> 2 **tablespoons unsalted butter**
> 2 **10-inch Chocolate Wafers (page 79)**
> 1 **ounce unsweetened chocolate, grated**

It is important that your chocolate sponge be moist, so be sure you don't overbake it. When it has cooled completely, trim the top and bottom as directed on page 95 and split it into two equal layers. You will use only one layer here; you can wrap the other in plastic wrap and freeze it. Trim the sides of the layer you're using to remove any dry, light-colored edges and expose the dark, moist cake inside.

Stir the sugar and water together in a saucepan. Scrape down any sugar that gets on the sides of the pan. Bring to a boil and cook without stirring to 240°. (Be sure you don't touch the bottom of the pan with the thermometer; it's hotter than the caramel.) Remove from the heat and swirl in the butter. Set aside in the pan.

Center one chocolate wafer on a cake plate. Drizzle about ¼ cup of caramel over it. Spread the caramel as evenly as possible. Sprinkle on 1 tablespoon of grated chocolate. Center the sponge layer on top and press it down lightly. Drizzle on ¼ cup of caramel and spread it. Sprinkle on 1 tablespoon of chocolate. Place the second wafer on top upside down, so that the top surface is smooth. Press it down gently. Pour the remaining caramel on top. Spread it evenly, pushing it all the way to the edges so that it dribbles down the sides. Sprinkle the remaining chocolate on top. Serve at room temperature.

Chocolate Beret Cake

This is a cake for chocolate addicts. It delivers five different chocolate experiences in every bite.

SERVES 12

> 4 ounces bittersweet chocolate (room temperature)
> 1 recipe Chocolate Wafer Dough (page 79)
> 1 9-inch Chocolate Sponge Cake (page 95)
> 1 recipe Chocolate Cream (page 108)
> ⅛ cup unsweetened cocoa powder

With a vegetable peeler, cut one chocolate curl from the bittersweet chocolate. Coarsely grate the rest. Chill until needed.

Follow the chocolate wafers recipe but do not cut the dough in half before rolling. Instead, cut off about one-quarter of the dough and roll that into a 6-inch circle, following the recipe directions. Divide the remaining dough into two pieces, one a little larger than the other. Roll the larger piece into a 9-inch circle and the smaller piece into an 8-inch circle. Bake the wafers on parchment-lined cookie sheets as directed. Set aside to cool.

Trim the top and bottom of the chocolate sponge (see page 95) and set aside.

Center the 9-inch chocolate wafer on a cake plate. Spread the top with about ½ inch of the chocolate cream. Center the 8-inch wafer on top and spread it with another ½ inch of cream. Center the 6-inch wafer on top and spread it, too, with cream. Set aside about 1 cup of the remaining cream and use the rest to round out the shape of the cake into a smooth dome. Center the chocolate sponge on top and with your hands mold it gently against the sides of the cake so that it completely covers the wafers and cream. Don't worry if the sponge cracks—it will be covered. Spread the reserved cup of cream evenly over the cake. Cover the cream completely with the grated chocolate, pressing it gently onto the sides with the palm of your hand. Sift a thin layer of cocoa over the grated chocolate. Stand the chocolate curl on end in the center of the cake so that the finished cake resembles a French beret. Refrigerate until 15 minutes before serving.

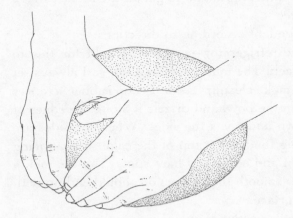

With your hands, mold the chocolate sponge against the sides of the cake.

Chocolate Fondant Cake

This is a very light and elegant three-layer chocolate cake. Iced with chocolate fondant, on top of a coating of butter cream, it gleams enticingly—and is quite rich and sweet. Remember, the fondant has to be made at least twenty-four hours before icing the cake. The chocolate sponge and ganache shells can also be made ahead if you like.

SERVES 12

    1 10-inch Chocolate Sponge Cake (page 95)
    1 recipe Egg White Butter Cream (page 109)
    ½ cup (4 ounces) unsweetened chocolate, melted and cooled
    1 recipe Chocolate Fondant (page 114)
    16 Chocolate Ganache Shells (page 125)

Trim the chocolate sponge and split it into three equal layers (see page 95). Prepare the butter cream and stir ½ cup of the melted chocolate into it thoroughly.

Center one sponge layer on a cake plate. Spread on ¼ inch of butter cream. Add the second sponge layer and another layer of butter cream. Add the third sponge layer. Cover the top and sides of the cake with the remaining butter cream. Use an icing spatula to get all the surfaces very smooth and even. Refrigerate.

Prepare the chocolate fondant according to directions.

Take the cake from the refrigerator—it must be cold for this to work—and set it on a wire rack. The fondant drips a lot, so I always set the rack on a cookie sheet to make cleanup easier. Scoop rubber scrapers full of chocolate fondant from the bowl and drizzle it along the edges of the cake so that it drips down and coats the sides. When the sides are covered, drizzle the remaining fondant on top of the cake. Use an icing spatula to smooth the fondant and cover any bare spots. Tap the rack a few times on the table to help smooth the sides. You should end up with a gleaming, mirror-smooth surface.

Arrange the ganache shells on top of the cake in an evenly spaced circle close to the edges, with their points toward the center. Let the cake sit at room temperature until the fondant sets up (that is, forms a crust), about 15 minutes, then refrigerate the cake until 15 minutes before serving.

Chocolate Cassis Cake

This traditional, extravagantly rich chocolate cake combines flaky bitter-chocolate wafers with a light, liqueur-drenched chocolate sponge. Allow yourself several hours of preparation time or bake the sponge ahead and freeze it.

SERVES 12

1 **9-inch Chocolate Sponge Cake (page 95)**
2 **Chocolate Wafers (page 79)**

    1 recipe Chocolate Butter Cream (page 108)
   ½ cup crème de cassis
   ½ cup currant jelly
    2 ounces bittersweet chocolate, grated

Trim the top and bottom of the chocolate sponge (see page 95) and set aside.

Center one chocolate wafer on a cake plate. Cover with about ½ inch of chocolate butter cream. Place the chocolate sponge on top of the cream and moisten it with the crème de cassis. Add another ½ inch of butter cream and place the second wafer on top. Use the remaining butter cream to cover (and smooth out) the sides of the cake. Melt the currant jelly over a low flame and brush it over the top of the cake. Cover the sides with the grated chocolate, pressing it on gently with the palm of your hand. Chill until 15 minutes before serving.

Chocolate Sunburst Cake

Thick, moist layers of chocolate cake combined with a rich chocolate butter cream make this a classic American chocolate cake. A sunburst pattern on top gives it a festive air.

SERVES 12

  4½ ounces unsweetened chocolate
  24 tablespoons (¾ pound) unsalted butter (soft)
   ¾ cup powdered sugar
   1 9-inch Chocolate Sponge Cake (page 95)
   2 ounces bittersweet chocolate, coarsely grated

Melt the unsweetened chocolate in the top of a double boiler and let it cool to room temperature. Using the whisk attachment on an electric mixer (see page 58), whip the butter and sugar at high speed until thick and white. Add the cooled chocolate and mix until smooth.

Trim the top and bottom of the chocolate sponge cake and split it into two equal layers (see page 95). Place one layer on a cake plate.

Spread 1 cup of butter cream evenly over the layer. Top with the second cake layer. Cover the sides and top with a thin layer of butter cream. Cover the sides of the cake with the grated chocolate by gently pressing it on with your open palm.

Put the remaining butter cream in a pastry bag with a #3 star tip. To make the sunburst pattern, start about 1 inch from the edge and pipe out a straight line to about 1½ inches from the center (pull up on the bag as you stop, to curl the end of the line). Make 11 more lines evenly spaced around the cake. In the spaces between these lines pipe out 12 new lines starting 1½ inches from the center but running only half the length of the first set. Now, starting again 1½ inches from the center, pipe out lines one-fourth the length of the first lines in every second space. Finally, pipe out tiny lines between the one-fourth- and one-half-length lines. (This is not as complicated as it may sound at first.) Chill the cake until 15 minutes before serving.

Orange-Zested Chocolate Cake

This light, moist cake is based on one of the all-time great flavor combinations, chocolate and orange. The tang of fresh oranges is both emphasized and smoothed by the richness of the chocolate. The whipped butter icing melts in your mouth.

SERVES 12

    1 9-inch Chocolate Sponge Cake (page 95)
    3 eating oranges (preferably seedless)
   24 tablespoons (¾ pound) unsalted butter (soft)
    ½ cup powdered sugar
    4 ounces (about ½ cup) unsweetened chocolate, melted
    4 ounces bittersweet chocolate, coarsely grated
    2 tablespoons Candied Orange Peel (page 124)

Trim the top and bottom of the sponge and split it into two equal layers (see page 95). Zest all of the oranges. Cut one orange in half and set it aside. Peel the others. Cut them into ½-inch slices and cut the slices into 1-inch wedges.

Using the paddle attachment on an electric mixer (see page 58), beat the butter and sugar at medium speed until white. Switch to the whisk attachment and beat at high speed until very light and airy. Test by tasting a bit on your finger. The sugar should be completely dissolved and the butter should seem to evaporate on your tongue. Beat the melted chocolate and the orange zest into the butter.

Center one sponge layer on a cake plate. Squeeze the juice from one orange half over it. Arrange the orange wedges in a single layer covering the sponge layer. Cover the oranges with a layer of chocolate butter icing. Smooth the surface with an icing spatula or long-bladed knife. Center the second sponge layer on top, making sure it lines up with the bottom layer. Squeeze the juice from the second orange half over the top. Cover the top and sides of the cake with the butter icing, spreading it on as smoothly as possible.

Cover the sides of the cake with the grated chocolate by pressing it on gently with your open palm. Make a decorative line pattern on top by gently touching the blade of a long knife or icing spatula to the icing. Make lines about 1 inch apart across the entire top of the cake, then give the cake a quarter turn and repeat. Scatter pieces of candied orange peel in a loose circle around the perimeter of the cake. Refrigerate at least 2 hours before serving.

Chocolate and Butter Cake

This is a rich and elegant cake. Its three chocolate layers are enclosed in sweet butter whipped to airy lightness. The top is randomly crisscrossed with lines of chocolate, making it look like a dessert by Jackson Pollock.

SERVES 12

1 10-inch Chocolate Sponge Cake (page 95)
4 ounces bittersweet chocolate
1 pound unsalted butter (soft)
1½ cups powdered sugar

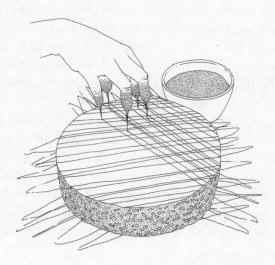

Dip your fingers into the melted chocolate, then wave them back and forth over the cake, spraying lines of chocolate across the top.

Trim the top and bottom of the chocolate sponge and split it into three equal layers (see page 95). Coarsely grate the chocolate and put it in the refrigerator to chill.

Using the paddle attachment on an electric mixer (see page 58), beat the butter and sugar together. When the butter is soft, switch to the whisk attachment and whip at medium speed until white and very light in texture, about 20 minutes. Stop several times to scrape the sides and bottom of the bowl. Check to see if the butter is ready by tasting a little. It should taste like air on your tongue (it just disappears in your mouth) with absolutely no graininess, and it will look like whipped cream. Turn the mixer up to medium-high and whip a few minutes more, until fluffy. Do not beat more than a few minutes at this stage; overbeating will make the butter runny and reduce its volume.

Center one sponge layer on a cake plate. Spread a ¼-inch layer of butter over it. Make the surface as even as possible. Add the second sponge layer, pressing it gently into the butter. Spread on another even layer of butter, then add the top sponge layer, pressing it gently. Cover the top and sides of the cake with the remaining butter. (*Note:* If you have overbeaten the butter and do not have enough to cover the cake, spread it on the sides somewhat skimpily. The grated chocolate will cover it.) Cover the sides of the cake with grated chocolate, pressing it on gently with your open palm. Refrigerate for 15 minutes.

Meanwhile, melt the excess grated chocolate over boiled (not boiling) water. Stir with a spoon to smooth. Cool slightly, then scrape it into a puddle in the bottom of the bowl. Set the cake close to the bowl. Dip the fingers of one hand into the chocolate (it's a bit hot) and wave them back and forth over the cake, spraying lines of chocolate across the top. Give the cake a half turn and make lines in the other direction. When your "canvas" is completed, chill the cake at least 2 hours to firm the butter.

Black Forest Cake

I love cherries, and this cake is one of the best ways I know to show them off. Choose cherries that are ripe but tart (try to get Montmorencies). If all you can find are dark, sweet Bings, boost their acidity by adding 2 teaspoons of lemon juice to the kirsch.

You need a cherry pitter to do this cake right. If you don't already own one, it's well worth the small investment (see page 50).

SERVES 12

    1½ pounds fresh cherries
    ½ cup kirsch
    ⅓ cup plus 1 tablespoon sugar
    1 10-inch Chocolate Sponge Cake (page 95)
    3 cups whipping cream
    ½ teaspoon vanilla extract
    5 ounces bittersweet chocolate (coarsely grate 3 ounces)
    1 teaspoon powdered sugar

Rinse and remove the stems from the cherries. Set aside 12 beautiful ones for decorating the finished cake. Remove the pits from the rest of the cherries and put them in a bowl. Add the kirsch and ⅓ cup of sugar. (If you're using Bings, add 2 teaspoons of lemon juice.) Stir together and let stand at room temperature at least 2 hours, stirring occasionally.

Prepare a chocolate sponge according to directions. When the cake has cooled to room temperature, trim the top and bottom and split it into two equal layers (see page 95).

Combine the cream, vanilla extract, and 1 tablespoon of sugar. Whip at high speed to stiff peaks.

Remove the cherries from their marinating liquid, reserving the liquid. Center one layer of chocolate sponge on a cake plate. Brush on half the marinating liquid. Mix 2 cups of whipped cream with the cherries and spread evenly on the sponge layer. Use an icing spatula or the back of a spoon to make the surface as smooth as possible, then place the second sponge layer on top. (Make sure it lines up with the bottom layer.) Brush on the remaining marinating liquid.

Set aside 1½ cups of whipped cream for decorating. Spread the rest evenly over the top and sides of the cake. Cover the sides with the coarsely grated chocolate by pressing it gently into the cream with your open palm.

Put the reserved cream into a pastry bag with a *#7* plain tip. Holding the tip about ½ inch above the cake, make a small circular mound, about 1½ inches in diameter, close to the edge of the cake. Make 12 mounds in all, evenly spaced around the perimeter of the cake. Top each with a cherry.

There are two ways to make the "raked" chocolate curls that complete the decoration of the cake. If you have a large block of chocolate, you can rake off about 2 ounces by repeatedly drawing the blade of a knife or cleaver across the surface of the block (see page 37). Or you can simply take a 2-ounce hunk of chocolate and peel off curls with a vegetable peeler. Pile the chocolate curls in the center of the cake and sprinkle them with powdered sugar.

Chill at least 30 minutes before serving.

German Chocolate Cake

A light chocolate sponge, unsweetened coconut, and water in place of milk make this cake less rich and sweet than the traditional German Chocolate Cake. Still, it is for people who like sweet desserts.

SERVES 12

   1   9-inch Chocolate Sponge Cake (page 95)
   1   pound (2¼ cups) light brown sugar
 1½   cups water
   2   large eggs
 24   tablespoons (¾ pound) unsalted butter (soft)
   2   teaspoons cider vinegar
   1   tablespoon vanilla extract
   3   cups unsweetened coconut, preferably flakes (see footnote, page 78)
   3   cups walnuts, chopped to ½-inch pieces
  ¼   cup powdered sugar
   2   ounces unsweetened chocolate, melted and cooled
   2   ounces bittersweet chocolate, grated

Trim the top and bottom of the chocolate sponge and split it into two equal layers (see page 95). Set aside.

Combine the brown sugar and ½ cup of water in a 2-quart saucepan. Bring to a boil over high heat. After a few seconds, scrape down any sugar that has stuck to the sides of the pan. Boil vigorously until the caramel smokes, about 5 minutes. Meanwhile, beat the eggs with ⅓ cup of water in a bowl. When the caramel starts to smoke, remove it from the heat and carefully pour ⅔ cup of water through a colander into the pan. Stir with a metal spoon. Bring back to a boil. Pour the eggs into the pan, stir, and bring back to a boil. Remove from the heat and whisk in 8 tablespoons of butter. Stir in the cider vinegar and vanilla extract. Fold in the coconut and walnuts.

Center one sponge layer on a cake plate. Spread a little more than half the caramel mixture over it. Smooth the surface with an icing spatula or the back of a spoon. Center the second sponge layer on top and spread the remaining caramel mixture over it, leaving about ½ inch around the edges.

Sift the powdered sugar. Using the paddle attachment on an electric mixer (see page 58), combine the powdered sugar with the remaining 16 tablespoons of butter. Add the melted unsweetened chocolate and mix until smooth and creamy (it will look like chocolate whipped cream). Cover the sides of the cake with a thin, smooth layer of the butter cream, then cover the butter cream with the grated bittersweet chocolate, pressing it gently against the cake with your open palm. Spoon the rest of the butter cream into a pastry bag with a #7 star tip. Make 16 rosettes around the rim of the cake. Refrigerate until 15 minutes before serving.

Cappuccino Cake

This is a chocolate cake robed in espresso-flavored whipped cream. It's richly satisfying at the end of a meal.

SERVES 12

  1 **9-inch Chocolate Sponge Cake (page 95)**
¼ **cup roasted espresso beans**
  4 **cups whipping cream**
  1 **tablespoon sugar**
  1 **tablespoon instant coffee powder**
  1 **teaspoon hot water**
  2 **ounces bittersweet chocolate, coarsely grated**

Trim the top and bottom of the chocolate sponge and split it into two equal layers (see page 95).

Warm the espresso beans in a 350° oven to bring out their flavor, then finely grind them. Whip 3 cups of cream with the sugar. When half whipped, add the espresso beans and the instant coffee powder dissolved in the hot water. Continue whipping to soft peaks.

Center one sponge layer on a cake plate. Spread a ½-inch layer of coffee cream over it. Add the second sponge layer, being sure to line it up with the bottom layer. Spread the top and sides of the cake with the rest of the coffee cream. Cover the sides with the grated chocolate, pressing it on gently with your open palm.

Whip the remaining cup of cream to soft peaks and spoon it into a pastry bag with a #7 plain tip. Hold the tip about 1 inch above the edge of the cake and make a pointed dome (like a Russian onion dome) about 1½ inches across by moving the tip in a circle, then lifting it up. Make 12 domes in all, evenly spaced around the perimeter of the cake. Refrigerate until ready to serve.

Chocolate Lemon Cake

The chocolate and lemon flavors both come through clearly in this smooth and rich-tasting cake. It is surprising to many people that the light sponge layers can drink in the juice of two lemons without making the cake sour and that the finished cake can be robed in unsweetened chocolate without becoming bitter.

SERVES 12

    1 10-inch Chocolate Sponge Cake (page 95)
    1 cup powdered sugar
    1 pound unsalted butter (soft)
    ½ cup Lemon Cream (page 107)
    4 ounces unsweetened chocolate, melted and cooled
    2 medium-size lemons
    3 ounces unsweetened chocolate, finely grated
    ½ cup Candied Lemon Peel, dipped in chocolate (page 125)

Trim the top and bottom of the chocolate sponge and split it into three equal layers (see page 95). Set aside.

Sift the powdered sugar. Combine it with the butter and whip at high speed with the whisk attachment on an electric mixer (see page 58) until very light. Beat in the lemon cream and then the melted unsweetened chocolate. Zest the lemons. Chop the zest very fine and stir it into the butter cream.

Center one sponge layer on a cake plate. Squeeze the juice of ½ lemon over it. Spread on 1½ cups of butter cream. Make the surface as even as possible with an icing spatula or the back of a spoon. Put on the second sponge layer and squeeze the juice of a whole lemon over it. Spread another layer of butter cream on top and smooth it. Place the last sponge layer on top and squeeze the juice from the remaining ½ lemon over it. Cover the sides and top of the cake with the remaining butter cream.

Cover the sides of the cake with grated chocolate, pressing it gently against the butter cream with an open palm. Sprinkle the rest of the chocolate over the top. Decorate the top of the cake with a circle of candied lemon peel. Refrigerate until ready to serve.

Chocolate Amaretto Cake

This is my interpretation of a classic Italian cake. It brings together three main ingredients that have a great affinity for one another—chocolate, Amaretto, and raspberries.

SERVES 12

    1   9-inch Chocolate Sponge Cake (page 95)
    1   recipe Chocolate Sauce (page 115)
    3   cups whipping cream
    12 tablespoons Amaretto liqueur
    ½   pint raspberries
    1   cup (about 4 ounces) bittersweet chocolate, coarsely grated

Trim the top and bottom of the sponge and split it into two equal layers (see page 95).

Using the whisk attachment on an electric mixer (see page 58), beat together the chocolate sauce, 2½ cups of whipping cream, and 6 tablespoons of Amaretto. Beat at medium speed until the cream starts to thicken, then switch to high speed and beat to stiff peaks.

Center one sponge layer on a cake plate. With a pastry brush, dab 3 tablespoons of Amaretto evenly over the layer. Spread 1½ cups of the chocolate cream over the layer. Use an icing spatula or long knife to make sure it is smooth and flat. Set aside 12 perfect raspberries and spread the rest in a single layer over the chocolate cream. Press the berries gently into the cream. Spread another cup of cream as smoothly as possible over the berries.

Center the other sponge layer on top of the cake (make sure it lines up with the bottom layer) and brush it with the remaining 3 tablespoons of Amaretto. Run your spatula around the sides of the cake to smooth out any cream that has squeezed out from inside, then spread a thin layer of chocolate cream evenly and smoothly over the top and sides of the cake (it should take about 2 cups).

Cover the sides of the cake with the grated chocolate by pressing it on gently with your open palm.

Put the rest of the chocolate cream in a pastry bag with a #7 plain tip. Holding the tip about 1 inch above the cake, make a large comma (about 2¼ inches long) 1 inch from the edge, its curve approximating the curve of the cake. Make 12 commas altogether, end to end, around the perimeter of the cake. Place one of the reserved raspberries inside the curve of each comma.

Beat the remaining ½ cup of cream to stiff peaks. Put the cream in the pastry bag (wash out the chocolate first) with the same tip. Make a large white dot of cream close to each of the raspberries, forming a ring of white dots inside the ring of commas.

Refrigerate the cake until 15 minutes before serving.

Blueberry-Lemon Cake

This striking cake is a study in blue and white. Its lively flavor comes from the simple combination of lemony whipped cream and fresh blueberries.

SERVES 12

5 **large eggs**
¾ **cup sugar**
¾ **cup fresh lemon juice (about 6 lemons)**
8 **tablespoons (¼ pound) unsalted butter**
2 **cups whipping cream**
2 **pints blueberries (the spicier the better)**
1 **9-inch White Sponge Cake (page 93)**

In a bowl, whisk together the eggs and sugar until light. Add the lemon juice and continue mixing until well blended. Pour into the top of a double boiler and stir constantly over simmering water until very thick. Remove from the heat and stir in the butter. Transfer to a bowl and refrigerate until cold. (*Note:* You can do this step a day ahead. Cover the bowl with plastic wrap and keep refrigerated until needed.)

Whip the cream to soft peaks. Fold in the lemon cream until smooth and evenly colored.

Wash and drain the blueberries. Spread them on a towel to dry. Trim the top and bottom of the sponge and split it into two equal layers (see page 95). Place one sponge layer on a cake plate and spread about ¼ inch of lemon cream evenly over the top. Cover the cream with a layer of blueberries; gently press the berries into the cream. Cover the berries with another layer of cream. Place the second sponge layer on top. Set aside about 1 cup of cream for decorating and spread the rest evenly over the top and sides of the cake. Spoon the reserved cream into a pastry bag with a #7 plain tip and pipe out 12 dome-shaped mounds evenly spaced around the perimeter of the cake (see page 54). Heap the remaining blueberries in the center. Refrigerate until 30 minutes before serving.

Lemon-Layered Ice Cream Cake

This is a lavish cake—alternate layers of lemon curd and vanilla ice cream crowned with golden meringue—guaranteed to add to the festive mood of birthdays and other special occasions. Because it needs to be frozen in stages, allow two days to prepare it. The results will amply reward your effort.

SERVES 12

> 1 layer cut from a 10-inch White Sponge Cake (page 93)
> 6 large eggs
> 2¾ cups sugar
> Zest of 1 lemon
> 1 cup fresh lemon juice
> ½ cup water
> 1 recipe Vanilla Ice Cream (page 305)
> 7 egg whites (reserved from ice cream recipe)
> ¼ teaspoon cream of tartar

Lightly oil the inside of a 10-inch springform pan. Cut a 10-inch parchment circle and a strip that will fit along the inside wall of the pan. Line the bottom of the pan with the circle and the sides with the strip, pressing the paper on so that it sticks to the oil. Cut a ½-inch-thick layer from the white sponge (see page 95) and lay it in the bottom of the pan. Freeze until needed.

Make a lemon curd as follows: Mix 6 eggs and 1¼ cups of sugar in the top of a double boiler until thoroughly combined. Add the lemon zest, lemon juice, and water. Cook for about 20 minutes over medium-high heat, stirring occasionally to prevent browning on the bottom. When the curd looks like soft custard, pour it into a bowl and chill completely.

Put a medium-size bowl, preferably stainless steel, in the freezer. Make the vanilla ice cream as directed. Scoop half the ice cream into the frozen bowl. Return it to the freezer until needed. Press the rest of the ice cream into the springform pan, covering the cake evenly. Pour half of the lemon curd over the ice cream. Spread it evenly and freeze until firm, about 6 hours.

Make two more layers with the remaining ice cream and lemon curd. Freeze at least 6 hours more.

Make the meringue by whipping the egg whites left over from the ice cream, the remaining 1½ cups of sugar, and the cream of tartar to stiff peaks. Cover the top of the cake with half of the meringue. Use the remaining half to decorate the top, using a pastry bag and a #7 star tip (see page 54), or mound and swirl the meringue with a knife.

To brown the meringue, light a propane torch (see page 175) and adjust the flame to medium. Move the tip of the flame with a circular motion over the surface of the meringue until it is golden brown. Be careful to keep the torch moving so as not to burn the meringue. Freeze the cake until 10 minutes before serving. Take it from the pan and carefully remove the paper from the sides and bottom. Set it on a cake plate and let it stand at room temperature until served.

Chiffon Cake with Boysenberries and English Cream

This is a tall, delicate, airy cake that drinks in the flavor of its two contrasting sauces—one vanilla-rich, the other slightly tart. It has an "elegant presentation," meaning it will look great on your dessert plates, and it's relatively low-fat (no butter or cream, although there are eggs and a little oil).

SERVES 12

Chiffon Cake:

- 1⅔ cups cake flour
- 1⅓ cups sugar
- ¼ teaspoon kosher salt (see page 42)
- 2 teaspoons baking powder
- ¼ cup water
- ¼ cup vegetable oil

6 **large eggs, separated**°
½ **teaspoon vanilla extract**
½ **teaspoon grated lemon zest**
¼ **teaspoon cream of tartar**
2 **teaspoons powdered sugar**

Boysenberry Sauce:

1 **pint fresh boysenberries**
2 **tablespoons sugar**
¼ **teaspoon grated lemon zest**

1 **recipe English Custard (page 106)**

Preheat the oven to 350°.

Butter the bottom and sides of a 10-inch springform pan. Line the bottom with a circle of parchment, then flour the sides.

Sift the flour, ⅔ cup of sugar, the salt, and baking powder into the bowl of an electric mixer fitted with the paddle attachment (see page 58). Combine the water and oil and pour into the dry ingredients. Mix to combine. Add the egg yolks, mix just a little, and stop the mixer to scrape the sides and bottom of the bowl. Mix at low speed only until smooth (you don't want to add air). The mixture will be thick, yellow, and kind of pasty. Add the vanilla and lemon zest. Set aside.

In a separate bowl, whip the egg whites at high speed until frothy. (If you have only one mixing bowl, transfer the yolk mixture to another bowl, wash and dry the mixing bowl, and use it for the whites.) Stir the cream of tartar and the remaining ⅔ cup of sugar together. With the mixer running, add the sugar in a *very* slow stream—it should take about 1 minute to add it all. Continue whipping to form soft peaks.

Pour the yolk mixture immediately into the beaten egg whites. Fold in with a rubber spatula until completely combined. The batter should be nice and smooth, with no streaks. Pour into the prepared pan and bake until the top springs back when touched lightly, about 40 minutes. This

---

° The right amount of egg is essential to the cake's texture. Do not substitute extra-large or medium eggs.

cake rises high, and sometimes the top cracks. Let the cake cool to room temperature, then sift the powdered sugar over the top.

Boysenberry Sauce: Wash the berries in a strainer. Put them in a food processor with the sugar and lemon zest, and process to a smooth liquid. Pour through a fine sieve into a serving boat.

To serve: Spoon about ¼ cup of English Custard onto each dessert plate. Stand a wedge of cake on the cream and pour about ⅛ cup of berry sauce over the top.

Blackberry Cake

This beautiful cake is very easy to make. You scatter dark, plump berries over the batter, and it rises and browns around them. The cake is intentionally dry because it's meant to be topped with ice cream or, as I prefer, a big dollop of lightly whipped cream.

SERVES 12

- 2½ cups cake flour
- 2 teaspoons baking soda
- 2 teaspoons cream of tartar
- 12 tablespoons unsalted butter (soft)
- 1¼ cups sugar
- 3 large eggs
- 1 pint blackberries, ripe and sweet

Preheat the oven to 375°.

Butter the sides and bottom of a 10-inch springform pan and line the bottom with a circle of parchment.

Combine the flour, baking soda, and cream of tartar; set aside. With the paddle attachment on an electric mixer (see page 58), cream the butter and sugar until white and fluffy. Add 1 egg and mix at medium speed until smooth. Stop the mixer and scrape down the sides and bottom of the bowl. Add one-third of the flour mixture, then the second egg, another third of the flour, the last egg, and the rest of the flour, stopping to scrape the bowl after each addition. Continue mixing at medium speed until the batter is very smooth, about 10 minutes. (It's important to beat enough air into the batter to make it very light. If you skimp on the mixing time, your cake will be too dense and won't rise to its potential.)

Pour the batter into the prepared pan. Smooth the surface with a rubber scraper or the back of a spoon, then scatter the berries on top in a single layer. Bake for 50 minutes to 1 hour. The cake is done when the top is golden brown and firm to the touch, and the sides have pulled away from the pan. A knife inserted in the cake should come out clean except for berry juice. Turn the cake out of the pan immediately and cool on a wire rack.

You can sift a little powdered sugar on top before serving, but I don't think this cake needs it. Serve topped with softly whipped, unsweetened cream or Vanilla Ice Cream (page 305).

Variations: This cake is just as good with boysenberries, loganberries, olallie berries, red currants, or a mixture. Choose the variety that is the plumpest and sweetest on the day you want to bake.

Peach and Pistachio Cake

This colorful, festive cake is based on one of my favorite flavor combinations. Try it when peaches are at their peak. Buy the pistachios raw and toast them yourself in the oven.

SERVES 12

- 2 cups pistachios, shelled
- 5 ripe peaches (don't peel them; there's lots of good flavor in the skin)
- ¼ cup sugar
- ¼ cup fresh lemon juice (about 2 lemons)
- 1 9-inch White Sponge Cake (page 93)
- 2 cups whipping cream

Toast the pistachios in a 375° oven until fragrant, about 10 minutes. Set aside to cool.

Wash the peaches, cut them in half, and discard the pits. Puree six of the halves with the sugar in a blender or food processor. Stop once or twice to scrape down the sides of the container to make sure you get a smooth puree. Transfer to a heavy-bottomed saucepan and simmer until thick, about 5 minutes. The puree should darken to the color of apricots and become glossy. Transfer to a bowl and refrigerate until cool.

Cut the remaining four peach halves vertically into ¼-inch slices. Toss them in a bowl with the lemon juice. (This will accentuate their fresh taste and prevent them from turning brown.) Drain the slices and stir the drained liquid into the puree.

Trim the top and bottom of the sponge and slice it evenly into two layers (see page 95). Whip the cream to soft peaks and fold the cooled puree into it until smooth and evenly colored. Place one sponge layer on a cake plate. Spread it with about ¼ inch of cream. Arrange the sliced peaches on top of the cream, leaving about ½ inch around the edge. Cover the peaches with another layer of cream and place the remaining half of the sponge on top. Spread the rest of the cream smoothly over the top and sides of the cake (see page 198), then completely cover the cake with pistachios. (To put nuts on the sides of the cake, hold them in the open palm of your hand and press them quickly and gently against the cake.) Chill until 15 minutes before serving.

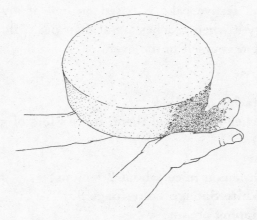

To put nuts on the sides of a cake, hold them in your
open palm, and press them quickly and gently against the cake.

Apple Walnut Cake with Light Bourbon Sauce

This moist, light cake has lots of apple. The bourbon sauce is surprisingly mild and makes a simple cake dramatic.

SERVES 12

    3 medium-size green apples
  ⅔ cup plus 1 tablespoon sugar
  ¼ cup plus 2 tablespoons dark brown sugar
1½ cups cake flour
  ½ teaspoon baking powder
2½ teaspoons cinnamon
  ½ cup milk
   6 tablespoons unsalted butter
   1 large egg
  ¼ teaspoon baking soda
   1 teaspoon grated lemon zest
  ¾ cup toasted walnut pieces

Preheat the oven to 375°.

Butter a 9-inch cake pan and line the bottom with a circle of parchment.

Peel and core the apples. Cut them into chunks about 1 inch square and set them aside.

Place ⅔ cup of sugar, the dark brown sugar, cake flour, baking powder, and 2 teaspoons of cinnamon in the bowl of an electric mixer and mix with the paddle attachment (see page 58) until well blended.

Scald the milk. Remove from the heat and stir in the butter until melted. Pour into the dry mixture and mix until smooth. Mix in the egg. Add the baking soda and mix at medium speed until smooth and light, about 5 minutes. Remove from the mixer and stir in by hand the lemon zest, apples, and walnuts. Pour into the prepared pan. Even out the top with a wooden spoon or rubber spatula. Mix together 1 tablespoon of sugar and ½ teaspoon of cinnamon and sprinkle over the batter.

Bake until the center springs back when touched lightly and the sides of the cake have begun to pull away from the pan, about 45 minutes. Cool in the pan on a wire rack for 30 minutes before transferring to a cake plate.

Light Bourbon Sauce:

If you make the lemon cream ahead, you can whip up this delicious sauce in less than one minute.

2 cups whipping cream
1 recipe Lemon Cream (page 107)
½ cup bourbon

Whip the cream to soft peaks. Stir in the lemon cream and bourbon. Serve in a bowl alongside the cake.

Red Currant and Orange Cake

Fresh red currants don't show up in the markets very often. When they do, it's nice to have a special dessert to show them off. This cake takes 3 cups of currants, which is about two baskets. Serve with unsweetened whipped cream.

SERVES 12

3 cups fresh red currants
Zest of 2 oranges
4 tablespoons unsalted butter (soft)
1 cup sugar
¼ cup vegetable oil
2 large eggs
1 tablespoon baking powder
3 cups cake flour
1 cup milk

Pull the currants gently off their stems. Rinse them and set aside. Finely chop the zest. Set aside. Butter the sides and bottom of a 10-inch cake pan; line the bottom with a circle of parchment.

Preheat the oven to 350°.

Using the paddle attachment on an electric mixer (see page 58), cream the butter and sugar until light. Mix in the oil. Add the eggs and mix until smooth. Scrape the sides and bottom of the bowl.

With the mixer on low speed, add the baking powder and 1 cup of flour. When well combined, add half the milk, another cup of flour, the rest of the milk, and the rest of the flour, mixing well after each addition. Stop to scrape the bowl as necessary. Remove the bowl from the mixer and gently fold in the currants and orange zest. Pour the batter into the prepared pan and bake until golden brown and firm on top, about 50 minutes. Cool on a rack to room temperature. Serve with lightly whipped unsweetened cream.

Gingered Peach Cake

Thanks to the popularity of Asian cooking, fresh ginger is now available in most American supermarkets. Its unmistakable sparkle both underscores and balances the richness of this lush, peach-filled cake.

SERVES 12

4 ounces fresh ginger
2 cups sugar
2 cups water
5 medium-size peaches, ripe and firm
1 9-inch White Sponge Cake (page 93)
3 large eggs
1 pound unsalted butter (soft)
12 slices crystallized ginger

Peel the ginger and cut it into ¼-inch-thick slices. Make a sugar syrup by bringing the sugar and water to a boil in a large, heavy-bottomed saucepan (the pan must be big enough to hold the peaches too). Add the ginger to the syrup, lower the heat, and simmer for 10 minutes. Meanwhile, peel and halve the peaches; discard the pits. Cut each half in quarters lengthwise, then across into quarters. Add the peach chunks to the syrup and simmer until tender, about 5 minutes.

Remove the peaches and ginger from the syrup with a slotted spoon. When the ginger is cool enough to handle, cut it into ¼-inch cubes and return it to the syrup. Also pour back any syrup that gathered around the peaches. Continue cooking the syrup to 235°, about 35 to 40 minutes.

Trim the top and bottom of the sponge and split it into two equal layers (see page 95).

Whip the eggs at high speed until thick and white. Turn the mixer down to low and slowly add the hot syrup to the eggs. Mix at medium speed until cool. Cut the butter into pieces and add a few pieces at a time. Stop the mixer to scrape the sides and bottom of the bowl. Continue beating until the butter cream is thick and creamy.

Center one sponge layer on a cake plate. Spread the peach chunks on top of the layer, leaving 1 inch around the edge. Fold the butter cream to mix in any ginger that has stuck to the bottom of the bowl and spread a ½-inch layer of it over the peaches. Place the second sponge layer on top, pressing it gently into the butter cream. Set aside 1 cup of butter cream and use the rest to cover the top and sides of the cake. Smooth all the surfaces with an icing spatula.

Put the reserved butter cream in a pastry bag with a #9 plain tip. Pipe out a mound shaped like an onion dome on top of the cake, close to the edge. Pipe out 12 domes in all, evenly spaced around the perimeter of the cake. Top each dome with a slice of crystallized ginger. (The slices should be about 1 inch in diameter; if some are too big, break them or cut them to size.) Refrigerate the cake at least 2 hours before serving.

Buttermilk Cake

I created this recipe specifically to fill the need for a low-fat cake that is light, fresh tasting, and sophisticated enough for any dinner party. This cake is even lighter than the Chiffon Cake on page 216 because it has no egg yolks. I serve it with Raspberry Sauce (page 118).

SERVES 12

 1⅔ cups cake flour
 1⅓ cups sugar
 ⅛ teaspoon kosher salt (see page 42)
 2 teaspoons baking soda
 ¼ cup vegetable oil
 ¾ cup buttermilk
 1 teaspoon vanilla extract
 6 large egg whites
 ¼ teaspoon cream of tartar

Preheat the oven to 350°. Butter the sides and bottom of a 10-inch cake pan. Line the bottom with a circle of parchment.

Using the paddle attachment on an electric mixer (see page 58), blend the flour, ⅔ cup of sugar, the salt, and baking soda. With the mixer on low speed, add the oil, buttermilk, and vanilla. Mix until smooth; the batter will feel very soft.

With a clean mixing bowl and the whisk attachment, beat the egg whites, the remaining ⅔ cup of sugar, and the cream of tartar to soft peaks. Pour the batter evenly over the egg whites so that it does not get too heavy in one spot and fall through. Fold in gently. Pour the batter into the prepared pan and bake until the center springs back when touched lightly, about 35 minutes. Serve at room temperature with raspberry sauce or any other fresh fruit sauce.

Fresh Fruit Pound Cake

This unusual cake is simple to prepare and practically goofproof. Even if you do something wrong, it always comes out great. Serve it with Lemon Cream (page 107) or unsweetened softly whipped cream flavored with orange zest.

SERVES 12

       2 medium-size firm green apples
       2 medium-size ripe pears
   1½ cups cranberries
       8 tablespoons (¼ pound) unsalted butter (soft)
   1¼ cups sugar
       ¼ cup buttermilk
   2½ cups all-purpose flour
       1 tablespoon baking powder
       4 large eggs

Preheat the oven to 350°. Butter and flour a 10-inch springform pan.

Peel and quarter the apples and pears. Cut them into ½-inch cubes. Wash and towel-dry the cranberries.

Using the paddle attachment on an electric mixer (see page 58), cream the butter, sugar, and buttermilk until light. Sift the flour and baking powder together. Mix half the flour mixture into the batter. Add 2 eggs. Blend well. Add the remaining 2 eggs and blend well. Add the remaining flour and beat until light.

Stir the apples, pears, and cranberries into the batter with a wooden spoon. Pour immediately into the prepared pan and bake until the center is firm, about 1 hour and 10 minutes. Allow the cake to cool 15 minutes in the pan, then remove it from the pan and let it cool completely on a wire rack. Serve at room temperature.

Note: This cake stores very well. Double wrap in plastic wrap, then refrigerate or freeze.

Coconut Flair Cake

Fresh coconut is moist, chewy, and delicious—nothing at all like processed coconut. I like it coarsely chopped, to emphasize its nutlike texture. The addition of white chocolate brings out the coconut's soft, mellow flavor.

SERVES 12

> 1 **small coconut**
> 1 **cup milk**
> 12 **ounces white chocolate**
> 1 **9-inch White Sponge Cake (page 93)**
> 2 **cups whipping cream**
> 2 **pints fresh strawberries***

Every professional cook has a favorite way of attacking a coconut. This is mine: Heat the coconut on a sheet pan in a 450° oven until it splits open, about 15 minutes. Insert a knife through the crack to poke a hole into the center of the coconut. The juice inside should smell sweet. (If it smells rancid, the coconut is bad. Don't use it.) Drain the coconut juice into a bowl. If it has picked up brown particles from the shell, filter it through cheesecloth or a paper coffee filter. Set aside. When the coconut is cool enough to handle, break it open and remove the meat. (Try an oyster knife to pry the meat away from the shell if your coconut is especially stubborn.) By hand or in a food processor, chop the meat, with brown skin attached, into ¼-inch chunks.

Combine the coconut, milk, and coconut juice in a heavy-bottomed saucepan. (Use up to ⅓ cup of coconut juice; if your coconut has more, discard the excess.) Bring to a boil, then reduce the heat and simmer for 5 minutes. Transfer to a bowl. Break up 8 ounces of the chocolate, add it to the coconut, and stir until melted. Refrigerate until cool. (This mixture must be completely cooled before you add it to the cream, or the cream will run.)

Trim the top and bottom of the sponge and split it evenly in half (see page 95), so that you have two thin layers. Whip the cream to soft peaks. Remove the coconut mixture from the refrigerator, stir it to incorporate any cocoa butter that has separated, and fold it into the cream.

---

* If strawberries are not in season or you can't find luscious, ripe ones at a reasonable price, you can cover the entire cake, top and sides, with grated chocolate and serve it with a strawberry sauce. We do this often at The Stanford Court, even when good strawberries are available. You'll need an additional 2 ounces of grated chocolate. For the sauce, thaw 1 pound of frozen, unsweetened strawberries and puree in a blender or food processor. If the taste is a little watery, add a tiny bit of sugar to bring out the fruitiness. Serve in a sauce boat alongside the cake.

Arrange the strawberries in concentric circles on top of the cake. Use the largest, best-looking berries, with their leaves on, for the outside circle.

Place one of the sponge layers on a cake plate. Spread it with about ½ inch of coconut cream. Lay the other sponge layer on top. Cover the top and sides of the cake with the rest of the cream. Coarsely grate the remaining chocolate. Cover the sides of the cake with the grated chocolate by pressing it on gently with the palm of your hand. Chill the cake in the freezer for 15 minutes.

Wash the strawberries and pat them dry. Arrange them decoratively on top of the cake. (I like to use the largest, best-shaped berries and the very small ones whole, with the leaves left on the large ones. I cut middle-sized berries in half.) Refrigerate the cake until 15 minutes before serving.

Cheesecake

Cheesecake is lighter and much less sweet without a crust. Here, in place of a crust, a thin layer of chopped almonds provides a surprising counterpoint and a welcome toastiness.

SERVES 12

   1 **pound 10 ounces cream cheese**
1¼ **cups plus 1 tablespoon sugar**
   3 **large eggs**
⅔ **cup half-and-half**
   1 **teaspoon vanilla extract**
   1 **teaspoon grated lemon zest**
⅓ **cup toasted almonds, chopped**

Preheat the oven to 350°.

Oil a 9-inch cake pan and line the bottom with a circle of parchment, making sure the parchment lies flat.

Using the paddle attachment on an electric mixer° and the lowest speed, mix together the cream cheese and 1¼ cups of sugar until smooth and free of lumps. If necessary, stop and scrape down the bowl and paddle to help break up the cheese. Add the eggs one at a time; mix each egg in completely and scrape down the sides of the bowl before adding the next.

Add half of the half-and-half to the cheese batter and blend it in well. Scrape down the bowl and the paddle. Add the remaining half and mix until smooth. Mix in the vanilla and lemon zest.

Pour the batter into the prepared pan. Place it inside a larger pan and pour ½ inch of water into the outer pan. Bake until the center is firm and the top is golden brown, about 2 hours. Add more water during baking if the outer pan goes dry.

Cool the cake in the pan on a wire rack. When completely cool, dust the top with 1 tablespoon of sugar. Turn the cake over onto a plate and remove the parchment. Sprinkle the bottom of the cake with the toasted almonds. Turn over onto a cake plate and lightly brush any excess sugar off the top of the cake. Chill at least 2 hours before serving.

° To make a perfectly smooth, evenly crusted cake, you must mix slowly and carefully throughout, using the paddle attachment on an electric mixer (see page 58). If your mixer has only beaters, you can still make this delicious cheesecake, but because of the air the beaters add to the batter, the crust will probably crack.

Pear and Cream Cake

This is a delicate cake, pale in color and subtle in flavor. You can use any kind of pears as long as they are flavorful, ripe, and firm.

SERVES 12

> 1 **lemon**
> 6 **medium-size pears**
> 3 **cups water**
> 1½ **cups sugar**
> 1 **vanilla bean, split**
> 1 **9-inch White Sponge Cake (page 93)**
> 3 **cups whipping cream**

Squeeze the juice of the lemon into a bowl. Peel the pears, cut them in quarters, and remove the cores. Toss the pears in the lemon juice.

Bring the water, sugar, and vanilla bean to a boil in a heavy-bottomed saucepan. Add the pears and simmer until the tip of a knife easily pierces the fruit (see footnote, page 323). Use a slotted spoon to transfer the pears to a bowl. Let them and the cooking liquid cool to room temperature. (You don't need the liquid, but you do need the vanilla bean.)

Trim the top and bottom of the sponge and split it into two equal layers (see page 95). Puree 8 of the pear quarters in a food processor until smooth. Scrape the pulp inside the vanilla bean into the puree. Cut the remaining 16 pear quarters in half lengthwise and then across into ½-inch chunks.

Center one sponge layer on a cake plate. Spread half the pear chunks evenly on top of it. Whip the cream to soft peaks. Set aside 1½ cups, then stir the pear puree into the rest. Spread 1½ cups of pear cream evenly over the pear chunks. Place the second sponge layer on top, making sure it lines up with the bottom layer. Spread the remaining pear chunks on top. Cover the top and sides of the cake with pear cream. Smooth the sides as much as possible; they're not going to be covered.

Spoon the reserved whipped cream into a pastry bag with a #7 plain tip. Holding the tip about 1 inch above the cake, close to the edge, make a teardrop mound about 1½ inches across (pipe on a round mound, then lift the tip up to one side). Make 16 teardrops in all around the edge of the cake. Refrigerate until ready to serve.

Hazelnut Torte

Not exactly a cake, this is a layered extravaganza of crisp hazelnut Vienna dough, apricot glaze, and rich chocolate butter cream. The elements are assembled into a 16-inch-long bar, which is then glazed with chocolate, cut into slices, and served cold. The bar has to be refrigerated overnight, so begin the day before you want to serve it.

SERVES 16

Double recipe Vienna Dough (page 80)
½ **recipe Apricot Glaze (page 122)**
1 **recipe Custard Butter Cream (page 109)**
2 **ounces unsweetened chocolate, melted and cooled**
Double recipe Chocolate Glaze (page 123)
2 **ounces bittersweet chocolate**

Prepare the Vienna dough as directed, but instead of rolling it into a circle, divide it in half and roll each half into an 11 × 17-inch rectangle (to fit the bottom of a standard cookie sheet). Line 2 cookie sheets with parchment. Roll each rectangle carefully around your rolling pin and unroll it onto a cookie sheet. Brush off any excess flour. With a pastry wheel trim the edges to make them perfectly straight. Cut each rectangle into three 17 × 3⅔-inch strips. (Separate them a little so they won't fuse together during baking.) Chill the dough until firm, about 20 minutes.

Prepare the apricot glaze. Set aside to cool.

Preheat the oven to 350°. Bake the Vienna dough strips until golden brown, dry, and firm, about 20 minutes. Cool to room temperature.

Gently heat the apricot glaze to liquefy. Turn over one Vienna dough strip (that will be the top layer), then coat all the strips with apricot glaze. Set aside.

Prepare the custard butter cream. Add the melted chocolate and stir until smooth. Put the butter cream into a pastry bag with a #7 plain tip. Pipe a ¼-inch-thick layer of butter cream onto one of the strips. Place another strip on top; press down gently. Repeat until all the butter cream and all the Vienna dough strips have been used (with the reversed strip on top). Smooth the butter cream on the sides of the bar with a knife or icing spatula. Refrigerate overnight.

Prepare the chocolate glaze. Let it cool about 10 minutes. Place the bar on a cooling rack set on a parchment-lined cookie sheet. Spoon a generous amount of glaze along the top edges of the bar so that it drips down and completely covers the sides. When the sides are covered, evenly spread the glaze remaining on top. Tap the rack a few times on the table to even out the coating of glaze on the sides of the bar. Grate the chocolate into curls with a vegetable peeler. Sprinkle the curls in a stripe down the middle of the bar. Refrigerate until 10 minutes before serving. To serve, cut into 1-inch slices.

Marjolaine

This is my interpretation of French Chef Fernand Point's famous Gateau Marjolaine, a lavish dessert consisting of two rich cream layers and three layers of crisp meringue. It took me three years to figure out how to make it. In this version I have used hazelnut meringues with layers of chocolate and coffee cream.

SERVES 8

- ¾ cup ground hazelnuts (measure after grinding)
- 1 tablespoon cornstarch
- 1¼ cups plus 2 tablespoons sugar
- 7 large egg whites
- 5 ounces bittersweet chocolate

¼ **cup milk**
3 **cups whipping cream**
1 **tablespoon instant coffee powder**
1 **teaspoon hot water**
2 **tablespoons powdered sugar**
16 **Chocolate Butterfly wings (page 126)**

For the meringues: Preheat the oven to 225°. Cut a piece of parchment to fit a cookie sheet. Draw three 16 × 3-inch rectangles on the parchment, then place the paper, lined side down, on the cookie sheet. Set aside.

Rub the hazelnuts, cornstarch, and 2 tablespoons of sugar together with your fingertips. Combine the egg whites and the rest of the sugar in the top of a double boiler. Heat over slow-boiling water, whisking continuously, to body temperature. Transfer to an electric mixer and beat at high speed to soft peaks. Fold in the dry ingredients immediately and spoon the meringue into a pastry bag with a #4 plain tip. Pipe out the meringue in long lines, close together, filling in the outlines on the parchment so that you have three 16 × 3-inch strips. Bake until firm to the touch, about 1 hour. Cool.

For the chocolate cream: Cut 3 ounces of the chocolate into small chunks. Bring the milk to a boil in a small saucepan. Turn off the heat. Add the chocolate and stir until melted. Transfer to a bowl and refrigerate until the mixture is cool and coats a spoon.

Using the paddle attachment on an electric mixer (see page 58), beat the chocolate mixture at medium-high speed for about 30 seconds. Add ½ cup of whipping cream. Mix at low speed until smooth. Stop the mixer and scrape the sides and bottom of the bowl. Add another ½ cup of cream. Replace the paddle with the whisk attachment and whip at medium speed to soft peaks. Refrigerate.

For the coffee cream: Dissolve the instant coffee powder in the hot water. Whip 1½ cups of whipping cream to soft peaks. Fold in the coffee. Refrigerate.

To assemble the marjolaine: Gently remove the three meringue strips from the parchment. (Don't worry if a strip breaks; you can piece it back together as you work.) Place one meringue strip, flat side down, on a sheet of parchment. Spoon the chocolate cream into a pastry bag with a #8 plain tip. Tube the chocolate cream out in long lines to cover the meringue. Place the second meringue on top of the cream, flat side up. Press it down gently so that some of the cream oozes out the sides.

Rinse the pastry bag and fill it with the coffee cream. Tube out the coffee cream as you did the chocolate and place the last meringue on top, flat side up. Press it gently into the cream. Using an icing spatula or a knife, smooth the cream that has oozed out to cover the sides of the marjolaine. Coarsely grate the remaining 2 ounces of chocolate. Coat the sides but not the ends of the marjolaine with the grated chocolate by pressing it against the cream with an open palm. Wrap the marjolaine in plastic wrap and freeze.

When the cream is frozen, cut the marjolaine into 8 pieces. Sprinkle powdered sugar over the top of each and arrange the pieces on a serving tray. Whip the remaining ½ cup of cream to soft peaks and spoon it into a pastry bag with a #7 star tip. Pipe out a rosette in the center of each piece. Decorate each rosette with a pair of chocolate butterfly wings. Refrigerate at least 1 hour before serving.

Carrot Cake

This is a moist, dense cake, filled with bits of chewy coconut, fresh pineapple, walnuts, and raisins. It really doesn't need any icing. Serve it with a dollop of Lemon Cream (page 107) or lemon-flavored whipped cream.

SERVES 12

- 2½ cups finely grated carrots (3 large carrots)
- 1½ cups walnut quarters
- 1 cup fresh pineapple chunks (about 1 × ½ × ½ inch)
- 1 cup golden raisins

  1 **cup unsweetened coconut flakes (see footnote, page 78)**
  2 **cups cake flour**
  2 **teaspoons cinnamon**
  2 **teaspoons baking soda**
  1 **teaspoon kosher salt (see page 42)**
  4 **large eggs**
1½ **cups sugar**
1½ **cups vegetable oil**

Preheat the oven to 375°.

Grease the sides and bottom of a 10-inch springform pan. Line the bottom with a circle of parchment, then dust the sides with flour.

Have all your ingredients measured out before you start combining them.

In a large bowl mix together the carrots, nuts, pineapple, raisins, and coconut. Sift all the dry ingredients except the sugar into another bowl. Toss about ½ cup of the dry ingredient mixture with the carrot mixture.

Beat the eggs and sugar at high speed until they form a ribbon. Continue mixing at low speed while you slowly add the oil. Remove from the mixer and fold in the dry ingredients. Pour the batter over the carrot mixture and gently fold it in. Pour into the prepared pan and bake until a toothpick inserted in the center comes out dry, about 1 hour and 15 minutes. Cool on a rack. When cool, remove from the pan, strip off the parchment, and set on a cake plate. Serve at room temperature.

Quince and Ginger Cake

This dark, moist cake, studded with chunks of exotic fruit, is best served with a dollop of softly whipped cream. When quince is out of season, use your favorite pears instead.

SERVES 12

>   2 medium-size ripe quinces
>   5 tablespoons unsalted butter (soft)
>   ½ cup plus 2 tablespoons sugar
>   1 large egg
>   ¾ cup dark molasses
>   2 cups plus 2 tablespoons cake flour
>   1½ teaspoons baking soda
>   1½ teaspoons grated fresh ginger *or* ¾ teaspoon powdered ginger
>   1 cup buttermilk

Preheat the oven to 375°.

Butter the sides and bottom of a 9-inch cake pan. Line the bottom with a circle of parchment, then flour the sides.

Peel the quinces with a vegetable peeler or knife and remove the cores. Cut into 1-inch cubes. Set aside.

Using the paddle attachment on an electric mixer (see page 58), cream the butter and sugar at medium-high speed until light and smooth. Stop two or three times to scrape down the bowl and paddle. Beat in the egg. Scrape the bowl and paddle. Beat at medium-high speed, letting the molasses trickle slowly into the batter. Stop halfway through to scrape the bowl and paddle. The batter will be smooth and a rich toffee color. Let it continue mixing while you sift together the flour and baking soda. Beat in the ginger and then half of the flour (lower the mixer speed enough to keep the flour from splashing out of the bowl). Beat in the buttermilk, then the remaining flour. Remove the bowl from the mixer and fold in the quinces. Pour into the prepared pan. Bake until the center of the cake is firm to the touch, about 1 hour and 20 minutes. Cool in the pan on a wire rack.

Strawberry Grand Marnier Cake

This is a cake of many parts, but it's well worth the time it takes to prepare all the elements. The sponge cake and candied orange peel can be made days ahead and stored.

SERVES 12

 2 10-inch Butter Wafer circles (page 80)
 1 layer from 10-inch White Sponge Cake (page 93)
16 strips Candied Orange Peel, ½ × 2 inches (page 124)
24 tablespoons (¾ pound) unsalted butter (soft)
1½ cups powdered sugar
1½ pints large strawberries, ripe and firm
 ¼ cup Grand Marnier
 ½ cup sliced almonds, toasted
 1 tablespoon sugar

Have the butter wafers, white sponge cake, and candied orange peel prepared.

Using the paddle attachment on an electric mixer (see page 58), cream the butter and powdered sugar at medium speed until light. Scrape the sides and bottom of the bowl. Switch to the whisk attachment and whip until the butter is fluffy.

Wash the strawberries and cut off the tops. Set aside ½ pint. Slice the remaining strawberries vertically into ¼-inch-thick slices (5 pieces if the berries are large, 4 pieces if they are medium).

Trim the edges of the butter wafer circles by placing a 10-inch cardboard circle on each and cutting away the excess wafer with a sharp knife.

Center one wafer on a cake plate. Spread ⅓ cup of the butter cream evenly over it. Set the white sponge layer on top. Sprinkle the Grand Marnier over the sponge. Cover the sponge with the sliced strawberries, leaving ½ inch around the edges. Carefully spread ⅔ cup of the butter cream over the berries. Place the second butter wafer on top and gently press it down—press with your hands open and flat to distribute the pressure evenly; otherwise, the wafer will crack. Spread a thin coating of butter cream evenly over the sides of the cake.

Crush the toasted almonds and cover the sides of the cake with them, pressing them on gently with your open palm.

Toss the candied orange peel strips in the sugar. Arrange the strips on top of the cake, close to the edge, points toward the center but at a slight angle, about 1 inch apart.

Put the remaining butter cream in a pastry bag with a #7 plain tip. Pipe a candy kiss-shaped mound of butter cream between each 2 orange peel strips. Slice the reserved strawberries in half vertically. Lean a strawberry half against the inner side of each mound. Refrigerate until ready to serve.

Strawberry-Orange Cake

This is a light and lively cake. Sponge layers drenched with fresh orange juice are heaped with ripe strawberries and crowned with whipped cream. Candied orange peel adds a decorative finishing touch.

SERVES 12

1 9-inch White Sponge Cake (page 93)
2 juice oranges ⎫
¾ cup sugar ⎬ *or* ½ recipe Candied
1 cup water ⎭   Orange Peel (page 124)
2 pints large strawberries
3 cups whipping cream
½ cup sliced almonds, toasted
½ recipe Currant Glaze (page 122)

Trim the top and bottom of the sponge and split it into two equal layers (see page 95). Set aside.

If you have candied orange peel on hand, you can use that to decorate the cake. If not, use the peel from the 2 oranges, the sugar, and water to make a half recipe (see instructions, page 125).

Cut the oranges in half. Wash the strawberries. Set one pint aside. Cut the tops off the other pint and cut the berries into quarters vertically. (If your berries aren't very large, cut them into thirds. If they are small, leave them whole. You want pieces that are about 1½ inches at the widest part.) Whip 1½ cups of cream to soft peaks and fold it into the cut strawberries.

Center one sponge layer on a cake plate. Squeeze the juice of one orange over it. Spread the strawberry cream on the layer, pushing the strawberries back ½ inch or so from the edges. (It's all right, in fact, it's preferable, to have some of the cream spill over the edges.) Smooth the surface with a rubber scraper or icing spatula. Add the second sponge layer and press it gently into the cream. Spread the cream that has oozed out between layers, plus any cream left in the bowl, to cover the sides of the cake. Crush the almonds with a rolling pin, then press them onto the sides of the cake with your open palm. (If you do this over a sheet of parchment, you'll be able to retrieve the almond pieces you drop and use them.)

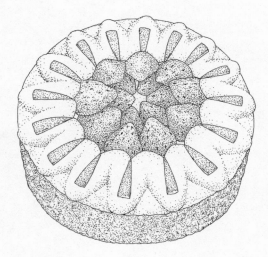

A zigzag border of whipped cream fills the area between the strawberries and the edge of the cake. A strip of candied orange peel is nestled in the center of each zigzag.

Squeeze the juice of the second orange over the top sponge layer. Cut the tops off the remaining pint of strawberries and cut the berries in half vertically. Arrange the berries in two concentric circles in the center of the cake. The tips of the strawberries should point toward the center and the circles should overlap slightly. Gently heat the currant glaze to liquefy. Brush a thin layer over the strawberries.

Whip the remaining cream to soft peaks. Put it in a pastry bag with a #9 plain tip. Using an up and back motion, make a tight zigzag border of cream, filling the area between the strawberries and the edge of the cake (see illustration). You'll need one piece of candied orange peel for each zigzag of cream. Cut the pieces of peel to a uniform length. Place one piece in the crease between the zig and the zag of each mound of cream, with the points toward the center of the cake. Refrigerate until ready to serve.

10
Puddings

Just about everyone has fond memories of the puddings Mother used to make. They were always rich and creamy, and always a special treat. The puddings in this chapter add some new twists to those sumptuous memories.

Bread pudding used to be a way of using up stale odds and ends of bread. The bread pudding that has become most popular at The Stanford Court is quite different. It is made from a buttery brioche loaf specially baked for the purpose. Slices of the fine-textured bread are layered with sliced apples and whole raspberries, then soaked with a rich cream custard.

Personally, I'm just as fond of the Apple and Rye Bread Pudding on page 245. The truth is I love rye bread, and this dessert is the only way I've found to sneak it onto the menu. This pudding uses store-bought bread, so it's a simpler approach than baking your own brioche. My co-author is as partial to rice pudding as I am to bread pudding. She contributed the recipe for the lively Gingered Rice Pudding on page 246.

Custards are always wonderful—smooth and deeply satisfying. They are especially good for busy home cooks because they are comparatively fast and easy to make, and they keep well in the refrigerator. Although custards are about as basic as a dessert can be, that does not mean they have to be plain, or predictable. Whenever possible (that is, whenever they are available and affordable) I bake raspberries into my Crème Brulée to give it added dimensions of color, texture, and flavor; they add just the right contrast to the very rich, smooth custard. I serve my Caramel Custard with slices of ripe papaya, which brings out the flavors and textures of both the custard itself and its bittersweet caramel sauce.

You don't see steamed puddings on menus or dinner tables very often anymore, except perhaps at Christmas, but I like them too much to save them just for the holidays. Steamed puddings are denser and moister than cakes, and are richly flavorful. They satisfy in a very homey and old-fashioned way. If you don't know what I mean, just try one and you'll see.

Many people cook steamed puddings on top of the stove. I find it works just as well to make some in the oven, immersed in a water bath. Confining the moist heat is the key to success. The steam created and trapped around the pudding is what cooks it and gives it its distinctive texture. The best known and most traditional steamed pudding is, of course, plum pudding. For many families the name is practically synonymous with Christmas. A recipe for New England Plum Pudding is included in this chapter, and so is a recipe for Date and Cranberry Steamed Pudding, a more up-to-date dessert cooked in individual servings and suitable for any time of the year and any occasion.

Brioche Bread Pudding

This is not the bread pudding your mother used to make. Between layers of butter-rich brioche loaf are a dense, smooth custard, tart apple chunks, and succulent raspberries. It's a Stanford Court favorite.

SERVES 10

    1 **Brioche loaf, page 83**
    6 **large eggs**
 ¼ **cup bread flour**
 ⅓ **cup sugar**
    1 **quart whipping cream**
    1 **medium-size tart apple**
 ½ **pint raspberries**

Preheat the oven to 375°.

Trim the crust off the brioche loaf and cut it into ½-inch slices. Cut each slice diagonally into two triangles. Set aside.

Using the paddle attachment on an electric mixer (see page 58), beat the eggs, flour, and sugar for about 1 minute at medium speed. Add the cream and mix just enough to combine.

Arrange 8 brioche triangles to cover the bottom of a 2½-quart soufflé dish. Do not overlap them. Peel, quarter, and core the apple. Cut each quarter lengthwise in half and then crosswise into pieces about twice the size of the raspberries. Scatter the apple chunks and the raspberries over the bread. Pour in half of the custard. Arrange 12 brioche triangles on top, slightly overlapping in a circle around the edge, leaving a hole in the center. Pour on the rest of the custard. Bake for 30 minutes, then cover the top loosely with a sheet of parchment. Continue baking until the custard is set, about 20 minutes.

Serve with Raspberry Sauce (page 118) and lightly whipped, unsweetened cream.

Apple and Rye Bread Pudding

The distinctive, hearty flavor of rye permeates this unusual bread pudding. You can use either home-baked or store-bought rye bread. In either case, trim and cut the bread the day before, and leave it out to get stale. Serve the pudding with lightly whipped, unsweetened cream.

SERVES 12

12–14 slices unseeded rye bread
   2 medium-size tart apples
  ½ cup golden raisins
   6 large eggs
  ½ cup sugar
   1 teaspoon ground cardamom
   3 cups half-and-half
   1 tablespoon powdered sugar

A day ahead, remove the crust from the bread (cutting the slices approximately square if the loaf is rounded). Cut each slice diagonally in half. Leave uncovered to get stale.

The second day, preheat the oven to 375°. Butter the bottom of a 2½-quart shallow earthenware baking dish. Cover the bottom with triangles of bread. Do not overlap.

Peel, quarter, and core the apples. Cut each quarter vertically into 6 slices. Arrange the slices on the bread, starting with a circle close to the rim of the dish, points toward the center, then filling in with the remaining slices. Scatter the raisins over the apples. Arrange the remaining bread triangles in a circle around the edge of the dish. They should overlap, flat sides against the side of the dish and points toward the center, leaving a hole in the middle.

Using the whisk attachment on an electric mixer (see page 58), beat the eggs for about 1 minute. Beat in the sugar, cardamom, and half-and-half. Pour the egg mixture into the baking dish. Bake until the bread on top springs back when touched lightly, about 1 hour and 5 minutes. Don't worry if the custard seems a little runny; the bread will absorb any excess liquid.

Before serving, sprinkle the top with powdered sugar. Serve with lightly whipped, unsweetened cream.

Gingered Rice Pudding

Elaine Ratner developed this recipe by first trying to duplicate the rice pudding her grandmother used to make and then adding some of her own favorite ingredients—ginger and currants.

SERVES 8

   1 cup Cal Rose or other medium-grain rice
   2 cups water
   ½ teaspoon kosher salt (see page 42)
      Bread crumbs
   4 large eggs

⅓ **cup milk**
1 **cup buttermilk**
3 **tablespoons plus 1½ teaspoons sugar**
2 **teaspoons unsalted butter (soft), cut into pieces**
¾ **teaspoon vanilla extract**
1½ **ounces crystallized ginger, minced (about ¼ cup before**
  mincing)
⅓ **cup currants**
1 **medium-size tart green apple**
¼ **teaspoon cinnamon**

Combine the rice, water, and salt in a covered heavy-bottomed saucepan. Bring to a boil, then lower the heat and simmer until all the water is absorbed, about 15 minutes. Remove from the heat. Toss the rice a little with a wooden spoon to fluff it, then re-cover the pot and allow the rice to cool.

Preheat the oven to 325°.

Butter a 6-cup baking dish. Cover the bottom and sides with fine bread crumbs.

Lightly beat together the eggs, milk, buttermilk, 3 tablespoons of sugar, butter, and vanilla. Add the cooled rice and mix well with a wooden spoon. Stir in the ginger and currants. Pour into the prepared dish.

Peel, quarter, and core the apple. Cut it into thin slices. Arrange the slices on top of the rice. Combine 1½ teaspoons of sugar with the cinnamon and sprinkle it over the apples. Bake until set, about 50 minutes. Serve warm.

Caramel Custard with Papaya

This is my version of the classic crème caramel. A cool, smooth custard is bathed in slightly bitter caramel and served with slices of fresh papaya. Be sure to start the custard the day before you want to serve it; it must be refrigerated overnight.

SERVES 8

   1⅔ **cups sugar**
    7 **large eggs**
    1 **teaspoon vanilla extract**
    1 **quart milk**
    1 **papaya, ripe and firm (about 5 inches long)**

Preheat the oven to 325°.

Heat 1 cup of sugar in a heavy-bottomed saucepan over medium heat to caramelize. Shake the pan occasionally to help dissolve the sugar, but do not stir. Cook to a rich mahogany color. Divide the caramel among eight 5-ounce custard cups.

Using the whisk attachment on an electric mixer (see page 58), mix the eggs and ⅔ cup of sugar at medium speed. Add the vanilla and milk, and mix until smooth. Pour through a strainer into custard cups, stopping about ½ inch from the top. (You may have some left over.)

Put the cups in a roasting or lasagne pan. Place the pan on a shelf in the oven and pour in about 1 inch of water. Bake until the custard "sets up"—until it does not stick to your finger when touched and a knife inserted in the center comes out dry. Baking time can vary greatly but will probably be 1 to 1½ hours. All 8 cups may not be done at once. As each is done, remove it from the pan of water and set it aside to cool. When cool, refrigerate overnight.

To serve: Have 8 shallow bowls ready. To remove a custard from its baking cup, gently press with your thumbs around the edges of the custard to release it, then turn the cup over onto a bowl. Shake the cup if necessary. The caramel is partly liquid; it will form a pool around the custard.

Peel the papaya and cut it in half. Discard the seeds. Cut each half crosswise into twenty ¼-inch slices. Pick up five slices at a time and fan them out. Place them on the plate beside the custard.

Raspberry Crème Brulée

Crème Brulée is a rich egg custard topped with a brittle layer of caramel that shatters like glass when you plunge in your spoon. Inside this version are ripe, tart raspberries to add color and offer contrast to the richness that is sometimes too wonderful to bear. Crème Brulée is made in individual servings, so you will need ten 4-ounce (or 5-ounce) ramekins. You will also need a propane torch, the pastry chef's secret weapon, to caramelize the sugar (see Tools, page 56).

SERVES 10

> 9 large egg yolks
> ¾ cup plus 2 tablespoons sugar (preferably superfine)
> 1 quart whipping cream
> 1 pint raspberries (you will need 100 berries)

Preheat the oven to 325°.

Using the paddle attachment on an electric mixer (see page 58) and low speed, beat the egg yolks. Add ¼ cup of sugar and mix until smooth. Scrape the sides and bottom of the bowl. Add the cream and mix until all the ingredients are combined. Pour through a fine strainer into a bowl or pitcher.

Put 10 raspberries into each ramekin. Pour the custard over the raspberries, filling the ramekins to the top. Place the ramekins inside a shallow pan—lasagne, jelly roll, and roasting pans all work well. Place the pan on the oven shelf, then pour in ½ inch of hot water. Bake until the custard is set but not browned, about 50 minutes. Remove the ramekins from the pan and cool to room temperature, then refrigerate until firm. The custards will keep for a couple of days in the refrigerator.

Just before serving, remove as many custards as you are going to serve from the refrigerator and spread ½ to 1 tablespoon of sugar evenly over the surface of each. You want a solid layer of sugar, thick enough to completely cover the surface. The size and shape of your ramekins will determine how much sugar you need. Light your propane torch and adjust it to a medium flame. Move the flame in a circular pattern over each ramekin so that the tip of the flame touches the sugar, melts it, and turns it a rich, dark brown. You'll get a splotchy brown crust, not a perfectly even colored one. Be sure you caramelize all the sugar. Let the sugar cool for 1 or 2 minutes, then serve at once.

New England Plum Pudding

This is a traditional plum pudding to which cranberries add a bit of contemporary color and sparkle. They also cut the sweetness. The pudding is cooked in a towel immersed in water rather than a pudding mold. Serve with unsweetened whipped cream or Vanilla Ice Cream (page 305).

SERVES 8

- 2¼ cups stale bread crumbs
- 1 cup sugar
- 2 cups currants
- 1 cup raisins
- 1½ cups cranberries
- ½ cup Candied Orange Peel (page 124)
- ½ cup Candied Lemon Peel (page 125)
- 8 ounces veal suet* (2 cups chopped)
- 5 large eggs, well beaten
- 1½ cups good brandy
- 2 tablespoons unsalted butter

In a large bowl, combine the dry ingredients, the fruit, and the suet. Toss until well blended. Stir in the eggs and brandy; mix well.

Coat the center of a white kitchen towel with the butter, covering about half the towel's surface. Line a bowl with the towel, buttered side

---

* Ask your butcher for the suet that surrounds the kidneys; it is the whitest and flakiest. Freeze the suet overnight. While it is still frozen, chop it very fine.

up; the edges of the towel should drape over the sides of the bowl. Spoon the pudding into the towel. Gather the ends of the towel just above the pudding and tie it closed with string.

Fill a large pot with enough water to completely cover the pudding. Bring to a boil. Set a plate in the bottom of the pot and drop the pudding gently onto it. The pudding will float a little. Lower to a simmer. Cover the pot and simmer for 4 hours. Add more water if needed to keep the pudding covered.

When done, remove from the pot. If you are going to serve the pudding immediately, dip the towel in cold water and then remove it. If you are not going to serve the pudding immediately, leave the towel on and refrigerate. Before serving, immerse the pudding in boiling water for 20 minutes to heat it thoroughly, then dip the towel in cold water and remove it. Serve warm with unsweetened whipped cream or Vanilla Ice Cream (page 305).

Date and Cranberry Steamed Pudding

This steamed pudding is not cooked in a pudding mold but in individual custard cups. It is served with English Custard and Poached Cranberries.

SERVES 10

12 tablespoons unsalted butter (soft)
 1 cup chopped dates
 ¾ cup cake flour
 ½ teaspoon baking powder
 2 large eggs
 ½ cup milk
 1 tablespoon all-purpose flour
 2 bags (24 ounces) cranberries
 1½ cups sugar
 1 cup water
 1 recipe English Custard (page 106)

Preheat the oven to 375°. Butter 10 custard cups.

Using the paddle attachment on an electric mixer (see page 58), cream the butter and dates until light. Meanwhile, sift the cake flour and baking powder together. Add the eggs to the butter one at a time, beating well after each addition. Add half the flour mixture and mix well. Add the milk and then the rest of the flour, mixing well after each addition.

Toss the all-purpose flour with one bag of cranberries and stir them into the batter. Spoon the batter into the prepared custard cups. Place the cups in a roasting, lasagne, or other large pan and pour about 1 inch of hot water into the pan. Bake until the center of each pudding springs back when touched lightly and a knife inserted comes out clean, about 45 minutes. Remove the cups from the water bath and cool to room temperature.

Poached Cranberries: Bring the sugar and water to a fast boil. Add the remaining bag of cranberries. Remove from the heat and stir gently until all the cranberries are coated with syrup. Allow the berries to cool in the syrup.

To serve: To unmold the puddings, run cold water on the bottom of each custard cup, then tap out the pudding onto a dessert plate. Pour English Custard over the pudding. Drain the syrup from the poached cranberries and spoon them on top of the custard.

11
Pastries

Classical pastries carry with them the pride of a long and much-loved European baking tradition. For many people they are obviously also tangible reminders of past enjoyments—a pleasant trip to Europe, a special French or Swiss pastry shop they visited there. Some people love pastries because they bring back the joys of a treasured childhood reward or a surprise gift that arrived in a square pink box. On the other hand, even those who don't have any special memories of their first eclair or napoleon usually agree that the smooth, rich taste and abundance of creamy filling are reason enough to love them.

Every day at The Stanford Court we offer trays of assorted pastries at meals and at afternoon tea. The selection always includes napoleons, eclairs, tartlets, and one or two other "pastries of the day," which vary with the season, the availability of ingredients, and the mood of the cooks in the pastry shop. Pastries tend to be rich, so we keep ours small. An eclair that is only two or three bites leaves room for a lemon tartlet too.

Making some pastries involves special techniques, and some require extra time. Before you can make eclairs and napoleons, you have to learn to make cream puff pastry dough and puff pastry dough. Then the napoleons, because of their thick pastry cream filling, have to be frozen solid before you can cut them. You can't just come home from the office and decide to whip up a batch. The Chocolate Pastries and Mocha Slice in this chapter have to be made in stages and refrigerated in between. Fondant, the shiny icing that sets many pastries gleaming, must be made at least a day before you want to use it and allowed to mellow. Still, most cooks who attempt traditional pastries agree that the challenge of mastering classical techniques and the pure ecstasy of eating the results make it well worth learning the routines.

For the most dramatic presentation, I suggest you make several different pastries and arrange an assortment on a silver tray. You don't have to make them all the same day. Napoleons need to be frozen before serving anyway. The puffs for eclairs can be made ahead, then filled and iced when you're ready to use them. The dough for tartlet shells can also be made ahead and rolled out, baked, and filled in just an hour or so.

To really get in the spirit of pastry making, plan to make several varieties in easy stages over the course of several days. It will be an interesting and enjoyable project. At the end you'll have an impressive array of very professional-looking desserts, the pride of being able to say you made them, and a depth of new knowledge that will make it all faster and easier next time.

In addition to miniature classical pastries, this chapter contains some new miniatures of my own invention, such as Pistachio Lemon Tartlets, and a number of full-sized desserts that are not meant for a pastry tray but command the spotlight on their own. One of my favorites in the latter category is a tangy Cranberry Turnover I like to serve topped with Caramel Ice Cream and a smooth Cranberry Sauce.

You will find the Mocha Slice and Chocolate Slice very similar to the rich multilayer cakes that are very thinly sliced and served with coffee in continental cafes and bakeries. Which brings us full circle, back to memories of long afternoons in romantic places. Fine pastries have a way of doing that.

Napoleons

These are miniature napoleons, perfectly suited for pastry trays and eating out of hand. About an inch of rich pastry cream is sandwiched between two flaky puff pastry layers. On top, a glistening coat of white fondant and the distinctive geometric pattern of chocolate lines. The only way to cut napoleons into individual pieces without losing most of the pastry cream filling is to freeze them first, so be sure to allow enough time.

Note: Both the Puff Pastry Dough and the Fondant are time-consuming recipes and should be made well ahead.

MAKES 40 (2 × 1 INCH)

¼ **recipe Puff Pastry Dough (page 84)**
1 **recipe Pastry Cream (page 105)**
⅓ **cup sugar**
⅓ **cup water**
1 **ounce unsweetened chocolate, melted and cooled**
1½ **cups Fondant (page 110)**

Line a cookie sheet with parchment.

Place the puff pastry dough on a floured table and sprinkle flour on top. Roll out to the dimensions of the cookie sheet (about 11 × 17 inches). Roll the dough as you did in making it, first the center, then the ends. Lift the dough by winding it around your rolling pin, then unwind it onto the cookie sheet (don't fold the dough to move it). Prick the dough every ½ inch over its entire surface with a fork. Chill for 30 minutes.

Preheat the oven to 400°.

Cut the dough in half crosswise and bake it until golden brown, about 10 minutes. Cool to room temperature.

Spoon the pastry cream into a pastry bag with a #5 plain tip. Using a back and forth motion, pipe out "logs" of pastry cream, close together, covering the entire surface of one piece of pastry. Go back and fill in any gaps you leave so that you have a thick, solid covering of cream. Set the second piece of pastry on top and press it down gently. Freeze until firm.

Make chocolate fondant for decorating, using the sugar, water, chocolate, and ½ cup of the fondant. Follow the technique described on page 114. Put the warm fondant in a parchment cone (see pages 62–63) and fold the top down tightly.

Heat the remaining cup of fondant in a saucepan, stirring occasionally, until it reaches body temperature and turns glossy. It should coat a spoon and be just starting to turn transparent. If the fondant is too thick, add water 1 teaspoon at a time until it reaches the right consistency.

Set the frozen napoleon on a work table with one long edge toward you. Pour the fondant over the top and spread it smooth with an icing spatula, using as few strokes as possible. With scissors, cut a fine hole in the parchment cone so the chocolate can flow out. Using a back and forth motion, make chocolate lines the length of the napoleon, about ¼ inch apart. (Don't worry how the edges look; you're going to trim them off later.)

Draw the tip of a paring knife at a 30-degree angle from the upper left corner to the bottom. This will put a wave in the chocolate lines. Repeat every inch along the length of the napoleon, then reverse the process and draw the knife from the bottom to top between each two lines, at the same angle. This will create the traditional napoleon pattern. Allow the napoleon to stand for 5 minutes so the fondant can dry, then return it to the freezer until 10 minutes before serving (it must freeze for at least 15 minutes).

Place the frozen napoleon on a work table and trim off all the edges with a sharp knife or cleaver (it will take some work to get through all the frozen layers). While cutting, have a damp towel close by and wipe the knife frequently; otherwise, fondant and pastry cream will build up on the knife and transfer back to the top of the pastry. Turn the block so that one long end is toward you. Cut it lengthwise into 2-inch strips, then cut each strip into 1-inch slices. If it is too hard to cut, let it stand a few minutes to soften slightly.

Eclairs

These are small, two-bite eclairs, but in every other way they're just like the torpedo-size treats you remember from your childhood. Light, tender pastry puffs are filled with pastry cream and topped with gleaming chocolate fondant. I use eclairs on assorted pastry trays for dessert and afternoon tea. If you want to serve them alone, serve each person several.

Note: The fondant must be made at least one day ahead. The cream puff pastry can also be made ahead, then wrapped in plastic wrap and frozen.

MAKES 80 (2¼ INCH)

> 1 recipe Cream Puff Pastry (page 87)
> 1 recipe Pastry Cream (page 105)
> ⅓ recipe Chocolate Fondant (page 114)

Poke a hole in the bottom of each pastry with your finger. (If you have kept the pastry frozen, defrost it in a 375° oven for 5 minutes.) Spoon the pastry cream into a pastry bag with a #5 plain tip. Fill each eclair with pastry cream by piping it in through the hole.

Prepare the chocolate fondant according to directions. Dip the top of each eclair into the fondant. As you take it out, scrape it lightly against the edge of the bowl to remove the excess fondant.

Stand the eclairs close together on a parchment-lined cookie sheet to keep them from rolling over before the fondant is set. Refrigerate until 15 minutes before serving.

Almond Cups

These tender almond pastry cups are filled with almond butter cream and topped with a glistening layer of coffee fondant. They're a wonderful accompaniment to an afternoon cup of tea or coffee, or an elegant addition to a tray of assorted pastries for any occasion.

MAKES 24

> 1 recipe Vienna Dough (page 80) made with ⅓ cup whole natural (skin on) almonds instead of filberts and omitting the cornstarch
> 1 cup whole natural almonds, toasted
> ¼ teaspoon almond extract
> 16 tablespoons (½ pound) unsalted butter (soft)
> ½ cup superfine sugar
> 1 cup Fondant (page 110)
> 1 tablespoon instant coffee powder
> ½ tablespoon hot water

Prepare the Vienna dough as directed, using almonds instead of filberts and eliminating the cornstarch. When the dough is ready to roll out, arrange 24 tartlet molds on your work surface in 6 rows close together. From top to bottom the rows should have 3, 4, 5, 5, 4, and 3 molds respectively. Roll the dough into the same shape formed by the molds but a little bigger. Lift the dough by carefully rolling it up on your rolling pin, then unroll it over the tartlet molds. Press the dough gently into the molds and cut off the excess by rolling a cutting pin (see page 51) over the surface. Press the dough gently against the sides and bottom of each mold. Place the molds on a cookie sheet and chill until firm, about 20 minutes.

Preheat the oven to 350°. Put a small paper baking cup inside each tartlet mold and fill it with beans or pie weights (a spoon makes filling the cups easy). Bake until the edges just start to turn brown, about 20 minutes. Take the molds out of the oven and remove the beans and paper liners. Return to the oven and bake about 5 minutes more, until the dough is golden brown. Remove the almond cups from the tartlet molds and place them on a parchment-lined cookie sheet to cool.

To make almond butter cream, finely grind the toasted almonds with the almond extract in a food processor. Using the paddle attachment on an electric mixer (see page 58), cream the butter and sugar until smooth. Stop the mixer and scrape the sides and bottom of the bowl. Switch to the whisk attachment and mix at high speed until light in color and texture. Add the almonds and mix until smooth.

When the almond cups are fully cooled, fill them with almond butter cream. Use a small icing spatula to smooth the surface of the butter cream even with the top of the cup. Refrigerate until firm, about 15 minutes.

Place the fondant in a heavy-bottomed saucepan. Dissolve the coffee powder in the hot water and stir it into the fondant. Warm over medium heat until the fondant reaches body temperature and turns glossy. Remove from the heat. Scoop up some fondant with a small icing spatula and transfer it to the top of a tartlet, drawing the spatula across the edge of the shell. Spread the fondant evenly, scraping the spatula against the edge of the shell with each stroke. If the fondant begins to thicken before all the tartlets are iced, put it back on the heat and warm it again to body temperature.

Chocolate Cups

This is a quadruple chocolate pastry—a chocolate crust filled with chocolate ganache, iced with chocolate fondant, and topped with a chocolate truffle. It's intense but not too sweet. This recipe really contains four separate recipes, so be sure you allow several hours of preparation time.

MAKES 25

Chocolate Sweet Dough:

  1½ **ounces unsweetened chocolate**
    1 **cup all-purpose flour**
   ½ **cup plus 2 tablespoons powdered sugar**
    6 **tablespoons unsalted butter (cold)**
    1 **large egg white**

Chocolate Ganache:

   ¾ **cup whipping cream**
  12 **ounces bittersweet chocolate**
   ⅛ **cup unsweetened cocoa**

Chocolate Fondant:

   ½ **cup Fondant (page 110)**
    1 **ounce unsweetened chocolate, melted and cooled**
    1 **tablespoon water**

Chocolate Sweet Dough: Melt the chocolate and set it aside to cool. Using the paddle attachment on an electric mixer (see page 58), combine the flour and sugar. Cut the butter into about 10 pieces and add it. Mix on low speed to the texture of coarse meal. Add the egg white and melted chocolate, and mix on medium-low speed until the dough comes together.

    Turn out the dough onto a table and knead it a few times. Sprinkle the table and the top of the dough lightly with flour. Form the dough into a thick patty, about 6 inches in diameter, then roll it out into an oblong 12 × 16 inches.

Arrange 20 tartlet molds close together to form an oblong about the same size as the dough. Roll the dough around your rolling pin to lift it, then unroll it over the tartlet pans. Press the dough gently into the cups and cut off the excess by rolling a cutting pin (see page 51) over the surface. Transfer the molds to a cookie sheet.

Gather the remaining dough, press it together into a patty, and roll it out. Use it to line the remaining 5 tartlet molds. Add them to the cookie sheet. Refrigerate until firm, about 20 minutes.

Preheat the oven to 350°. Place a paper liner (small muffin cup) inside each tartlet shell and fill it with dry beans or pie weights. Bake until firm, about 25 minutes. Remove the paper liners and beans and set aside to cool. When cool, remove the chocolate cups from the molds and place them on a parchment-lined cookie sheet.

Chocolate Ganache: Bring the cream to a simmer in a saucepan. Turn off the heat. Cut the chocolate into small pieces and add it to the cream. Stir until smooth. Set aside to cool. When cool, use half of the ganache to fill the chocolate cups. Smooth the top of each with a small icing spatula. Refrigerate the other half of the ganache to be used later (along with the cocoa) to make truffles.

Chocolate Fondant: In a heavy-bottomed saucepan, combine the fondant, chocolate, and water until well blended. Warm over low heat, stirring constantly, until a little warmer than body temperature. To ice a filled cup, hold it in your fingertips so that the top extends above your fingers. Dip your icing spatula into the fondant and scrape a little onto the surface of the cup at one side. Tip the cup and let the fondant spread, helping it along with the spatula so that it reaches all the edges. Remember, you want only a little fondant on each cup, first because it is sweet, and second because if you use too much, it will run down the edges and not give you a smooth surface. You will probably have some fondant left over.

Once the ganache in the refrigerator is set up (about the texture of soft fudge), cut and roll it into twenty-five ½-inch balls. Roll the balls in cocoa and return them to the refrigerator to chill. When they are solid and no longer sticky, set one on top of each chocolate cup and serve.

Peanut Butter Cups

Everyone knows that peanuts and chocolate are a great combination. These tartlets have peanuts baked into their shells as well as peanuts in the filling and on top. Bittersweet chocolate flavors the ganache filling and the smooth glaze. The children will love these—and so will you.

MAKES 30

> 1¼ cups raw peanuts
> ½ recipe Sugar Dough (page 76)
> 12 ounces bittersweet chocolate
> ⅔ cup whipping cream
> ½ cup smooth, unsalted peanut butter (available in health food stores)
> 8 tablespoons (¼ pound) unsalted butter

Toast the peanuts in a 350° oven until fragrant, about 10 minutes. Finely grind ¼ cup plus 2 tablespoons.

Prepare the sugar dough as directed, using half of a lightly beaten egg and just 1 teaspoon of milk. Add the ground peanuts with the flour. Roll the dough out to a rectangle about 13 × 14 inches. Arrange 25 tartlet molds on the table in the shape of a rectangle. Lift the dough by winding it around your rolling pin, then unwind it over the molds. Press the dough gently into the molds and cut off the excess by rolling a cutting pin (see page 51) over the molds. Press the scraps of dough together and roll out; line 5 more tartlet molds. Place the molds on a cookie sheet and refrigerate until the dough is firm, about 20 minutes.

Prebake the dough as directed. Cool to room temperature. Remove the tartlet shells from the molds and put 1 teaspoon of whole peanuts in each.

Make a chocolate-peanut butter ganache to fill the shells: Chop 8 ounces of chocolate. Bring the cream to a boil in a saucepan. Add the peanut butter and the chopped chocolate. Remove from the heat and stir until smooth. Spoon the ganache into the shells. Fill even with the top of the cups. Smooth with a small icing spatula. Refrigerate.

Prepare a glaze by melting the remaining 4 ounces of chocolate with the butter in the top of a double boiler. Stir until smooth. Using the small icing spatula, spread 2 teaspoons of glaze on each tartlet. Coarsely chop the remaining ¼ cup of peanuts. Sprinkle a 1-inch circle of chopped peanuts in the center of each tartlet. Refrigerate until 15 minutes before serving.

Chocolate Slice

This is an intensely chocolate dessert but not an overly sweet one. Three unsweetened chocolate wafers are stacked with layers of chocolate butter cream and coated with a bittersweet chocolate glaze.

MAKES 13 (1 × 3-INCH) SLICES

 1 recipe Chocolate Wafer Dough (page 79)
 ½ recipe Egg White Butter Cream (page 109)
 3 ounces unsweetened chocolate, melted and cooled
 7 ounces bittersweet or semisweet chocolate
12 tablespoons unsalted butter

Make the chocolate wafer dough according to directions, but instead of cutting it into circles, roll it out into one 11 × 15-inch rectangle. Place the rectangle on a parchment-lined cookie sheet. Just before baking, trim the dough to make the edges as straight as possible and cut it into three 3½ × 15-inch strips. Bake as directed.

Make the butter cream, adding 1 ounce (⅛ cup) of melted unsweetened chocolate after the butter is incorporated.

When the chocolate wafer strips are cool, brush them with the remaining 2 ounces of unsweetened chocolate (on 1 side only). Lay 1 wafer strip on a parchment-lined cookie sheet. Spread half the butter cream on it, covering the entire surface. Top with the second strip, pressing it gently into the butter cream. Add the rest of the butter cream and the final strip, again pressing it down gently. Smooth the butter cream that has been squeezed out on the sides with a knife or icing spatula. Refrigerate until firm.

Meanwhile, make a chocolate glaze by melting 6 ounces of bittersweet chocolate and the butter together over boiled (not boiling) water. Remove from the heat and stir until smooth.

Transfer the wafer bar to a wire rack over a sheet of parchment or wax paper to catch the drips. Spoon a generous amount of glaze along the edges of the bar so that it drips down and completely covers the sides. Pour the rest of the glaze on top and spread it smooth with an icing spatula. Grate the remaining bittersweet chocolate and sprinkle it in a 1-inch-wide stripe down the center of the bar. Transfer to a clean parchment-lined cookie sheet and refrigerate until 10 minutes before serving. Using a serrated knife, trim off the ends of the bar and cut the remainder into 1-inch slices. Saw through the top layer, then press the knife straight down through the rest. Wipe the knife on a damp cloth after each slice.

Mocha Slice

This is an elegant, deliciously rich pastry. Two strips of crisp Vienna dough sandwich a thick layer of coffee butter cream. On top is an apricot glaze, topped in turn with glossy chocolate fondant and a decorative spray of chopped toasted hazelnuts.

MAKES 14 (1 × 3-INCH) SLICES

½ recipe Vienna Dough (page 80)
⅛ cup hazelnuts
½ recipe Apricot Glaze (page 122)
16 tablespoons (½ pound) unsalted butter (soft)
¾ cup powdered sugar
1 tablespoon espresso powder *or* 1 heaping tablespoon instant coffee powder
1 teaspoon hot water
½ cup Fondant (page 110)
2 tablespoons unsweetened chocolate, melted
1 tablespoon water

Prepare the Vienna dough according to directions. When the dough is mixed, form it into a patty. Roll it out on a floured table to a rectangle 7 × 16 inches. Nudge the edges straight with a yardstick. Line a cookie sheet with parchment. Lift the dough by carefully rolling it around a rolling pin, then unroll it onto the lined cookie sheet. Using the yardstick and a pastry wheel, trim the sides and the ends so that they are straight. Cut the dough in half lengthwise. Refrigerate for 20 minutes.

Preheat the oven to 375°. Bake the strips until lightly browned, 20 to 25 minutes. Set aside to cool.

Toast the hazelnuts in the oven until fragrant, about 5 minutes. While still warm, put them in a towel, fold it over once, and rub off the skin. Coarsely chop the nuts with a knife or cleaver and set aside.

Prepare the apricot glaze according to directions and set aside to cool.

Using the paddle attachment on an electric mixer (see page 58), cream the butter and powdered sugar until light. Dissolve the espresso or instant coffee powder in the hot water and add it to the butter mixture. Mix until smooth. Spoon the butter cream into a pastry bag with a #5 plain tip. Pipe it all out onto one Vienna dough strip, completely covering the strip. Place the second strip on top, carefully lining it up. Press down gently on the top strip to eliminate any air pockets—they can make the pastry split when you slice it. Use a knife to smooth the butter cream on the sides. Wipe the top clean.

Gently heat the apricot glaze to liquefy. Brush a layer of glaze onto the top strip. Be sure to fill in any holes so that the surface is level and smooth. Refrigerate for 10 to 15 minutes.

Meanwhile, combine the fondant, melted chocolate, and water in the top of a double boiler. Stir together well. Heat, stirring constantly, until hot to the touch. Spoon the fondant onto the glazed surface of the strip and spread it evenly with an icing spatula. Use a knife to clean the edges. While the surface is still wet, sprinkle on the chopped hazelnuts in a 1-inch-wide strip down the middle. Gently press them into the fondant. Refrigerate until firm, about 30 minutes.

Cut the strip crosswise into 1-inch slices. A serrated knife works best. Saw through the top layer, then press the knife straight down through the rest. Wipe the knife on a damp cloth after each slice. Refrigerate until 10 minutes before serving.

Toasted Walnut Squares

This rich and crunchy pastry has a thick layer of toasted walnuts and caramel butter cream sandwiched between crisp walnut Vienna dough wafers. It needs to sit overnight in the refrigerator, so start a day ahead.

MAKES 24

  1 **recipe Vienna Dough (page 80)**
1⅓ **cups toasted walnuts**
16 **tablespoons (½ pound) unsalted butter (soft)**
  1 **recipe Caramel Sauce (page 118)**
24 **toasted walnut halves**

Prepare the Vienna dough as directed, substituting ⅓ cup of toasted walnuts for the filberts. Instead of rolling the dough into a circle, roll it out into a 10 × 16-inch rectangle. Transfer the rectangle to a parchment-lined cookie sheet and chill until firm.

Preheat the oven to 375°. Before baking, trim the edges of the dough as straight as possible and cut it into two 10 × 8-inch halves. Bake until lightly browned, 20 to 25 minutes. Set aside to cool.

Coarsely chop the remaining cup of toasted walnuts.

Using the whisk attachment on an electric mixer (see page 58) and high speed, beat the butter until very light. Beat in 4 tablespoons of the caramel syrup. Fold in the chopped nuts.

Spread 2 tablespoons of caramel syrup over one of the Vienna dough wafers. Spread all of the butter cream evenly on top. Spread 2 tablespoons of caramel syrup on the second wafer and place it, caramel side down, over the butter cream. Press the wafer down gently. Smooth the butter cream that has been squeezed out on the sides with a knife or icing spatula. Spread 3 tablespoons of caramel syrup over the top wafer. Allow the caramel to set, then wrap the pastry in plastic wrap and refrigerate overnight.

The next day, arrange the walnut halves evenly on top of the pastry in 4 rows of 6. Wrap and freeze. Remove from the freezer about 30 minutes before serving. Trim the edges with a sharp knife or cleaver. Cut the pastry into 24 pieces, each with a walnut half in the center.

Rum Corks

Rum corks get their name from the cork-shaped piece of almond cake that is cut out of the center and replaced jauntily on top—and from the rum that flavors the pastry cream filling. They look like small cupcakes but are moister, more flavorful, and much more sophisticated.

MAKES 30

   1 recipe Shortbread Dough (page 76)
   1 recipe Pastry Cream (page 105)
   2 tablespoons good rum
   ½ recipe Apricot Glaze (page 122)
   ¾ cup natural (skin on) almonds
   ¼ cup sugar
   ¼ teaspoon almond extract
   1½ tablespoons water
   7 tablespoons unsalted butter (soft)
   ⅓ cup sugar
   2 large eggs
   ¼ cup plus 2 tablespoons cake flour
   ⅛ cup powdered sugar

Arrange 30 tartlet molds close together on the table to form a rectangle. Prepare the shortbread dough and roll it out into a rectangle slightly larger than the one made by the molds. Roll the dough around your rolling pin to lift it, then unroll it over the molds. Press the dough gently into the molds and trim off the excess with a cutting pin (see page 51). Transfer the molds to a cookie sheet and refrigerate until needed.

Prepare the pastry cream according to directions. Stir in the rum. Refrigerate. Prepare the apricot glaze. Set aside to cool.

Preheat the oven to 400°. Toast the almonds on a cookie sheet in the oven for about 5 minutes. Lower the oven temperature to 375°. Finely grind the almonds in a food processor. Add ¼ cup of sugar and the almond extract. Process. Add the water and process until the ingredients come together into a firm paste.

Using the paddle attachment on an electric mixer (see page 58), beat the butter and ⅓ cup of sugar at high speed until light. Reduce the speed to medium and add the almond paste in four portions, mixing well after each addition. Add 1 egg; mix well. Add half of the flour, the other egg, and the rest of the flour, mixing well after each addition. Mix until very smooth.

Fill the tartlet molds with the almond batter. Bake until the shells are golden brown and the filling is firm, about 25 minutes. Cool for 10 minutes in the molds. Hold each tartlet in turn in your hand to give it support and cut a cork-shaped piece out of the center with a 1-inch pastry cutter. (If you don't have a pastry cutter, carefully cut a 1-inch circle with a sharp paring knife.) Do not cut through to the bottom crust. Rock the cork gently to loosen it, then remove it. Take the pastries out of the tartlet molds.

Spoon the pastry cream into a pastry bag with a #4 plain tip. Fill the hole in each tartlet with pastry cream. Sprinkle the cake surrounding the hole generously with powdered sugar.

Gently heat the apricot glaze to liquefy. Glaze the top of each "cork" and set the corks over the pastry cream.

Pistachio Lemon Tartlets

Pistachio nuts in the crust add texture, color, and a nutty flavor to these always popular lemon tartlets. We serve them on trays of assorted pastries after meals and at afternoon tea.

MAKES 25

    ½ cup plus 2 tablespoons shelled pistachios
1¼ cups cake flour
    ¼ cup plus 2 tablespoons sugar
    6 tablespoons unsalted butter (soft)
    1 large egg
    Double recipe Lemon Cream (page 107)

Preheat the oven to 350°. Toast the pistachios in the oven until fragrant, about 10 minutes. Chop them to about ⅛-inch nuggets (small enough that they won't stick out when you roll out the dough). Set aside 2 tablespoons of chopped nuts for decorating the finished tartlets.

Using the paddle attachment on an electric mixer (see page 58), mix the rest of the pistachios with the flour, sugar, and butter until smooth. Add the egg and mix well. On a lightly floured surface, roll the dough into a 14-inch square. Arrange 25 tartlet molds on the table in 5 rows of 5 (they should form a square about 13 inches across). Lift the dough by rolling it up carefully around your rolling pin, then unroll it over the tartlet molds. Press the dough gently into the molds and cut off the excess dough by rolling a cutting pin (see page 51) over the surface.

Transfer the tartlet molds to a cookie sheet. Put a paper baking cup inside each mold and fill it with beans or pie weights. Bake until the shells are golden brown, 25 to 30 minutes. Remove the paper liners and beans and allow the shells to cool to room temperature, then remove them from the molds.

Prepare the lemon cream. When both it and the tartlet shells are cool, put the lemon cream in a pastry bag with a #4 plain tip. Fill the shells generously. Sprinkle a few pieces of the reserved chopped pistachios in the center of each tartlet. Serve immediately or refrigerate until 10 minutes before serving.

Lemon and Chocolate Tartlets

Chocolate and lemon is a wonderful combination, but for some reason it often ends up too sweet for my taste. Unsweetened chocolate solves the problem. Here it is brushed inside tartlet shells, which are then filled with rich lemon cream.

MAKES 28 TO 30

½ **recipe Sugar Dough (page 76)**
2 **ounces unsweetened chocolate**
1½ **recipes Lemon Cream (page 107)**

Prepare the sugar dough as directed, using only the white of the egg. Refrigerate the dough for about 20 minutes before rolling it out.

Group 24 tartlet molds about ½ inch apart in a square or rectangle on your work surface. Roll the dough out to approximately the same size and shape. Lift the dough by winding it around a rolling pin, then unwind it over the tartlet molds. Gently press the dough into the molds, cutting the excess off against the rims. Set up 4 to 6 more molds. Press the dough scraps together and roll them out in a shape to cover the new molds. Line the molds with dough as above. Place the molds on a cookie sheet and refrigerate until firm. Fill with beans and prebake as directed. Cool to room temperature.

Melt the chocolate in the top of a double boiler. Paint the inside of the tartlet shells with it. Cool. Fill the shells with lemon cream, leaving a ¼-inch rim of chocolate showing around the edges. Do not heap up the filling; bring the cream just level with the top of the shells in the center. Refrigerate until 15 minutes before serving.

Chocolate Pastries

These moist double-layer squares get their rich flavor from chocolate, chocolate, chocolate, chocolate, and almond. Inside is a classic chocolate-almond *frangipane* (pastry). Outside, a chocolate glaze is topped with grated chocolate and then dusted with cocoa.

MAKES 17 (1½-INCH) SQUARES

- 8 ounces almond paste
- ¾ cup sugar
- 12 tablespoons unsalted butter (soft)
- ½ cup plus 2 tablespoons unsweetened cocoa powder
- 4 large eggs
- 8 ounces bittersweet or semisweet chocolate°
- ¼ cup milk

° If you like a more assertive chocolate flavor, you can substitute unsweetened chocolate for the bittersweet or semisweet.

Begin with the *frangipane*. Preheat the oven to 350°. Butter or oil a 7½ × 11-inch baking pan and line the bottom with parchment.

Using the paddle attachment on an electric mixer (see page 58) and low speed, combine the almond paste, sugar, butter, and ½ cup of cocoa. Increase the mixer speed to medium and mix until well blended. Add 2 eggs and mix until smooth. Stop the mixer and scrape the sides and bottom of the bowl. Add the remaining 2 eggs and mix until smooth. Spread the batter in the baking pan with a rubber scraper, making sure to get it into all the corners. Smooth the top with a dough scraper; make it as level as possible. Bake until the cake is lightly firm, about 35 minutes. Cool to room temperature, then cover with plastic wrap and refrigerate until completely firm, 1 to 2 hours.

Cut the *frangipane* in the pan into thirty-five 1½-inch squares. Melt 4 ounces of the chocolate over boiled (not boiling) water. Stir in the milk until smooth. Hold one square in the palm of your hand. Using a small icing spatula, spread a thin layer of melted chocolate over it. Keep the chocolate sitting over the hot water as you work so that it stays soft. Place a second square on top of the first. Spread a thin layer of the chocolate over the sides and then the top of the double square, filling in any cracks and smoothing the edges as you go. Repeat with the rest of the squares.

Finely grate the remaining chocolate and put it into a bowl. Drop each square in turn into the bowl upside down and lightly press grated chocolate onto its sides so that top and sides are coated with grated chocolate. Place the finished squares on a parchment-lined cookie sheet. Sift or sprinkle the remaining cocoa over the tops. Refrigerate until 10 minutes before serving.

Apple Turnovers

These light, crisp turnovers are simple to make once you have the Puff Pastry Dough on hand. They're fruity, not sweet. They make a wonderful dessert or snack all by themselves and, of course, can be dressed up with a scoop of ice cream or a dollop of whipped cream.

MAKES 24

- ½ **recipe Puff Pastry Dough (page 84)**
- 4 **medium-size green apples**
- 2 **tablespoons cornstarch**
- 4 **tablespoons sugar**
- 2 **teaspoons lemon juice**

On a floured surface, roll the puff pastry dough out to a rectangle 16 × 24 inches. Using a yardstick as a guide, cut the rectangle into thirds, each 16 × 8 inches. Lay out the pastry on parchment-lined cookie sheets and let it rest in the refrigerator for 30 minutes.

Peel, quarter, and core the apples. Cut the quarters into ⅛-inch cubes. Rub the cornstarch and 2 tablespoons of sugar together, then toss with the apples in a bowl. Add the lemon juice and toss again.

Take the dough from the refrigerator and cut it into 4 × 4-inch squares. Brush the squares lightly with water and press a diagonal crease in each one with a stiff rubber scraper or any stiff straight edge (don't cut through).

Spoon 1½ tablespoons of apple filling onto each square, centering it on one of the triangles created by the crease. Spread the filling gently with a spoon, leaving about 1 inch on all three sides. Brush a little water along the outside edges of the empty triangle, then fold it over the filled half and press the edges together with your fingers. Pierce each triangle once with a fork. Chill for 30 minutes.

Preheat the oven to 400°. Brush the turnovers lightly with water and sprinkle ¼ teaspoon of sugar over each. Bake until golden brown, about 35 minutes. Cool. Serve at room temperature.

Cranberry Turnovers

These plump and flaky turnovers are slightly tart and very flavorful. You can use them on a pastry tray just as they are or top them with ice cream and a light cranberry sauce for a festive dessert.

MAKES 24

1 **package (12 ounces) cranberries, fresh or frozen (not defrosted)**
½ **cup seedless raspberry preserves**
¼ **cup water**
¼ **cup sugar**
½ **recipe Puff Pastry Dough (page 84)**

Wash the cranberries. Combine the preserves, water, and sugar in a saucepan. Bring to a boil over high heat. Add the cranberries and cook, stirring constantly, until the mixture starts to thicken; the cranberries will pop loudly as they cook. Turn down the heat to medium and continue cooking until the mixture is very thick but still has some whole berries in it. Transfer to a bowl and allow to cool.

On a floured surface, roll the puff pastry dough out to a rectangle 16 × 24 inches. Using a yardstick as a guide, cut the rectangle into thirds, each 16 × 8 inches. Lay out the pastry on parchment-lined cookie sheets and let it rest in the refrigerator for 30 minutes, then cut it into 4 × 4-inch squares. Brush the squares lightly with water and press a diagonal crease in each one with a stiff rubber scraper or any stiff straight edge (don't cut through).

Spoon about 1 tablespoon of cooled cranberry filling onto each square, centering it on one of the triangles created by the crease. Spread the filling gently with a spoon, leaving about 1 inch on all three sides. Brush a little water along the outside edges of the empty triangle, then fold it over the filled half and press the edges together with your fingers. Chill for 30 minutes.

Preheat the oven to 400°. Pierce the top of each turnover with the tip of a knife. Bake until crisp and golden, about 30 minutes. Serve warm from the oven or at room temperature, topped with a scoop of Caramel Ice Cream (page 304) and Cranberry Sauce (page 116).

Lemon Roll

This is a much smaller and more delicate "jelly" roll than those most of us remember from childhood. The sponge is lightly flavored with lemon zest, and the "jelly" is a rich, tart lemon cream. Be sure you have a yardstick handy; you will need it for the rolling process.

MAKES 30 (2-INCH) SLICES

1 **Jelly Roll Sponge Cake (page 97)**
⅔ **cup fresh lemon juice**
1 **recipe Lemon Cream (page 107)**
2 **tablespoons powdered sugar**

Have two 12 × 17-inch sheets of parchment and a yardstick close at hand.

Take the jelly roll sponge out of the refrigerator, unroll it on a table, and discard the parchment it was stored in. Cut the cake in half lengthwise so that you have two 5½ × 17-inch pieces. Sprinkle ⅓ cup of lemon juice over each half, then spread on an even layer of lemon cream (use half of what you have on each piece). Roll each sponge into a 17-inch-long log. As you roll, rub the brown skin off the bottom of the sponge with your fingers.

Now comes the tricky part, but it really isn't hard if you just follow along step by step. (See illustrations, page 276.) The idea is to tighten the roll with the help of a sheet of parchment. Lay a 12 × 17-inch sheet of parchment on the table with a 17-inch edge near you. Place one lemon roll, with the loose end down, in the middle of the sheet. Lift the near edge of parchment up and over the sponge roll and lay it down 1 inch short of the far edge. Your roll is now inside a loop of parchment. Take up the slack in the loop by placing your yardstick as close as possible to the sponge roll. Hold the yardstick at a 45-degree angle and press it down and toward the roll. Holding the bottom edge of the parchment with one hand (leaving the top edge free), keep pulling the yardstick toward you until the sponge has rolled together very tightly. Some of the filling will squeeze out of the ends of the roll; that's okay. Keeping the pressure on with the stick so the roll won't loosen, roll the sponge toward the far edge of the parchment, trapping the yardstick. Pull out the stick, roll the sponge up completely in the rest of the sheet, and tape it securely. Freeze until firm.

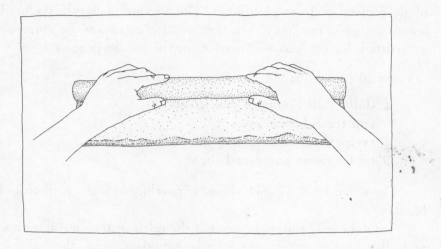

Roll the sponge into a log.

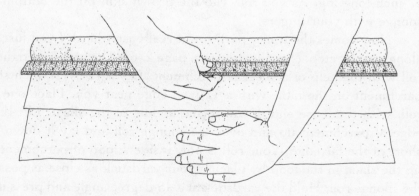

Hold the yardstick at a 45-degree angle and press it down and toward the roll. Keep pulling the yardstick toward you until the sponge has rolled together very tightly.

Repeat the same tightening procedure with the second roll.

When the rolls are frozen firm, take them out, unwrap them, and sprinkle them with the powdered sugar. Rub the sugar smooth with your hands—I think it makes a much more interesting finish. Cut off the ends of the rolls on a diagonal (about 30 degrees). Cutting on the same diagonal, slice each roll into fifteen 1-inch slices. Allow the slices to come to room temperature before serving.

Chocolate-Filled Apricots

Chocolate ganache is a traditional cream filling for candy. Here it is sandwiched between tangy apricot halves. You bite through the chewy fruit and suddenly your teeth sink into the soft, rich filling. It's fun.

MAKES 40

12 ounces dried apricot halves
¼ cup whipping cream
4 ounces bittersweet chocolate
Zest from ½ orange

Sort through the apricot halves and select 80 that are soft and moist (look for the ones that have a strong orange color). Push open any that are closed. Line a cookie sheet or tray with parchment and lay out the apricots in rows, skin side down.

To make a ganache, bring the cream to a boil in a very small saucepan over medium-low heat. Remove from the heat and add 3 ounces of chocolate and the orange zest. Stir with a spoon until smooth and glossy. Transfer to a bowl and allow to cool.

The ganache is "set up" when it is no longer warm and will hold a crease. Put it into a pastry bag with a #4 plain tip. Pipe a dollop of ganache onto 40 of the apricot halves. Top each with another half, skin side up, to form a sandwich. Match sizes and shapes as much as possible. Chill until firm.

Remove the apricot sandwiches from the refrigerator and let them sit for 10 minutes at room temperature. Meanwhile, temper the remaining chocolate (see page 37). Move the apricots very close together on the tray. Dip the three middle fingers of one hand into the tempered chocolate, then wave your hand back and forth over the apricots, spraying them with lines of chocolate. Keep at room temperature until ready to use.

12
Cookies

I think cookies should be small, perhaps an inch across, so that as you pick up each one you can't help but look at it and pause in conversation to see how it tastes.

I like a cookie that creates a taste explosion in the mouth, an intense experience of chocolate or toasted hazelnuts or almond. In two bites, at the most, it's gone and you're hooked, already searching for the next great taste.

I almost never serve just one kind of cookie. I arrange four or five different kinds in neat rows on a small, round, silver pedestal tray and invite guests to pick and choose. In The Stanford Court's restaurants an assortment of cookies (called by their French name, *petits fours sec*) is often brought out at the very end of a dinner, after dessert is finished. The assorted trays are also popular with after-theater parties who come in late for cookies and a round of coffee or port.

Many of my cookies are made from refrigerator doughs, that is, doughs that must be well chilled before slicing and baking. Those doughs can be made hours or even days ahead if you don't have time for the whole operation at once. Once they're baked, of course, cookies keep well at room temperature (except for their extreme susceptibility to nibbling). Our hotel pastry shop has a metal cabinet about 5 feet tall, affectionately known as the cookie box. In it there are always a dozen or so pans of cookies ready to be arranged on a tray and presented. At home you can store cookies on stacked trays (or cookie sheets) or in tins, in a cool, dry place.

This chapter also includes bars (Currant and Coconut Meringue) that are richer and chewier than cookies but are equally well suited to after-dinner or late-night munching. I cut them into bite-size pieces and serve them on my cookie trays as another sort of tiny cookie. You can, of course, cut them in larger pieces and serve them by themselves or with ice cream. They are somewhat moister than cookies, and they don't keep fresh as long as cookies do.

Nut Sables

These are small, crisp, spicy hazelnut cookies, dipped in bittersweet chocolate.

MAKES 9 DOZEN

      16 tablespoons (½ pound) unsalted butter (soft)
       1 cup powdered sugar
      ⅔ cup toasted hazelnuts, crushed
      2½ cups cake flour
      ½ teaspoon vanilla extract
      ½ teaspoon ground cloves
      ½ teaspoon cinnamon
      ¼ teaspoon kosher salt (see page 42)
       1 large egg white
      ½ recipe Chocolate Glaze (page 123)

Using the paddle attachment on an electric mixer (see page 58), cream the butter and sugar until light. Add the hazelnuts, flour, vanilla, cloves, cinnamon, salt, and egg white, and mix to a moist, thick dough. Turn the dough out onto a sheet of parchment and shape it into a block 4½ × 9 inches (it will be about 1 inch thick). Make the edges as straight as possible—a yardstick is a good straightening tool. Wrap the dough in the parchment and refrigerate until it is firm enough to slice, about 2 hours.

Preheat the oven to 325°. Line 2 cookie sheets with parchment. With a sharp knife and a yardstick, cut the dough into three 9 × 1½-inch bars. Cut each bar into ¼-inch slices. Bake the cookies on the parchment-lined cookie sheets, 1 inch apart, until the edges turn golden brown, about 18 to 20 minutes. You will be able to bake only 40 cookies at a time on a cookie sheet. Keep the remaining dough refrigerated until ready to bake. As each sheet comes out of the oven, slide the parchment onto a table or counter to cool, replace it with a new sheet of parchment, and lay out the next batch of cookies to be baked.

When all the cookies are baked and cooled, prepare the chocolate glaze. Dip each cookie into the glaze diagonally so that a triangular half of the cookie, from corner to opposite corner, is chocolate coated. After dipping each cookie, scrape the bottom against the rim of the pan to remove the excess chocolate. Lay the cookies out on a clean sheet of parchment to dry. Store at room temperature.

Chocolate Mounds

These are fez-shaped rather than flat cookies. Dense but lightly flavored, they are dipped after baking in a rich chocolate glaze.

MAKES ABOUT 4 DOZEN

>   2 ounces unsweetened chocolate
>   10 tablespoons unsalted butter (cold), cut into 4 pieces
>   ½ cup powdered sugar
>   1½ cups cake flour
>   ½ recipe Chocolate Glaze (page 123)

Melt the unsweetened chocolate in the top of a double boiler. Using the paddle attachment on an electric mixer (see page 58), mix the butter, sugar, and flour at low speed to the consistency of coarse meal. Add the melted chocolate and mix just until the dough comes together.

Remove the dough from the mixer and divide it into 4 equal pieces. On a lightly floured table, roll each piece with your hands into a cylinder

10 inches long and ¾ inch in diameter. Lay the cylinders on a parchment-lined cookie sheet and refrigerate until firm, about 1 hour.

Preheat the oven to 325°. Line another cookie sheet with parchment. Slice the cylinders into ¾-inch pieces. Stand them, cut end down, on the cookie sheet about 1½ inches apart. Bake until the middle of the top feels firm, about 15 minutes. Remove from the oven and immediately slide the parchment onto a counter or table. Cool.

Line a tray or cookie sheet with parchment. Dip each cookie halfway into the chocolate glaze. As you bring it out, scrape the bottom against the rim of the bowl. Place it on the parchment and nudge it slightly in the direction of its dipped side. This will prevent a ridge of glaze from forming at the bottom edge. Let stand at room temperature until the glaze has hardened.

Lemon Mounds

These pale, fez-shaped cookies have a light lemony flavor and a pleasant crunch. They are dipped after baking in lemon icing. For a different, richer effect, you can dip them instead in white chocolate that has been slowly melted.

MAKES ABOUT 4 DOZEN

   10 tablespoons unsalted butter (cold), cut into 4 pieces
1½ cups cake flour
1½ cups powdered sugar
      Zest of 2 lemons, finely chopped
    3 tablespoons plus 1 teaspoon lemon juice

Using the paddle attachment on an electric mixer (see page 58) and low speed, mix the butter, flour, and ½ cup of sugar to a coarse meal. Add the lemon zest and 1 teaspoon of lemon juice and mix just until the dough comes together.

Remove the dough from the mixer and divide it into 4 equal pieces. On a lightly floured table, roll each piece with your hands into a cylinder

10 inches long and ¾ inch in diameter. Lay the cylinders on a parchment-lined cookie sheet and refrigerate until firm, about 1 hour.

Preheat the oven to 325°. Line another cookie sheet with parchment. Slice the cylinders into ¾-inch pieces. Stand them, cut end down, on the cookie sheet about 1½ inches apart. Bake until the middle of the top feels firm and the cookies are lightly browned, about 15 minutes. Remove from the oven and immediately slide the parchment onto a counter or table. Cool.

Stir the remaining sugar and lemon juice together. Work out any lumps with the back of a spoon. Heat the icing over boiling water just to body temperature.

Line a tray or cookie sheet with parchment. Dip each cookie halfway into the icing. As you bring it out, scrape the bottom against the rim of the bowl. Place it on the parchment and nudge it slightly in the direction of its dipped side to prevent a ridge of icing from forming at the bottom edge. The icing should look translucent when it goes on the cookies. If it thickens and turns opaque, put it back over the boiling water to thin it. Let the dipped cookies stand at room temperature until the icing has hardened.

Hussar's Love

These are toasted hazelnut cookies dusted with sugar and topped with a dot of raspberry jam. I don't know where the name came from. Perhaps the Hussars, the elaborately uniformed Hungarian light cavalry of the fifteenth century, loved them. Or perhaps the cookie was first baked as a gift for a Hussar from his love.

MAKES 90 COOKIES

> ½ cup toasted hazelnuts (filberts)
> 7 tablespoons unsalted butter (room temperature)
> 3 tablespoons sugar
> 1¼ cups cake flour
> 2 tablespoons powdered sugar
> ½ cup seedless red raspberry jam

Finely grind the nuts. Cut the butter into pieces. Place the filberts, butter, sugar, and flour in the bowl of an electric mixer. Using the paddle attachment (see page 58), mix at medium speed until combined and then at medium-high until the dough comes together. Remove the dough from the mixer and divide it into 4 equal parts. Roll each part with your hands into a cylinder 8 inches long and ¾ inch in diameter. Put the cylinders on a tray and refrigerate until firm, about 1 hour.

Preheat the oven to 325°. Line two cookie sheets with parchment.

Cut the cylinders into ¼-inch-thick slices. Place the slices on the cookie sheets and bake until golden brown, 10 to 15 minutes. Remove from the oven and immediately slide the parchment onto a counter or table. Cool to room temperature.

When cool, place the cookies very close together on one sheet. Put the powdered sugar in a shaker or a fine sieve; shake a thin coating of sugar over the cookies. Heat the jam gently until liquid. Pass it through a fine sieve, then spoon it into a parchment cone with a ¼-inch opening cut in the tip (see pages 62–63). Top each cookie with a dot of jam.

Almond Macaroons

These classic, delicate cookies are crisp on the outside, soft and moist on the inside.

MAKES ABOUT 5 DOZEN

    ⅔ cup powdered sugar
    ¼ cup granulated sugar
    8 ounces almond paste
    2 large egg whites

Line two cookie sheets with parchment.

Sift the powdered sugar. Using the paddle attachment on an electric mixer (see page 58), stir together both sugars and the almond paste until the almond paste breaks down and the mixture resembles coarse meal. Scrape the bowl and paddle. Add the egg whites one at a time, mixing each in thoroughly at medium speed. Scrape the bowl and paddle again. Mix at medium-high speed until all the lumps are gone and the dough is smooth and creamy. (Scrape the bowl often if the dough sticks to the sides.)

Spoon the dough into a pastry bag with a #5 plain tip. Hold the tip ¼ inch above the cookie sheet and pipe out mounds of dough about 1 inch in diameter and ¼ inch high (they will look a little like chocolate kisses). You should be able to fit 30 cookies, 1½ inches apart, on the first sheet. Pipe the remaining 25 or so cookies onto the second sheet.

Now wet a cotton (not terry cloth) dish towel with warm water and wring it out well. Fold it into quarters lengthwise and grasp an end in each hand, with your thumbs lying flat on top and your fingers curled tightly underneath. Slap the tops of the cookies gently with the towel until all the cookies are shiny and rounded (the shape of fried egg yolks).

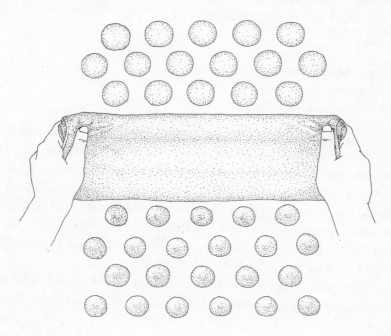

Slap the tops of the cookies gently with the towel until all the cookies are shiny and rounded.

Strange as it may seem, it's the best way to get the classic shape of macaroons. Refrigerate the trays of cookies for 30 minutes.

Preheat the oven to 325°. Bake the cookies for 5 minutes, then slip a second, room-temperature cookie sheet under each sheet. This will keep the bottoms of the cookies from getting too dark. Bake 12 to 15 minutes more, until the tops are light brown (the color of brown egg shells). Remove the sheets from the oven and immediately slide the parchment onto a table or counter. Allow the cookies to cool.

Meringues and White Chocolate

These light, airy cookies are simple to make. You don't bake them so much as dry them out in a very slow oven.

MAKES 50 (1-INCH) COOKIES

> 2 large egg whites
> ½ cup sugar
> 3 ounces white chocolate

Preheat the oven to 150°. Line a cookie sheet with parchment.

Using the whisk attachment on an electric mixer (see page 58), beat the egg whites and sugar at high speed until thick. Stop and scrape the sides and bottom of the bowl. Continue beating at high speed until the whites are very stiff and dry (their glossiness will disappear). Transfer the meringue into a pastry bag with a #3 star tip and pipe out fifty 1-inch rosettes on the cookie sheet. (You can put them quite close together; the cookies don't spread much in the oven.)

Place the cookie sheet on the lowest shelf in the oven and bake until the meringues are thoroughly dry but not brown, about 2 hours. Cool to room temperature.

Cut or grate the chocolate into small pieces and put it in the top of a double boiler. Bring the water in the bottom of the double boiler to a boil and turn off the heat *before* you put the top containing the chocolate on. White chocolate must be melted over relatively low heat; if the heat is too high, the chocolate will curdle instead of melting.

Dip the top of each meringue in the melted chocolate. Allow them to dry on a clean sheet of parchment. Store at room temperature.

Currant Bars

These are thick, crunchy bars rich with the taste of toasted nuts and coconut. The small amount of vinegar keeps them from being too sweet — be sure you use only cider vinegar in this or any other pastry recipe. Bake the bars a day ahead so they have plenty of time to cool and dry before you cut them.

MAKES 55 BARS

½ **recipe Shortbread Dough (page 76)**
2 **large eggs**
1¾ **cups sugar**
8 **tablespoons (¼ pound) unsalted butter, melted and cooled**
1⅓ **cups unsweetened medium or coarsely shredded coconut**
1 **cup currants**
1⅓ **cups chopped pecans**
3 **tablespoons apple cider vinegar**
⅓ **cup raspberry preserves**

Prepare the shortbread dough as directed and bake it in a 7½ × 11-inch (or equivalent) pan. Set aside to cool. Raise the oven temperature to 375°.

Mix the eggs and sugar until smooth. Add all the remaining ingredients except the preserves and mix well. Coat the shortbread crust with preserves (I find it easiest to do with my hands), then spread the currant mixture evenly on top. Bake until golden brown, about 30 minutes. Cool to room temperature and let stand overnight before cutting. Cut into 1 × 1½-inch bars.

Coconut Meringue Bars

Coconut combines with toasted pecans to give both chewiness and crunch to these light meringue bars. A thin layer of strawberry jam hidden between the meringue and the flaky crust adds an unexpected brightness to each bite.

MAKES 80 BARS

>   1 recipe Shortbread Dough (page 76)
>   2½ cups pecans
>   7 large egg whites
>   1½ cups sugar
>   1 teaspoon vanilla extract
>   3 cups unsweetened medium or coarsely shredded coconut
>   ½ cup strawberry jam

Preheat the oven to 325°.

Prepare the shortbread dough as directed. Roll it out and line the bottom and sides of a cookie sheet with it. Do not pierce or bake. Refrigerate the dough while you make the meringue.

Toast the pecans in the oven until fragrant, about 10 minutes. Coarsely chop them and set aside.

Combine the egg whites and sugar in a mixing bowl. Heat over simmering water to body temperature, then whip to stiff peaks. Add the vanilla. Mix the pecans with the coconut and fold them into the meringue.

Spread the strawberry jam over the shortbread dough with your hand. Spread the meringue mixture over it. Even out the surface as much as possible, pushing the meringue well into the corners. Bake until the meringue is lightly browned and the crust is golden and has pulled away from the sides of the pan, about 40 minutes. Cool to room temperature. Trim the edges by running a sharp knife about ½ inch from the sides of the pan, then cut into 1 × 2-inch bars.

Almond Blocks

These are thin, crisp, very almondy, rectangular cookies. The dough needs to be frozen overnight, so start it the day before you plan to bake.

MAKES 7 DOZEN

  8 **tablespoons (¼ pound) unsalted butter (soft)**
¼ **cup sugar**
½ **cup (firmly packed) light brown sugar**
  2 **large eggs**
¼ **teaspoon almond extract**
  2 **teaspoons unsweetened cocoa powder**
¼ **teaspoon baking soda**
1¾ **cups cake flour**
  2 **cups (about 6 ounces) sliced almonds (preferably blanched)**

Cut the butter into 8 pieces. Using the paddle attachment on an electric mixer (see page 58), cream the butter and both sugars at medium speed until smooth. Add 1 egg and mix until smooth. Scrape the sides and bottom of the bowl. Mix in the almond extract and then the second egg. Sift together the cocoa, soda, and flour; add and mix until smooth. Stir in 1¼ cups of the almonds, reserving the rest for decoration. Transfer the dough to a parchment-lined cookie sheet and refrigerate for 1 hour. When the dough is cold, use a rubber scraper or a spreader to form it into a block 7 inches long × 4½ inches wide × 1 inch deep. Wrap the parchment around the block and freeze the dough until firm, preferably overnight.

Preheat the oven to 300°.

Cut the frozen block lengthwise into three 1½-inch-wide strips. Return two strips to the freezer. Cut the third into ¼-inch-thick slices. Arrange the slices about 1½ inches apart on a parchment-lined cookie sheet. Bake until firm, about 15 minutes. Remove from the oven and immediately slide the parchment onto a counter or table. Cool to room temperature. Repeat with the other two strips of dough, removing each from the freezer when you are ready to slice and bake it.

When all the cookies are baked and cooled, brush their tops lightly with cold water and place an almond slice on each.

Peanut Butter Cookies Dipped in Chocolate

Peanut butter and chocolate is a surefire combination. These crunchy, very peanutty cookies are dipped in chocolate glaze after they are baked.

MAKES 5 DOZEN

>   1 **cup light brown sugar**
>   ½ **teaspoon kosher salt (see page 42)**
>   6 **tablespoons unsalted butter (soft)**
>   ½ **cup unsalted natural peanut butter (available at health food stores)**
>   1 **large egg**
>   1½ **teaspoons baking soda**
>   2 **tablespoons water**
>   1½ **cups cake flour**
>   ½ **recipe Chocolate Glaze (page 123)**

Using the paddle attachment on an electric mixer (see page 58), cream together the sugar, salt, butter, and peanut butter. Beat in the egg. Stir the baking soda into the water and slowly beat in. Slowly beat in the flour.

Line a cookie sheet with parchment. Spoon the cookie dough into a pastry bag with a #9 plain tip, then pipe it out onto the cookie sheet in 3 long logs. Freeze until firm, about 15 minutes.

Preheat the oven to 375°. Line a second cookie sheet with parchment. Cut the cookie dough into ¾-inch pieces and arrange the pieces, cut side down, on the cookie sheets, keeping them 1½ inches apart. Dip a fork in water and gently press the cookies down to about ¼ inch thick, making crosshatch marks with the tines of the fork. Keep the fork moist so the dough won't stick. Bake until the cookies are lightly browned, about 20 minutes. Remove from the oven and immediately slide the parchment onto a counter or table. Cool.

Line a tray or cookie sheet with parchment. Dip each cookie halfway into the chocolate glaze. As you bring it out, scrape the bottom against the rim of the bowl. Place it on the parchment and nudge it slightly in the direction of its dipped side to prevent a ridge of glaze from forming at the bottom edge. Let stand at room temperature until the glaze has hardened.

Lillian's Butter Cookies

Lillian Drake was the baker at my family's resort hotel in New Hampshire. I remember spending a lot of time in the kitchen when I was about 5 years old, watching her make these tender, buttery cookies and eating them by the handful.

MAKES 5 DOZEN

16 tablespoons (½ pound) unsalted butter (soft)
½ cup sugar
1 egg yolk
½ teaspoon vanilla extract
2 cups cake flour, sifted

Preheat the oven to 375°.

Using the paddle attachment on an electric mixer (see page 58), beat the butter until it is light. Add the sugar and beat until smooth. Beat in the egg yolk and vanilla. Add the flour ½ cup at a time, beating well after each addition. The batter will be soft and smooth.

Use a cookie press to make rows of cookies on a parchment-lined cookie sheet. Or make small balls of dough, about ½ inch in diameter, arrange them in rows on a parchment-lined cookie sheet, and gently press them with the tines of a fork.

Bake until lightly browned, about 12 minutes. Remove the pan from the oven and immediately slide the parchment onto a counter or table to cool.

Scottish Shortbread

Shortbread is a very buttery cookie, traditional in Scotland and popular at The Stanford Court. These are hard and crumbly, and not too sweet. The dough keeps well; it can be made ahead, refrigerated, and baked later.

MAKES 112

> 1 **cup cake flour**
> 1¾ **cups bread flour**
> 1 **cup powdered sugar**
> **Pinch of kosher salt (see page 42)**
> 20 **tablespoons unsalted butter (cold)**
> ¼ **teaspoon vanilla extract**

Preheat the oven to 400°.

Using low speed and the paddle attachment on an electric mixer (see page 58), combine the flours, sugar, salt, and butter (broken into pieces). Add the vanilla. Mix until the dough is smooth and comes together.

Turn the dough out onto a floured board and roll it into a 14-inch square. Use a yardstick to gently nudge the sides into straight lines. Pierce the dough lightly all over with a fork. Lay the yardstick along one edge of the dough and cut along it with a pastry wheel to make a 1 × 14-inch strip (assuming your yardstick is 1 inch wide, as mine is; if it is not, fudge a little). Repeat 12 more times. Cut each of the 14-inch strips crosswise into 1¾-inch rectangles.

Place the cookies about ½ inch apart on cookie sheets lined with parchment and bake until light brown, about 12 minutes.

Chocolate Rosettes

These small, easy-to-make, very chocolaty rosettes can be used as cake decorations or eaten as cookies.

MAKES 16

4 ounces bittersweet chocolate
⅓ cup sour cream (room temperature)

Melt the chocolate in a bowl over boiled (not boiling) water. Stir in the sour cream. Put the mixture in a pastry bag with a #3 star tip. Lay down a half sheet of parchment and pipe sixteen 1-inch rosettes onto it (see page 55). Leave the rosettes to dry at room temperature. Store as cookies.

13
Ice Creams, Sherbets, and Ices

Ice cream must certainly be the most popular dessert in the world. Every country I have ever visited has its own version. American ice cream now runs the gamut from not very rich supermarket varieties to the ultra-rich Italian-style *gelato* available in most major cities and even in some supermarkets. One reason *gelato* is so much richer than American-style ice cream is that it doesn't have so much air beaten into it; another, of course, is its cream content. I like ice creams that have a creamy, smooth richness carefully balanced with a pure, intense flavor. I often thin the cream with milk, even skimmed milk, to keep it from overwhelming the flavors. Sometimes it's a matter of adjusting the amount of sugar or the flavor ingredient until the balance is perfect.

The best ice creams, sherbets, and fruit ices are always the ones you make yourself. They're wonderful partly because they are fresh and flavored to your personal taste and partly because of the thrill of making them. Ice cream making is exciting, especially when a whole group of friends participates. I think it makes us all feel like children again.

To make good frozen desserts you have to have some kind of freezer because the mixture has to be stirred throughout the freezing process. But you don't need one of the those expensive push-button models. In the hotel pastry shop I have a sleek and efficient sorbet freezer worth thousands of dollars. At home I have a small motor-driven bucket-type freezer that works with ice cubes and table salt. The hotel freezer is faster and takes less effort, but they both make excellent ice creams, sherbets, and ices.

Like any other dessert, your ice cream is going to taste just as good and as balanced as the ingredients you put into it. You're not going to cover up the disappointing taste of underripe or overripe fruit by adding more sugar or cream. I make my Vanilla Ice Cream with a fresh vanilla bean to give it as much vanilla intensity as possible. I make my Chocolate Ice Cream with unsweetened cocoa so that I can control just how much sweetness it gets (from sugar) and how much fat (from fresh whipping cream). When ice cream gets too rich it can leave an unpleasant film on the roof of your mouth.

Beyond vanilla and chocolate there are unlimited possibilities for ice cream flavors. The great advantage of making ice cream at home is being able to experiment with flavor combinations and come up with your own unique favorites. Two of my favorites, bing cherry with lemon and peach with pistachio, are included in this chapter.

Sherbets, because they are made with milk instead of cream, are less rich than ice cream but every bit as delicious. I am particularly fond of citrus sherbets. This chapter includes a recipe for a very tangy Lime Sherbet and a less startling though wonderfully flavorful Zested Orange Sherbet.

Easiest of all to make and intensely flavorful are the fruit ices— frequently called by their French name, *sorbet*. Basically they consist of a fruit juice or puree mixed with a simple syrup (sugar and water) and frozen. Made well, they end up tasting like the fresh, ripe fruit that went into them. Ices are not only great warm-weather desserts, they're delicious at any season, especially after a big meal. During the summer months I make ices from melons or peaches or boysenberries or nectarines. When summer fruits are gone, my enthusiasm turns to grapefruit, pears, and oranges. Orange, especially, combines well with other flavors to offer surprising taste sensations; Orange and Anise Ice and Orange Caramel Ice are included in this chapter.

When freezing ice cream, sherbet, or ices, follow the instructions that came with your ice cream freezer. Each one is a little different, and each manufacturer knows how its machine works best. I always suggest that you have a frozen stainless steel bowl waiting to receive the dessert when it comes out of the machine. That way you won't have to worry about melting around the edges. Transfer the frozen dessert to the bowl, cover it with plastic wrap, and return it to the freezer until you are ready to serve it. To make scooping easier, dip your ice cream scoop in warm water before each serving.

Bing Cherry and Lemon Ice Cream

Fresh Bing cherries are one of the best things about summer. Nuggets of cherry turn this rich, creamy lemon ice cream pink and help create the delightful interplay of tangy and sweet in every bite. If you don't already own a cherry pitter, I suggest you get one; pitting cherries with a knife can turn you and your entire kitchen very red.

MAKES 1 QUART

Double recipe Lemon Cream (page 107)
1 **pound Bing cherries**
1 **lemon**
1 **cup skim milk**
1 **cup whipping cream**

Make the lemon cream far enough ahead so that it is completely cooled.

Wash and pit the cherries. Cut them in half. Put them in a bowl and squeeze the juice of the lemon over them. Toss to coat and set aside.

Stir the lemon cream with a whisk until smooth. Whisk in the milk and then the cream. Freeze in an ice cream freezer according to manufacturer's instructions.

While the ice cream is freezing, drain the cherries and towel-dry them. (Use a towel you don't care about staining.) Add the cherries to the ice cream just before it is completely frozen.

Fresh Mango Ice Cream

When mangoes are at their peak they're unbelievably sweet, juicy, and luscious—and I look for every way I can to use them. One of my favorites is this rich and smooth ice cream. You will need at least a 1-pound mango to give you 12 ounces of flesh. Let the fruit ripen in a sunny spot until it's very soft and fragrant.

MAKES 1½ PINTS

- 1 **large mango (to yield 12 ounces of flesh)**
- 2 **tablespoons lemon juice**
- 3 **large egg yolks**
- ⅓ **cup sugar**
- ¾ **cup milk**
- ¾ **cup whipping cream**

Peel the mango and cut the flesh away from the stone. (Be careful to avoid the hairs close to the stone.) Puree the mango with the lemon juice in a food processor until smooth.

Whip the yolks and sugar until light. Bring the milk to a boil in a heavy-bottomed saucepan. Add the egg mixture and cook, stirring constantly, until it boils. Remove from the heat. Stir in the cream and then the mango. Transfer to a stainless steel bowl and cool to room temperature. When cool, freeze in an ice cream freezer according to manufacturer's directions.

Peach and Pistachio Ice Cream

Peach and pistachio is one of my favorite combinations. This ice cream has it all—color, texture, and marvelous taste. It's rich and creamy and fun to eat.

MAKES 1 QUART

5 medium-size peaches, ripe and firm
1 orange
1½ cups sugar
7 large egg yolks
2 cups skim milk
2 cups whipping cream
4 ounces pistachios

Wash the peaches. Cut three of them into quarters and discard the pits. Then cut each quarter in half crosswise. Squeeze the juice of the orange over the peach chunks (to keep them from turning color), toss a little, and set aside.

Cut the remaining two peaches into 16 wedges each, then cut the wedges crosswise into sixths. Put the pieces in a bowl and drain the orange juice from the first bowl into this one. Toss.

In a food processor, puree the first batch of peach chunks (the three peaches) with ½ cup of the sugar until smooth. Transfer the puree to a heavy stainless steel saucepan. Bring to a boil over medium heat, then simmer, stirring frequently, until the puree is very thick and has been reduced to 1 cup, about 15 minutes. Cool.

Using the whisk attachment on your electric mixer (see page 58) and medium-high speed, beat the egg yolks with ½ cup of sugar until white, about 5 minutes.

Put the skim milk in a large saucepan. Stir in ½ cup of sugar and bring to a boil over medium heat. Stir a little of the hot milk into the yolks, then pour all of the yolk mixture into the milk. Stir vigorously with a whisk over medium heat until the mixture bubbles on the sides and in the middle. In stirring, be sure to scrape the sides of the pan and to zigzag over the bottom frequently. Any place you leave the eggs unmoved they will cook. Transfer the mixture back to the mixing bowl. Stir with the whisk, then allow the mixture to cool. When cool, whisk in the peach puree and the cream. Freeze in an ice cream freezer according to manufacturer's instructions.

While the ice cream is freezing, toast the pistachios for 10 minutes in a 350° oven. Coarsely chop the toasted nuts (once over with a knife).

Drain the juice from the peach chunks and towel-dry.

When the ice cream is almost frozen, fold in the nuts and the peach chunks. Store in a metal container in the freezer. (It's a good idea to have the container frozen before you put the ice cream in it.)

Caramel Ice Cream

Caramel ice cream is great with chocolate cake, with cranberry turnovers, and all by itself.

MAKES 1½ PINTS

> 6 **large egg yolks**
> ⅔ **cup sugar**
> 1½ **cups milk**
> 1½ **cups whipping cream**

Whip the egg yolks at high speed until light. While they are whipping, heat the sugar in a large saucepan (at least 4 quarts) over high heat, without stirring, until it turns dark amber in color and begins to smoke. Stir the milk into the caramelized sugar. Pour about ⅓ of the caramel into the egg yolks and let them continue whipping. Bring the rest of the caramel to a boil. Add the egg mixture and whisk over medium heat until thick. Transfer to a bowl.

Pour the cream into the saucepan and stir it with a rubber spatula, scraping any remaining caramel off the sides of the pan before it has a chance to harden. Add the cream to the egg mixture and let it cool.

Freeze in an ice cream freezer according to manufacturer's instructions.

Chocolate Ice Cream

This is a very chocolaty ice cream that is rich but not too rich. Because it is made with skim milk it doesn't have that too creamy texture that causes some ice creams to leave a film on the roof of your mouth.

MAKES 1½ PINTS

6 large egg yolks
¾ cup sugar
½ cup unsweetened cocoa powder
2 cups skim milk
1 cup whipping cream

Whip the egg yolks, sugar, and cocoa together until light. Bring the milk to a simmer in a large saucepan. Pour the milk into the whipped yolks, stir to combine, then pour the whole mixture back into the saucepan. Cook over medium heat, stirring constantly with a whisk, until the mixture begins to thicken. Be sure to scrape the bottom of the pan as you stir so that the egg does not cook. Remove from the heat and pour into a clean bowl. Stir in the whipping cream. Chill until cold, then freeze in an ice cream freezer according to manufacturer's directions.

Vanilla Ice Cream

This is a rich and creamy ice cream, alive with the taste of real vanilla. If you are making it as part of a Praline Ice Cream Pie (page 174) or Lemon-Layered Ice Cream Cake (page 215), separate the eggs and set aside the whites to be used in the meringue. Otherwise, you can freeze the whites for future use.

MAKES 1 QUART

7 large egg yolks
1 cup sugar
2 cups skim milk
1 vanilla bean, split in half
1 cup whipping cream

Beat the egg yolks and sugar together until pale yellow. In a 2-quart stainless steel saucepan bring the milk and vanilla bean to a simmer. Remove from the heat and stir in the egg yolks. Cook over medium-high heat, stirring continuously with a wire whisk, until the center bubbles and the mixture has thickened. Remove the vanilla bean, pour the mixture into a bowl, and cool to room temperature. Stir in the cream and chill completely. Freeze in an ice cream freezer according to manufacturer's instructions.

Zested Orange Sherbet

This sherbet has a full, well-rounded flavor and a creamy texture. Be sure to use juice oranges; eating oranges are often too sweet and can keep the sherbet from freezing.

MAKES 1½ PINTS

4–5 juice oranges (to yield 2¼ cups juice)
½ cup milk
1 cup sugar

Zest enough of the oranges to give you 1 tablespoon of zest. Set aside. Juice the oranges and pour 2¼ cups of juice through a fine strainer into a bowl. Finely chop the zest and add it to the juice.

Combine the milk and sugar in a heavy-bottomed saucepan. Scald the milk, heating it just enough to completely dissolve the sugar. Cool. Stir the cooled milk into the juice. Freeze in an ice cream freezer according to manufacturer's instructions.

Lime Sherbet

Although limes are available all year round, they vary in acidity according to the season and where they were grown. If your limes are very tart, they will make a very tart sherbet.

MAKES 1 QUART

  1½ **cups sugar**
  1½ **cups milk**
  16 **limes (or enough to yield 2 cups juice)**

Combine the sugar and milk in a heavy-bottomed saucepan. Scald the milk, heating it just enough to completely dissolve the sugar. Cool.

Zest two of the limes, then juice them all. Pour 2 cups of juice through a fine sieve into a bowl. Finely chop the zest and stir it in. Stir in the cooled milk. Freeze in an ice cream freezer according to manufacturer's instructions.

Pink Grapefruit Ice

The delicate color and flavor of pink grapefruit make this light dessert especially elegant. I like to serve it with orange or grapefruit sections, or raspberries. It can also stand alone nicely, garnished with a sprig of fresh mint.

MAKES 1½ PINTS

  1¾ **cups sugar**
  1¾ **cups water**
  4 **large pink grapefruits (or enough to yield 1 quart juice)**

Make a simple syrup by bringing the sugar and water to a boil, then allowing it to cool to room temperature.

Zest one grapefruit, then squeeze all four. Pour the juice through a sieve to strain out any seeds or pulp. Press any pulp left in the sieve with the back of a spoon to get out all the juice. Combine the simple syrup, juice, and zest. Stir well and freeze in an ice cream freezer according to manufacturer's instructions.

Pear Ice

This is a smooth, white, very fruity ice. The taste will vary, of course, according to the kind of pears you use. Any variety is fine as long as the pears are ripe and flavorful.

MAKES 1½ QUARTS

> 4 **pears**
> 2 **tablespoons lemon juice**
> 1¾ **cups sugar**
> 4 **cups water**
> ½ **vanilla bean**

Peel the pears and toss them in the lemon juice. Cut each pear in quarters lengthwise. Remove the cores, then cut each quarter crosswise into thirds. Put the pears in a heavy-bottomed saucepan with the sugar and 2½ cups of water. Split the ½ vanilla bean lengthwise and scrape out the seeds. Add both the seeds and the pod to the pan. Bring to a boil, reduce to a simmer, and cook until the pears are tender enough to be pierced easily with the tip of a knife.

Strain the syrup into a bowl. Puree the pieces of pear until smooth. Stir the puree and the remaining water into the syrup. Refrigerate until cold, then freeze in an ice cream freezer according to manufacturer's instructions.

Melons with Melon Ice

This is a colorful, light, and refreshing dessert, perfect after a big dinner or anytime on a warm day. Just about any melon will work, but the dish is most attractive when you use three melons of different colors. I like to use watermelon, honeydew, and either cantaloupe or casaba.

SERVES 8

2⅓ cups sugar
1⅚ cups water
2 medium-size melons (cantaloupe, honeydew, casaba, etc.)
1 small watermelon
2 teaspoons lemon juice
Mint sprigs for garnish

Make a simple syrup by bringing 1⅓ cups of sugar and 1⅓ cups of water to a boil in a saucepan. Cook only until the sugar dissolves. Cool to room temperature. You should have about 2 cups of syrup.

Cut the 2 medium-size melons in half and discard the seeds. Scoop out the flesh of one half of each melon and puree separately in a food processor until liquid. You need 1 cup of puree from each melon to make the ices (leftover puree is a refreshing drink — a bonus for the cook). To each puree add 1 cup of cooled sugar syrup and ½ teaspoon of lemon juice. Freeze separately in an ice cream freezer according to manufacturer's directions.

The watermelon needs less water in the syrup because the melon itself contains so much water. Make a sugar syrup, as above, using 1 cup of sugar and ½ cup of water. Cool. About ¼ of a small watermelon should yield the 1 cup of puree you need. Remove the seeds from the watermelon before you puree the flesh. Add the simple syrup and the remaining 1 teaspoon of lemon juice to the puree and freeze in an ice cream freezer according to manufacturer's instructions.

Cut the skin and rind from the remaining half melons. Cut each half in half vertically, then cut across at a slight angle into ½-inch-thick slices.

You'll need one slice from each melon for each serving. Cut slices of watermelon as close as possible in size and shape to the slices of the other melons.

To serve, arrange one slice from each melon on each plate, in a fan shape (touching at one end and well apart at the other). Place a scoop (preferably oval) of melon ice in the curve of each melon slice, matching the ice to the type of melon. Garnish with a mint sprig at the point where the melon slices come together.

Rhubarb Ice

When not oversweetened (which, unfortunately, it often is), rhubarb has an intriguing, slightly tart flavor. This ice comes out smooth, rich, and pink. Try it with something chocolate—cookies or chocolate-dipped candied ginger (page 125).

MAKES 1½ PINTS

¾ **cup sugar**
¾ **cup water**
1½ **pounds rhubarb**

Make a simple syrup by bringing the sugar and water to a boil in a saucepan. Cook only until the sugar dissolves. Cool to room temperature.

Wash the rhubarb. Using a sharp knife (to cut cleanly through the tough skin), trim off the top and bottom of each stalk, including any green. Cut the stalks into pieces and puree in a food processor until liquid. Strain through a fine sieve. Work the pulp against the sieve with the back of a spoon or a rubber spatula to get out all the liquid.

Stir the liquid rhubarb and simple syrup together and freeze in an ice cream freezer according to manufacturer's directions.

Apricot Ice

Make sure your apricots are fully ripe and tasty; unripe fruit simply can't deliver the delicate flavor that makes this dessert so memorable.

MAKES 1 PINT

> **8–10 medium-size apricots**
> ½ **cup sugar**
> ½ **cup water**

The more fruit you start with, the less sweet your ice will be, so use just 8 apricots if you want it on the sweet side and 9 or 10 if you want it less sweet. Of course, the size of the apricots makes a difference, too.

Wash and quarter the apricots and discard the pits. Puree in a food processsor until smooth. You should have at least 1½ cups of puree. Bring the sugar and water to a boil in a saucepan. Cook only until the sugar dissolves. Cool. When the syrup is cool, stir in the puree. Freeze in an ice cream freezer according to manufacturer's directions.

Boysenberry Ice with Orange-Berry Sauce

This dessert is special in at least three ways. First, it's so intense in flavor, it satisfies like a rich dessert without being either rich or sweet. Second, it's equally intense in color and looks stunning on clear glass or light-colored plates. Third, the orange-scented sauce has lots of texture because it's full of whole berries and chunks of orange.

SERVES 6

> **2 pints boysenberries**
> 1¼ **cups plus 2 tablespoons sugar**
> 1¼ **cups water**
> 1 **medium-size eating orange (preferably Valencia)**

For the ice: Rinse 1 pint of boysenberries and puree them in a food processor until smooth, about 5 minutes. Combine 1¼ cups of sugar with the water in a saucepan and bring to a boil. Cook only until all the sugar dissolves. Cool. Stir the cooled sugar syrup into the berries and strain through a fine sieve. Press the seeds against the sieve with a rubber scraper to make sure you get out all the liquid. Freeze in an ice cream freezer according to manufacturer's instructions. Makes about 1 quart.

For the sauce: Rinse the remaining pint of berries. Puree ½ pint with 2 tablespoons of sugar in a food processor until smooth. Meanwhile, zest the orange. Strain the pureed berries through a fine sieve. Stir in the orange zest. Peel the orange and cut it into 8 vertical wedges. Cut each wedge crosswise into quarters. Stir the orange pieces and the remaining ½ pint of whole berries into the puree. Refrigerate until ready to serve.

To serve: Spoon about ½ cup of sauce onto each dessert plate. Top with a scoop of boysenberry ice.

Note: If boysenberries are not available, blackberries work very well.

Elderberry Ice

By themselves, elderberries have an unpleasant, grassy taste, but they make a delicious, brightly colored, unusual ice.

MAKES 1 PINT

> 2 **pints elderberries**
> 1 **tablespoon lemon juice**
> ¾ **cup plus 1 tablespoon sugar**
> ¾ **cup plus 1 tablespoon water**

Wash the elderberries and remove as many of the stems as you can. Puree in a food processor with the lemon juice until liquid (lemon offsets the grassy taste of the berries). Strain through a fine sieve.

Combine the sugar and water in a saucepan and bring to a boil. Cook only until the sugar dissolves. Cool to room temperature, then stir in the berry puree. Freeze in an ice cream freezer according to manufacturer's instructions.

Nectarine Ice

When nectarines are picked ripe they are very smooth in texture and all but bursting with juicy sweetness. They make a particularly smooth, tasty, and beautiful ice that has a soft orange color flecked with red.

MAKES 1½ PINTS

5 medium-size nectarines, ripe and firm
1 cup sugar
1 cup water

Wash the nectarines and cut them into chunks. Puree until smooth in a food processor, then strain through a fine sieve.

Bring the sugar and water to a boil in a saucepan. Cook only until the sugar dissolves. Cool to room temperature, then stir in the puree. Freeze in an ice cream freezer according to manufacturer's instructions.

Peach Ice

Try this when peaches are ripe and plentiful. Delicate in flavor and not too sweet, peach ice makes a refreshing warm-weather dessert served by itself, with sliced fruit, or with cookies.

MAKES 1½ PINTS

5 medium-size peaches, ripe and firm
1 teaspoon lemon juice
¾ cup plus 2 tablespoons sugar
¾ cup plus 2 tablespoons water

Wash the peaches and cut them into chunks. Puree them in a food processor with the lemon juice until smooth. Strain through a fine sieve.

Work the puree against the sieve with a rubber scraper to force through as much of the flesh as possible.

Bring the sugar and water to a boil in a saucepan. Cook only until the sugar dissolves. Cool. Stir the puree into the sugar syrup and freeze in an ice cream freezer according to manufacturer's instructions.

Orange and Anise Ice

This bright yellow, very fruity ice has a pleasant hint of anise that comes through mostly as an aftertaste. Don't substitute navel oranges in this recipe. They have too much natural sugar, which keeps the ice from freezing well.

MAKES ABOUT 1 QUART

- 1 teaspoon anise seeds
- 1 cup plus 1 tablespoon sugar
- ½ cup water
- 3 cups fresh orange juice (about 8 juice oranges)

Crush the anise seeds with the flat side of a knife or a mortar and pestle. Combine them with the sugar and water in a saucepan. Bring to a boil. Remove from the heat and strain into a bowl. Cool. When the syrup has cooled to room temperature, stir in the orange juice and freeze in an ice cream freezer according to manufacturer's directions.

Orange Caramel Ice

Caramel and orange is a particularly happy combination. Here the slightly bitter caramel flavor is subtle, underscoring the sweetness of the oranges. The texture is smooth and rich, almost like ice cream. Don't substitute navel oranges for the juice oranges; they're too sweet and may keep the ice from freezing.

MAKES 1½ QUARTS

> **2 cups sugar**
> **2½ cups water**
> **3 cups fresh orange juice (about 8 juice oranges)**

Combine the sugar and ½ cup of water in a saucepan. Cook over medium-high heat, without stirring, until the mixture turns mahogany. If the sugar starts to darken unevenly, swirl the pan to even out the color.

Remove from heat and carefully stir in the orange juice (the hot caramel may spatter). If the caramel begins to solidify, heat the mixture until it liquefies again. Add the remaining 2 cups of water. Cool to room temperature, then freeze in an ice cream freezer according to manufacturer's instructions.

Tulip Wafer Cups

My favorite way to serve ices is in edible tulip-shaped cups. These are crisp and buttery, fragile during the shaping process but surprisingly sturdy in their role as temporary dishes. They are the perfect accompaniment to any fruit ice. So forget about cookies tonight; your guests will eat their cups.

MAKES 12

> **8 tablespoons (¼ pound) unsalted butter (soft)**
> **1 cup sugar**
> **1 teaspoon vanilla extract**
> **⅔ cup bread flour**
> **⅓ cup cake flour**
> **4 large egg whites**

Using the paddle attachment on an electric mixer (see page 58), whip the butter with ½ cup of sugar until light. Add the vanilla and the flours, and mix until smooth.

Combine the egg whites with the remaining ½ cup of sugar and heat in the top of a double boiler until warm to the touch. Add half of the egg whites to the batter and mix at high speed until thoroughly incorporated. Stop the mixer and scrape the sides and bottom of the bowl. Add the rest of the whites and mix at medium speed. Continue mixing for 10 minutes. The batter will be very light.

Preheat the oven to 325°. Grease a cookie sheet very well with vegetable oil. (If you have a coated cookie sheet, use that and grease it besides.)

Put the batter in a pastry bag with a #5 plain tip. Pipe out two 3-inch circles on the cookie sheet as follows: Hold the tip close to the pan. Start with a dot of batter, then move the bag in a spiral until you have a flat circle 3 inches in diameter. The wafers spread a lot during baking, so put only two on a cookie sheet. Leave about 3 inches between them and as much space as possible between the batter and the sides of the pan. Bake until an even golden brown, about 15 minutes.

Have two custard (or similarly shaped) cups upside down on the table when you take the wafers from the oven. Immediately lift each wafer carefully off the pan by slipping the blade of a metal scraper under it and lay it over an inverted cup. Gently press the wafer down around the sides of the cup to shape it. The sides of the wafer cup will be wavy. Be careful, the wafers are very fragile at this stage. Allow the wafer cup to cool slightly, then remove it from the cup and stand it right side up on a parchment-lined cookie sheet. Continue making wafers two at a time until all the batter is used. Cool them completely before using.

To serve, place one wafer cup on each dessert plate and fill with a scoop of fruit ice. Place the scoop gently in the cup; if you drop it in, it might shatter the wafer. Garnish, if you wish, with a sprig of mint. There's really no way to keep leftover wafers fresh and crisp. Eat them the day you make them; they'll be soft the next day.

14
Poached Fruit

The simplest way to serve ripe, fresh fruit is just to arrange it in a fruit bowl or basket. The next simplest way is to poach it and serve it with a light syrup or sauce. Poaching turns delicious seasonal fruit into an elegant dessert that is both refreshing and unusual. It provides the perfect ending for a rich or heavy meal.

Because the presentation is so simple and straightforward, the flavor combinations are the focus of poached fruit desserts. I have found to my delight that by combining seemingly ordinary flavors I can create exciting and often surprising effects. Honeydew in Chile, for instance, brings together three very different flavors—honeydew, chile, and lime—to create a perfect harmony of sweet, tart, and hot.

Plums in Rum and Vanilla, another unexpected combination, is wonderfully rich and smooth. The rum gives the plums an exotic flair but is gentled and rounded off by the addition of vanilla. Quince and Cranberries is lively and sparkling. Peppered Strawberries is a curiosity at first and a sure hit as soon as people taste it.

In all of these poached desserts, the fruit is cooked just enough to soften it. It must never be allowed to get mushy. Firm fruits such as pears are cooked for several minutes, until a knife pierces them easily. Softer fruits, such as strawberries, oranges, peaches, and grapes, don't get cooked at all. They are arranged in a serving bowl and hot syrup is poured over them. The syrup gently cooks the fruit as it cools.

Poached fruit keeps very well. It can be made hours or even a day ahead and stored, covered, in the refrigerator. I think it should always be served in a clear glass bowl because the colors of the fruit are too beautiful to hide. When the fruit is gone, leftover syrup can be used again to poach the same or similar fruits. Just add a little water because it tends to become concentrated.

Oranges in Cinnamon

On a dreary winter day, this dessert looks like a bowl of sunshine. It's the ideal light finish for a rich or spicy meal.

SERVES 8

> **8 medium-size eating oranges (preferably seedless)**
> **2 cups sugar**
> **3 cups water**
> **2 cinnamon sticks, broken in half**

Grate 1 tablespoon of orange zest before you start peeling the oranges. Set aside.

To peel an orange: Cut off the top and bottom with a sharp knife. Stand the orange on one cut end. Starting at the top, cut under the skin, following the curve of the fruit, removing a strip of peel about 1 inch wide. Be sure you cut off all of the bitter white pith beneath the skin. Turn the orange and repeat until all the skin and pith are removed.

Cut the peeled oranges horizontally into slices about ½ inch thick. Remove seeds, if any. Arrange the slices in a bowl. Sprinkle the zest on top.

In a heavy-bottomed saucepan, bring the sugar, water, and cinnamon to a boil. Boil for 5 minutes, then slowly pour into the bowl of orange slices and zest (be careful not to splash the hot syrup). Let stand until completely cool.

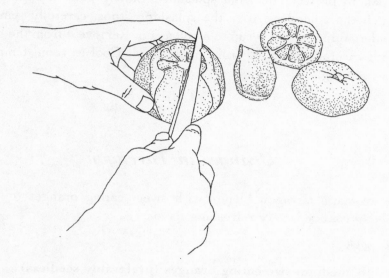

Zested Oranges in Caramel

This is a sophisticated caramel—light, fragrant, and just slightly bitter. All the sweetness comes from the oranges.

SERVES 8

8 medium-size eating oranges (preferably seedless)
1¼ **cups sugar**
3 **cups water**

Grate 1 tablespoon of orange zest and set it aside. Peel the oranges (see above) and cut them into horizontal slices about ½ inch thick. Arrange the slices in a 2-quart bowl and sprinkle the zest over them.

In a heavy-bottomed saucepan, bring the sugar and 1 cup of water to a boil over high heat. Allow the mixture to boil until it turns a rich mahogany color. Do not stir, but if the liquid begins to darken unevenly, swirl the pan to distribute the color throughout.

Remove from the heat and place a large metal colander or sieve over the pan to protect you from splashing. Slowly pour 2 cups of water through the colander. After the splashing stops, carefully remove the colander and bring the syrup to a boil again. Remove it from the heat and pour it carefully over the fruit in the bowl. Cool to room temperature before serving.

Oranges in Tarragon

Aromatic tarragon blends with sweet eating oranges to create a perfectly rounded, very refreshing flavor.

SERVES 8

> **8 medium-size eating oranges (preferably seedless)**
> **4 3-inch sprigs of tarragon**
> **1 cup sugar**
> **2½ cups water**

Peel the oranges (see page 321) and cut them horizontally into ½-inch slices. Arrange the slices in a 2-quart bowl and place the tarragon sprigs around the edges.

In a heavy-bottomed saucepan, bring the sugar and water to a boil. As soon as it boils, remove the syrup from the heat and pour it gently over the fruit. Let cool to room temperature before serving.

Pears in Anise

These pears are delicate in both flavor and appearance. They go well after a spicy meal and look best on bright, solid color dishes. They are the perfect partner for a plate of assorted cookies.

SERVES 8

   8 medium-size pears, ripe and firm
   1 cup fresh orange juice
1½ cups sugar
   1 teaspoon anise seed *or* 1 fresh anise blossom
   3 cups water

Cut a circle of parchment a little bigger than your heavy-bottomed saucepan.

Peel the pears. Cut them in half and remove the stems and cores (the small end of a melon baller is perfect for scooping out the core). In a bowl, toss the pears with the orange juice. Allow the pears to soak in the juice while you prepare the syrup.

In the saucepan, bring the sugar, anise, and water to a boil. Turn off the heat. Drain the pears and add them carefully to the syrup. Place the circle of parchment over the pears and press it down lightly with a spoon until the top is covered with a thin layer of liquid. The paper will keep the pears moist during poaching. Bring the syrup to a boil again, then turn down the heat and simmer until the pears are just tender.* Use a sharp knife to nudge the paper aside and test the fruit for doneness; if the tip of the knife goes through the pear with just a tiny bit of resistance, it is done. Remove the pears with a slotted spoon and arrange them in a bowl. Carefully pour the liquid over them. Cool to room temperature before serving.

---

* If some of your pears are less ripe than others, they will need to poach longer. Begin cooking the less ripe fruit first. Test it with the tip of a knife every few minutes. When the cooking fruit gives about the same amount of resistance to the knife as the ripe, uncooked fruit, add the ripe fruit and continue poaching until all are tender.

If you overcook pears, they will be mushy and may fall apart. You can often save slightly overcooked fruit by immediately icing it down. See page 337.

Pears in Port

This dessert is simple to make yet extravagant. Since it has only two ingredients, make sure both of them are of high quality.

SERVES 8

8 medium-size pears, ripe and firm
1 fifth good ruby port

Peel the pears. Cut them in half and remove the stems and cores with the small end of a melon baller.

In a heavy-bottomed saucepan, bring the port to a boil. Turn off the heat while you add the pears. If the liquid doesn't cover the pears, add 1 cup of water. Bring the liquid back to a boil and cook at a medium boil until a knife easily pierces the fruit, about 5 minutes.*

Remove the pears with a slotted spoon and arrange them in a bowl. Carefully pour the liquid over them. Cool to room temperature before serving.

Variations: The flavor of pears combines well with many liqueurs. I often substitute crème de cassis for port. Sometimes I use Zinfandel. You will probably come up with equally wonderful combinations of your own.

Pears and Blackberries

This is a festive dessert, colorful and very bright tasting. The slight tartness of the berries contrasts beautifully with the soft, round sweetness of the pears.

SERVES 8

1 pint fresh blackberries
8 medium-size pears, ripe and firm

---

*If some or all of your pears are not fully ripe, you will have to cook them longer and may have to add more water during poaching to keep them covered with liquid. See footnote on page 323, Pears in Anise.

1½ **cups sugar**

3 **cups water**

Puree ½ pint of the berries in a blender or food processor. Transfer the puree to a large bowl and set aside.

Peel the pears. Cut them in half and remove the stems and cores with the small end of a melon baller. Toss the pears in the berry puree to stain them with the bright berry color and keep them from turning brown. Let the pears stand in the puree for at least 5 minutes.

Meanwhile, combine the sugar and water in a heavy-bottomed saucepan and bring them to a boil. Turn off the heat while you add the pears and the berry puree. Bring back to a boil, then reduce the heat and simmer about 7 minutes, until a knife easily pierces the pears. (See footnote on page 323, Pears in Anise.)

Remove the pears with a slotted spoon and arrange them in a bowl. Scatter the remaining ½ pint of blackberries on top of the pears. Pour the poaching liquid through a fine sieve into the bowl. Cool to room temperature before serving.

Variations: This recipe is also excellent with raspberries, boysenberries, or olalaberries substituted for blackberries.

Strawberries and Oranges in Grand Marnier

Strawberries, like oranges, are available all year round. This dish is simple, elegant, and luscious any time you can find fruit that is ripe and sweet. (In the dead of winter most people find it a delightful surprise.)

SERVES 8

8 **medium-size eating oranges (preferably seedless)**

1 **cup sugar**

1½ **cups water**

1 **cup Grand Marnier**

1 **pint medium-size strawberries**

Peel the oranges (see page 321) and cut them horizontally into slices about 1 inch thick. Remove the seeds, if any.

In a heavy-bottomed saucepan, bring the sugar and water to a boil. Add the Grand Marnier and bring to a boil again. Remove from the heat and add the orange slices (be careful not to splash the hot syrup). Let cool 20 minutes.

Wash the strawberries and remove the stems. Add to the oranges, pushing them down into the liquid, and let stand at least 1 hour before serving. Serve at room temperature.

Pineapple with Lemon Cream

A light lemony sauce is poured hot over the pineapple so that the fruit doesn't absorb the lemon flavor but is gently surrounded by it.

SERVES 8

    1 **medium-size pineapple**
    1 **lemon**
  1½ **cups sugar**
    3 **cups water**
    1 **recipe Lemon Cream (page 107)**

Peel the pineapple (see page 32), quarter it, and remove the woody core. Cut each quarter into ½-inch slices and arrange the slices in a bowl.

Cut the lemon into thin slices. Combine the lemon slices, sugar, and water in a heavy-bottomed saucepan. Bring to a boil. Pour the hot liquid over the pineapple. Cool to room temperature before serving. Serve with a sauce boat of lemon cream.

Pineapple in Maple Syrup

This dessert is pure simplicity and pure elegance. Although real maple syrup is expensive, its incredibly rich taste is worth it. Serve topped with plain, unsweetened yogurt—the kind with no gelatin in it.

SERVES 8

> 1 medium-size ripe pineapple
> 2 cups maple syrup

Peel the pineapple (see page 32). Cut it vertically into quarters and remove the woody core. Cut each quarter crosswise into ½-inch slices.

In a heavy-bottomed saucepan, bring the maple syrup to a boil. Wait until it builds up a good head of golden froth, then turn off the heat. Add the pineapple and stir to coat each slice with syrup. Transfer to a bowl and cool to room temperature before serving.

Peaches and Green Grapes in Anise

The peaches are lush and soft; the grapes are firm and juicy. Together they make an unusual and very satisfying dessert. The anise adds a subtle licorice-like background that gently ties the fruit flavors together.

SERVES 8

> 6 medium-size peaches, ripe and firm
> ½ cup fresh orange juice
> 8 ounces seedless green grapes
> 1½ cups sugar
> 2 cups water
> 1 tablespoon anise seeds

Wash the peaches, cut them into quarters, and discard the pits. Cut each quarter lengthwise into thirds (or in half if the peaches are on the small side). Toss the peach wedges in the orange juice to keep them from turning color. Drain, reserving the liquid. Wash the grapes, discarding the stems, and put them in a glass bowl with the peaches.

Combine the sugar, water, anise seeds, and reserved orange juice in a heavy-bottomed saucepan. Bring to a boil. Pour the hot liquid over the fruit. Cool to room temperature before serving.

Plums in Port

Port is deep, rich, and smooth in both color and flavor. It is the perfect background for tender, slightly tart plums.

SERVES 8

16 plums (any kind), ripe and firm
3 cups good ruby port

Wash the plums, cut them in half, and remove the pits. Place them in a heavy-bottomed saucepan with the port. Bring to a boil, then lower the heat and simmer for 5 minutes. Transfer to a bowl and cool to room temperature before serving.

This is a recipe you can make ahead; once cool, cover with plastic wrap and refrigerate. Some people like the flavor even better the second day.

Plums in Rum and Vanilla

Any kind of plums will work in this bright and colorful dessert. Choose your favorites, ripe and firm. Tart skins will stay tart, so be sure the fruit you select is sweet enough for your personal taste. I prefer slightly sour plums for their contrast with the rich, smooth sauce.

SERVES 6

16 medium-size plums
2½ cups water
1½ cups sugar
1 cup rum
2 vanilla beans, split in half lengthwise

Wash the plums, cut them into quarters, and remove the pits. Set aside.

Combine ½ cup of water and the sugar in a large, heavy-bottomed saucepan (3-quart or 1-gallon size). Stir over medium heat until the mixture boils, then allow it to cook without stirring until it turns a dark caramel color, about 5 minutes.

Place a large metal colander or sieve over the top of the pan to protect you from splashing, and slowly pour 2 cups of water and 1 cup of rum through it. Be careful; sugar syrup is very hot. Remove the colander. Put the vanilla beans in the syrup and bring it to a boil.* Lower the heat and simmer for 5 minutes. Remove from the heat and add the plums (be careful not to splash yourself). Let the plums stand in the liquid until cool.

Raspberries and Pink Grapefruit

Ripe pink grapefruit can be surprisingly sweet. Its refreshing sparkle contrasts with the delicate smoothness of the raspberries. Since the berries aren't cooked, they stay plump and round.

SERVES 8

4 medium-large pink grapefruits
1½ cups sugar
3 cups water
½ pint raspberries

---

* If you are using gas, be sure the flame does not come up the sides of the pan. It could set the rum on fire.

Using a zester, cut half the skin of one grapefruit into julienne strips. (If you don't have a zester, remove the peel—but not the bitter white pith underneath—with a vegetable peeler and use a sharp knife to cut it into thin strips.) Set aside.

Peel the grapefruits as you would an orange (see page 321). Using the tip of a sharp knife, cut each section away from the membranes that separate them. Put the sections in a bowl and top them with the julienned zest.

In a heavy-bottomed saucepan, bring the sugar and water to a boil. Pour the hot liquid over the grapefruit sections. Allow the grapefruit to sit in the syrup for 5 minutes, then drop in the raspberries. Cool to room temperature before serving.

Raspberries in Honey

This is an intensely flavorful dish, created for true raspberry lovers. The taste varies slightly depending on the kind of honey you choose. I suggest a mild-flavored honey that won't upstage the delicate taste of the berries.

SERVES 6

1½ pints raspberries
⅓ cup honey

Puree ½ pint of the raspberries in a blender or food processor. Add the honey and process until smooth. Pour through a fine sieve to remove the seeds.

Divide the puree among six dessert plates; there should be about 2 tablespoons for each plate. Arrange one-sixth of the whole raspberries in a mound on top of the puree in each plate. That's all.

Cantaloupe in Honey

The fruity sweetness of ripe cantaloupe is highlighted by the deeper, richer sweetness of honey. Choose a fairly mild honey so it won't obscure the cantaloupe flavor.

SERVES 8

¼ **cup honey**
¼ **cup sugar**
2 **cups water**
1 **ripe cantaloupe, chilled**

Combine the honey, sugar, and water in a heavy-bottomed saucepan. Bring to a boil. Turn off the heat and skim off the foam. Transfer the syrup to a bowl or storage container and refrigerate until cold, about 30 minutes.

To peel the cantaloupe: Cut off the top and bottom. Stand the melon on one cut end. With a sharp knife cut off a strip of rind about 1 inch wide, following the curve of the fruit from top to bottom. Turn the melon a little and repeat. Continue until you have removed all of the rind.

Cut the melon into quarters vertically. Scrape out the seeds with a spoon and discard them. Cut each quarter in half crosswise. Each of the resulting eight pieces will be one serving. For each serving, cut the melon wedge crosswise into ½-inch slices. Arrange the slices on a shallow soup plate or dessert dish by starting with the largest slice near one edge of the plate, matching the curve of the plate. Center each slice, in descending order of size, overlapping the one before. The final shape will resemble a fan. Pour about ¼ cup of the chilled syrup over each portion just before serving.

Papaya in Lime

The smooth and subtle taste of papaya comes alive when combined with the acidity of lime. This tropical flavor combination is especially refreshing on a hot summer evening.

SERVES 8

> **4 medium-size papayas, ripe and firm**
> **5 limes**
> **1½ cups sugar**
> **3 cups water**

Peel the papayas, cut them into quarters vertically, and discard the seeds. Cut each quarter crosswise into ¾-inch slices. Put the slices in a bowl. Zest two of the limes and sprinkle the zest over the papaya. Squeeze the juice of four limes, including the two you have zested, into the bowl. (Cut the limes in half. Hold each half in turn over the bowl; stick a fork into the middle of the lime and squeeze. Move the fork to a new position and squeeze again.) Toss the papaya lightly in the lime juice and zest. Set aside.

Combine the sugar and water in a heavy-bottomed saucepan and bring it to a boil. Pour the hot liquid over the fruit. Slice the remaining lime very thin and stir the slices into the bowl. Chill well before serving. Before setting the bowl on the table, arrange the lime slices in a ring around the edge.

Honeydew in Chile

This unusual dessert always wins raves. Serve it well chilled to preserve the perfect balance of hot, sweet, and tart flavors. We tested the recipe with every chile available in California. Serrano won hands down for flavor and heat in just the right proportions to blend with the melon and lime.

SERVES 8

2 **medium-size serrano chiles**
3 **cups water**
2 **cups sugar**
1 **medium-size ripe honeydew melon**
3 **limes**

Rinse the chiles and cut off the tops. Slice the chiles open, discard the seeds and membranes (they're very hot), and chop coarsely. (Wash your hands immediately—and keep them away from your eyes.)

Bring the water and sugar to a boil. Cook only until the sugar dissolves. Turn off the heat and add the chopped chiles. Chill.

Cut the melon in half and discard the seeds. Cut each half into wedges about 1 inch wide in the middle. Cut away the skin and rind, leaving only the sweet, light-colored flesh. Cut each wedge crosswise into 3-inch pieces.

Cut one of the limes into thin slices and set aside. Zest the other two. Place the melon in a large glass bowl, add the zest, and squeeze in the juice from the zested limes. Toss lightly to coat the melon. Chill well.

When both the melon and the syrup are cold, pour the syrup over the melon. Arrange the lime slices decoratively on top.

Peppered Strawberries

This combination surprises many people. It's delicious. The pepper-corns add texture and spiciness to the soft, sweet berries. To add yet another contrast in taste and texture, serve with a scoop of orange sherbet.

SERVES 8

- **4 pints strawberries**
- **1 cup strawberry *eau de vie** (*eau de vie de fraise*)**
- **1 cup sugar**
- **½ cup water**
- **⅓ cup (6-ounce can) green peppercorns**
- **1 eating orange, for zest**

Wash the strawberries and cut off the tops. Put 3 pints in a large glass bowl. Puree the other pint in a food processor. Combine the puree in a heavy-bottomed saucepan with the *eau de vie*, sugar, and water. Bring to a boil. Turn off the heat. Drain the liquid from the canned peppercorns and add them to the hot syrup. Cool to room temperature. When cool, pour the syrup over the strawberries and stir to coat all the berries.

Using a zester, cut curls of zest from the orange. Scatter the curls over the strawberries and stir gently.

---

*Eaux de vie are clear distilled spirits made from various fruits. The best ones come from Alsace. You should be able to find *eau de vie de fraise* in any well-stocked liquor store.

Quince and Cranberries

A perfect combination of sweet and tart. The quinces are delicate in taste and texture. The cranberries plump up, and pop when you bite them.

SERVES 8

- 4 **medium-size ripe quinces**
- 1½ **cups sugar**
- 4 **cups water**
- 1 **cinnamon stick, split in half**
- 3 **whole cloves**
- 12 **ounces (1 bag) cranberries, fresh or frozen (*not* defrosted)**

Peel the quinces with a vegetable peeler or knife. Cut them in quarters and remove the cores. Cut each quarter in half lengthwise, then cut crosswise into ½-inch slices.

Bring the sugar, water, cinnamon, and cloves to a boil in a large, heavy-bottomed saucepan. Add the quinces and simmer until glossy and easily pierced with the tip of a knife, about 10 minutes (longer if the fruit is not fully ripe). Add the cranberries and simmer 2 minutes more. Remove from the heat and cool, stirring occasionally. Transfer to a serving bowl—clear glass, if you have it. Serve at room temperature.

Quince and Zested Oranges

Soft, translucent chunks of quince provide a visual and textural contrast to the bright, firm, juicy slices of orange. The flavors create their own delightful interplay of subtle sweetness and lively acid-sweet.

SERVES 8

- 6 **medium-size eating oranges (preferably seedless)**
- 3 **medium-size ripe quinces**
- 1 **cup sugar**
- 3 **cups water**

Remove the zest from two of the oranges and cut it into julienne strips, about 1 inch long. Then peel all the oranges (see page 321) and cut them crosswise into ½-inch slices. Place the orange slices in a serving bowl. Scatter the julienned zest on top.

Peel the quinces with a vegetable peeler or knife. Cut them into quarters and remove the cores. Cut each quarter in half lengthwise and then crosswise into thirds. Bring the sugar and water to a boil in a heavy-bottomed saucepan. Add the quinces and simmer until glossy and tender, 10 to 30 minutes (depending on the ripeness of the fruit). Pour the quinces and their poaching liquid over the oranges. Cool to room temperature before serving.

Appendix

Rescue Tips

Idon't know anyone who bakes or cooks who has not at some time
burned, overwhipped, or made some other mistake with what he was
cooking. If you make a mistake in one of the recipes in this book, don't
immediately despair and throw your dessert away. Evaluate what you
have left and decide if you can save it. Some of the ingredients you will
be using are very expensive, and you shouldn't throw anything away until
you are sure it is unusable. The following suggestions may help you to
save a dessert that has gone wrong. You may not end up with a cake you
want to bring to a friend's house for a special occasion, but you will
probably still have a dessert that you can enjoy with your family and very
close, understanding friends.

ICING DOWN OVERCOOKED FRUIT: If when you remove poached
fruit from the heat it is already perfectly cooked, by the time its poaching
liquid has cooled it will be overcooked. To prevent the fruit from
continuing to cook in the hot liquid, first get both fruit and syrup out of
their saucepan, which, of course, holds heat. Pour them into a cool bowl
and place the bowl in a sink of ice water or inside a larger bowl of ice
water. (Ice water cools faster than ice alone.) The ice water should come

up to the same level as the fruit and syrup. Very carefully stir the syrup and the fruit to release the heat and distribute the cold. Stir until both fruit and syrup feel cool.

PATCHING A HOLE IN A PIE OR TART SHELL: Sometimes when you blind bake a pie shell or tart shell it splits or develops a hole. It should be patched so that the crust won't leak. Roll out a very thin piece of unbaked dough, brush it with water, and gently press it over the crack or hole. Then continue with your recipe. (It's wise to save your dough trimmings at least until the dessert is done in case of such an emergency.) Don't patch a prebaked pie or tart shell that will not be going back into the oven. It's better to have a small crack or hole than a piece of raw dough in your dessert. If the damage to the shell is extensive, you should probably discard it and start again.

SAVING OVERWHIPPED CREAM: If you overwhip cream, pour in some unwhipped cream, a little at a time, and gently fold it in. It will take about 25 percent of the amount of cream you originally whipped to thin it back down. The resulting cream will be dense rather than light, but it will be usable.

TRIMMING A BURNED CAKE: If you burn the top of a cake, the best thing to do is just trim off the burned part. By removing all the dark areas, you can get rid of the bitter taste that comes from burning. Smell what's left. If it still smells burned or bitter, discard it. If it smells all right, go ahead and use it. It may look slightly lopsided, but it should taste fine.

TRIMMING A BURNED PIE OR TART SHELL: If you burn the edges of a pie or tart shell, scrape away the burned areas with a knife, then smell what's left. If it smells all right, it is. Don't ever serve a pie or tart with burned edges; it will taste unpleasantly bitter.

Index

ABOUT THE AUTHORS

Jim Dodge has been pastry chef at San Francisco's famed hotel The Stanford Court since 1978. His desserts have been featured in nearly every major food magazine in the United States and in the PBS television series "The Great Chefs of San Francisco." In 1983 he was the only pastry chef included in Food & Wine *magazine's Honor Roll of Outstanding American Chefs. In addition to heading a staff of seven bakers, he teaches extensively and trains apprentices in his hotel pastry shop.*

Elaine Ratner is a freelance writer and book editor and an avid amateur baker. She has written on such diverse subjects as fine printing, earthquake preparedness, and the treasures of King Tut's tomb. She now writes mostly about dessert.